BERNARD OF CLAIRVAUX

GREAT MEDIEVAL THINKERS

Series Editor
Brian Davies
Blackfriars, University of Oxford,
and Fordham University

DUNS SCOTUS
Richard Cross

BERNARD OF CLAIRVAUX
G. R. Evans

BERNARD OF CLAIRVAUX

G. R. Evans

NEW YORK   OXFORD

OXFORD UNIVERSITY PRESS

2000

Oxford University Press

Oxford   New York
Athens   Auckland   Bangkok   Bogotá   Buenos Aires   Calcutta
Cape Town   Chennai   Dar es Salaam   Delhi   Florence   Hong Kong   Istanbul
Karachi   Kuala Lumpur   Madrid   Melbourne   Mexico City   Mumbai
Nairobi   Paris   São Paulo   Singapore   Taipei   Tokyo   Toronto   Warsaw

and associated companies in
Berlin   Ibadan

Published by Oxford University Press, Inc.
198 Madison Avenue, New York, New York 10016

Oxford is a registered trademark of Oxford University Press

Library of Congress Cataloging-in-Publication Data
Evans, G. R. (Gillian Rosemary)
Bernard of Clairvaux / Gillian R. Evans.
p.   cm. — (Great medieval thinkers)
Includes bibliographical references and index.
ISBN 0-19-512525-8; ISBN 0-19-512526-6 (pbk.)
1. Bernard, of Clairvaux, Saint, 1090 or 91–1153.
I. Title.   II. Series.
BX4700.B5E89   2000
271'.1202—dc21   99-13708

1 3 5 7 9 8 6 4 2

Printed in the United States of America
on acid-free paper

SERIES FOREWORD

Many people would be surprised to be told that there *were* any great medieval thinkers. If a *great* thinker is one from whom we can learn today, and if "medieval" serves as an adjective for describing anything which existed from (roughly) the years A.D. 600 to 1500, then—so it is often supposed—medieval thinkers cannot be called 'great'.

Why not? One answer often given appeals to ways in which medieval authors with a taste for argument and speculation tend to invoke 'authorities', especially religious ones. Such invocation of authority is not the stuff of which great thought is made—so it is often said today. It is also frequently said that greatness is not to be found in the thinking of those who lived before the rise of modern science, not to mention that of modern philosophy and theology. Students of science are nowadays hardly ever referred to literature earlier than the seventeenth century. Students of philosophy in the twentieth century have often been taught nothing about the history of ideas between Aristotle (384–322 B.C.) and Descartes (A.D. 1596–1650). Modern students of theology have often been frequently encouraged to believe that significant theological thinking is a product of the nineteenth century.

Yet the origins of modern science lie in the conviction that the world is open to rational investigation and is orderly rather than chaotic—a conviction which came fully to birth, and was systematically explored and developed, during the Middle Ages. And it is in medieval thinking that we find

some of the most sophisticated and rigorous discussions in the areas of philosophy and theology ever offered for human consumption—not surpris-
ingly, perhaps, if we note that medieval philosophers and theologians, like
their counterparts today, were mostly university teachers participating in an
ongoing worldwide debate and were not (in contrast to many seventeenth-,
eighteenth-, and even nineteenth-century philosophers and theologians)
people working in relative isolation from a large community of teachers and
students with which they could be regularly involved. As for the question
of appeal to authority: It is certainly true that many medieval thinkers believed in authority (especially religious authority) as a serious court of appeal; and it is true that most people today would say that they cannot do this.
But as many contemporary philosophers are increasingly reminding us,
authority is as much an ingredient in our thinking as it was for medieval
thinkers (albeit, because of differences between thinkers, one might reason-
ably say that there is no such thing as 'medieval thought')—for most of what
we take ourselves to know derives from the trust we have reposed in our
various teachers, colleagues, friends, and general contacts. When it comes
to reliance on authority, the main difference between us and medieval thinkers lies in the fact that their reliance on authority (insofar as they had it) was
more often focused and explicitly acknowledged than ours. The difference
does not lie in the fact that their appeal to authority was uncritical and naive
in a way that ours is not.

    In recent years, such truths have come to be increasingly recognized at
what we might call the 'academic' level. No longer disposed to think of the
Middle Ages as 'dark' (meaning 'lacking in intellectual richness'), many university departments (and many publishers of books and journals) now devote a lot of their energy to the study of medieval thinking. And they do so
not simply on the assumption that it is historically significant but also in light
of the increasingly developed insight that medieval thinking is full of things
with which to dialogue and from which to learn. Following a long period in
which medieval thinking was thought to be of only antiquarian interest, we
are now witnessing its revival as a contemporary voice—one to converse
with, one from which we might learn

    The *Great Medieval Thinkers* series reflects and is part of this exciting
revival. Written by a distinguished team of experts, it aims to provide substantial introductions to a range of medieval authors. And it does so on the
assumption that they are as worth reading today as they were when they
wrote. Students of medieval 'literature' (e.g., the writings of Chaucer) are

currently well supplied (if not oversupplied) with secondary works to aid them when reading the objects of their concern. But those with an interest in medieval philosophy and theology are by no means so fortunate when it comes to reliable and accessible volumes to help them. The *Great Medieval Thinkers* series, therefore, aspires to remedy that deficiency by concentrating on medieval philosophers and theologians and by offering solid overviews of their lives and thought, coupled with contemporary reflections on what they had to say. Taken individually, the volumes in the series will provide valuable treatments of single thinkers, many of whom are not currently covered by any comparable works. Taken together, the volumes of the series will constitute a rich and distinguished history and discussion of medieval philosophy and theology considered as a whole. With an eye on college and university students, and with an eye on the general reader, the authors of the series strive to write in a clear and accessible manner, so that the medieval thinkers they take as their subjects can be learned about by those readers who have no previous knowledge in the field. But each contributor to the series also intends to inform, engage, and generally entertain even those readers with specialist knowledge in the area of medieval thinking. As well as surveying and introducing, volumes in the series will advance the state of medieval studies both at the historical and the speculative levels.

Bernard of Clairvaux, the subject of the present volume, was a theologian of a sort which was to grow rarer with the passing of his century. Bernard was above all a monk, and his thinking was chiefly practical. He wanted to bring people closer to God, to heighten their sense of the divine, and to activate them spiritually. He set about these tasks by persuasion and argument, leaning upon Scripture and the Fathers, rather than attempting to be up to the moment or to rival the scholars who were pursuing a different sort of enquiry in the schools of northern France. Yet he came into dispute with some of those scholars and was used by Church authorities to respond on the Church's behalf to the challenges of Peter Abelard and Gilbert of Poitiers. Looking at Bernard's engagement with these two contemporaries helps us to see with some clarity the contrast between different styles of medieval thinking.

In *The Mind of St. Bernard of Clairvaux* (Oxford, 1983), G. R. Evans offered a rounded account of Bernard's thinking. In the present book she takes a fresh look at the problems dealt with in her earlier study while also extending the range of topics discussed. Among other things, she focuses on Bernard's contribution to thinking about ecclesiology and ministry—which proved to be formative in the debates which eventually led to the divisions of the Reformation and their modern ecumenical aftermath.

Bernard was an immensely attractive figure to his contemporaries, and he remains so today. While, like St. Augustine, Bernard produced writings that can seem too dense and rich for modern tastes, readers of this book shall find an accessible Bernard—one whose thinking is clearly presented as something of modern and not just historical interest.

BRIAN DAVIES

CONTENTS

BERNARD OF CLAIRVAUX

INTRODUCTION

Bernard thought there was more than one way to heaven. There was, in his view, no better choice than to be a monk, for the monastic life was very heaven on earth; yet the ground rules of Christian living could—if with difficulty—be followed by all Christians, whatever their calling. Although Bernard wrote chiefly for a monastic readership, he spent a great deal of time chivvying persons in secular positions to establish the right Christian priorities in their lives and activities. In his mind, the whole body of the faithful stands behind his principally monastic audience.

Bernard's book *On Consideration* contains a metaphor of orientation.[1] Bernard invites Pope Eugenius, for whom he wrote it, to look around himself—to discover what is below him, what is at his side, and what is above him. Although he considers the pope uniquely placed in the world because of his high office, the general rules seem to Bernard to be sound. Christians should seek to get a sense of where they stand in relation to one another and to God.

Order is important. Without order there can be no pattern of conformity with the will of God. Everyone ought to have rules and follow them. When Bernard wrote to Cardinal Ivo to persuade him to give his support to the campaign to condemn Peter Abelard, he represented to the cardinal that Abelard's offence was a breach of *rectus ordo*. He is a monk without a rule. He is bound by no rules: *nec ordinem tenet, nec tenetur ab ordine*.[2] Bernard thought it no robbery to be hard on others. That would be regarded as an extension of his monastic duty?[3] He was hard on himself.

The idea of life as failure (*perdite vixi*)[4] was deeply attractive to him because it went with the sacrifice and struggle to which he believed Christ had called his people.

Bernard's idea of the norms by which he should live his life is familiar in Western Christian writing from the patristic period onwards. The conventions of Bernard's thinking are therefore unsurprising for his time. He argues for moderation and for patience in persecution; he gives us, for the most part, standard ideas about saints and heretics.

But he argues with a freshness which derives in part from his remarkable command of the expressive possibilities of the Latin language of his day, and in part from the passion for what he was saying, which took him again and again over the boundaries of the moderation he preached. The *exercitatio mentis*, the wandering, exploratory, digressive style of Bernards thought,[5] is often also an *excitatio mentis*. The biblical texts, read in a liturgical context in the monastic life, stimulate in Bernard's hands an exegesis sometimes baroque and decadent, sometimes full of contradiction, but always powerful.

Embedded in these patterns of life and thought are a theology and a philosophy. These are the principal subject of this study. But they have to be looked at in the context of the life and the times of Bernard himself. Bernard is not a great or pioneering theologian, but as Gregory the Great demonstrated, originality and influence do not always run together. Bernard, like Gregory, was read and listened to because he was a good communicator and seductively persuasive. What he had to say made its impact because he wrote for his times and for individuals whom he wished to affect, even to drive. In his richly embroidered webs of words are designs to please faithful souls, systems of thought and belief which he intended to be entirely orthodox, and here and there something quite new, a fresh insight of enduring value.

So we may read him as a man of his times who was important and had an influence beyond his day; as a figure who would stand out in any period because he has much to say that is of perennial relevance to the understanding of the human condition.

VITA BERNARDI

Bernard's contemporary life-story was written by people who knew him well. It was a joint enterprise.[1] Geoffrey of Auxerre began to prepare a *Vita* from the time Eugenius III was elected pope in 1145, for Eugenius had been a Cistercian monk and could be expected to look with favour in due course on a life history designed to win canonisation for Bernard. That was almost always the purpose of the writing of such a life story at this period. Indeed, it was possible to hire hagiographers who would devise an account for almost anyone according to the accepted canons of the genre.

Geoffrey of Auxerre probably had it in mind that Raynaud should do the actual writing. Raynaud had been abbot of Foigny from 1122, but ten years later he had returned to Clairvaux to a post as Bernard's secretary. He had a good working knowledge of Bernard's movements. He had travelled with Bernard a good deal between 1132 and 1138 and had accompanied him to Paris in 1140, when Bernard went to preach to the students there.[2] He had been eyewitness of numerous events which might usefully go into a biography; Raynaud lacked perhaps the combination of admiration and sturdy independence which makes a good biographer—an Eadmer writing about Anselm of Canterbury, or a Boswell writing about Dr. Johnson. (Indeed, Eadmer's *Life of Anselm*[3] would not have survived if Eadmer had not been too much of a historian to disobey Anselm's express instructions to destroy what he had written; Eadmer made a copy before he did so.) Raynaud had to be abandoned as author-in-charge, and it was Geoffrey who continued to set the biography's tone and purpose.

Geoffrey's instinct was for panegyric.[4] But he had the wit to choose others to write alongside him who might usefully say something he could not about Bernard the public figure. One of these was Arnaud de Bonneval, a Benedictine abbot about whom we know comparatively little and whose connections with Bernard are not always explicit, although he seems to have had knowledge of Bernard's involvement with the papal schism and of his support of the cause of Innocent II.[5] But Arnaud is important, because a letter purporting to have been written to him from Bernard's deathbed survives among the *Letters*. It describes Bernard's state of mind and his physical condition at his death.[6] But there is reason to suppose that it may have been written by Bernard's secretary Geoffrey of Auxerre himself after the event and not by Bernard at the time. To do that would not have seemed an act of forgery, for Geoffrey would frequently have written letters on Bernard's behalf in his own words, with a mere indication from Bernard of what to say.[7]

The intellectual giant among this party of biographers was William of St. Thierry. He has, as we shall see, some claims to rival and even on occasion to outstrip Bernard himself as a theologian. William was born at Liège in the late 1070s and studied there and at Reims and perhaps at Laon. He became a Benedictine monk. He had made a first visit to Clairvaux in 1115 when he was a monk of St. Nicaise and already forty-five years old, in contrast to Bernard's comparative youth; we shall hear more of that in a moment. For a decade, he and Bernard corresponded, and William made another visit to Bernard in the late 1120s. In 1121 he was elected abbot of St. Thierry. William of St. Thierry wrote on the nature of body and soul, on virtue and vice, on the moral exegesis of the Song of Songs, on grace and free will (in a book dedicated to Bernard). He longed to join Bernard at Cîteaux, but Bernard would not allow him to do so until, between 1135 and 1148, he became a Cistercian monk.[8]

So as a biographer William was strongly partisan and well informed about the mind and heart of his subject. He was a strong advocate in the biography of a view of the inner Bernard as pure and holy, and of the outer Bernard as a man whose deeds could only express an interior life which was beyond reproach and could not themselves be in error. His prologue to the first book of the *Vita Prima* says as much.[9]

A biography such as Bernard's had to fit certain contemporary expectations. It was intended not merely to be of interest to readers curious to know about an important figure, but to set before them an example of how to live a good Christian life. Bernard wrote that sort of biography himself, in his *Life* of the Irish saint Malachy. Yet although Bernard of Clairvaux had energetic and adulatory contemporary biographers, who made of his 'official' *Life* something far richer and more informative than the conventions demanded, this ambitious and innovative *Vita* was still a hagiography. In Bernard's time, hagiography had a purpose and an agenda; it set out to present its subject in a particular light; its canons of accuracy were not those of the historian, because it seeks to edify and to instruct, rather than simply to record.[10] It is more important to the author of a saint's 'life' to convey spiritual truths than historical facts.

It is time to come to the outline of events. Bernard was born in 1090 into a socially fairly well-placed family in northern France, at Fontaines near Dijon. The *Vita* says that his mother had a vision before he was born, but that is a commonplace of contemporary saints' 'lives', and may be a 'recollection' after the event, rather than *of* the event.

Bernard was educated as a small boy by the canons of St. Vorles de Châtillon. We do not know what he learned in their school, or what was the standard of his formal education, but it was clearly capable of taking this able child beyond the elements. They gave him a good command of Latin and either then or later he got to know the text of the Bible extraordinarily well.

By putting Bernard to school, his family was marking out a track for him which was likely to take him into the religious or the clerical life. Those, or the life of a soldier, were almost the only choices which lay before young men of good family at that time and place.

Bernard was born at a time of experimentation in the religious life. The anonymous 'Little Book on Different Orders' (*Libellus de diversis ordinibus*) describes the variety to be found at the time of its writing in the mid-twelfth century. It argues that monks and canons should be of one mind in their singleness of purpose in the Christian life, but that they need not adopt a single *style* or *form* of life. 'Different servants of God have arisen from the beginning of the early Church, and many kinds of callings have come into being,' says the author.[11] He wants to call them all good.[12] He begins with hermits, who lead the religious life in solitude, remote from the habitations of men and women. Then he describes monks, then canons, whom he deems their equals in the value of the lives they lead, although those lives have radically different assumptions at some points.[13] For example, monks should be primarily contemplatives, remaining in the house where they are professed. Canons may go out actively and serve as priests in the world. The *Libellus* thus seeks to present variety in styles of religious life as a desirable thing.

The choices open to Bernard were not so numerous. But there was one experiment to which he was drawn. When Bernard was eight years old, Robert of Molesme, with twenty companions, founded a house at Cîteaux, where the sixth-century Rule of Benedict was to be followed with severity, and in simplicity of life. Robert had himself been a monk at Marmoutier and abbot of St.-Michel-de-Tonnerre, and in both houses he had found it impossible to reform the lax way of life which he believed to have lost touch with the original spirit of the Benedictine Rule. The new house flourished. The movement grew. In 1100 Robert of Arbrissel founded Fontevrault, a house in the same tradition. In 1109, Alberic, who had been the founding prior of Cîteaux and its second abbot, died, and was succeeded as abbot by Stephen Harding, who had the qualities needed to sustain the experiment in the longer term.

In 1113 Bernard, drawn by the promise of an ascetic and truly dedicated life, which Cîteaux seemed to offer, became a monk at Cîteaux, taking thirty companions with him, many of them his kinsfolk. Their arrival gave the already thriving new 'Order' a strong boost, for Bernard was and remained an attractive figure. It became fashionable to become a Cistercian, just as it had been fashionable in an earlier generation to enter Cluny and was later, in the thirteenth century, to be the fashion to become a friar. In each period the best minds of the day have been drawn in succession to the mode of religious life then in vogue, and it was Bernard's achievement to win that pride of place for the Cistercians for a time.

The Cluniacs, hitherto the leading Benedictines of the day, had undergone a reform during the previous century, but it had led them into a pattern of heavily detailed observances in which the deep purpose of Benedict's Rule were easily lost sight of. And they had rich houses, with all the attendant dangers of moral corruption and decay of principle which go with an easy life. The kind of thing which offended Bernard was the observance of fasts at which the vegetarian dishes served were cooked to *cordon bleu* standards. One of the attractions of the Cistercian way of life was its simplicity, its emphasis on the self-denial the Benedictine Rule had intended.

The author of the *Libellus de Diversis Ordinibus* characterises the Cluniacs as monks who live close to human settlements and the Cistercians as monks who live in places remote from other people.[14] That is a striking image of the profounder difference. Cistercians lived lives both literally and metaphorically apart, dedicated to prayer and contemplation, their houses not only away from other human habitation but also plain, without adornment. They had no vessels of precious metal, and their vestments were simple. There were strict rules of silence and plain food, and the place of manual labour, which Benedict had considered important, was restored to the daily round. There were organisational differences from Benedict's plan, however, most notably in the introduction of a class of lay brothers alongside the choir monks, who were usually by this period drawn from noble families. That change gave individuals of lowlier social classes the opportunity to enter the religious life, although less was expected of the lay brothers by way of strictness and severity.

It took organisation to give the new Order a unified and distinctive character. Stephen Harding had composed the Charter of Love (*Carta Caritatis et Unanimitatis*) perhaps as early as 1113 or 1114, to encourage all Cistercians to follow the same customs. Each new house was free to regulate its own affairs, but it was expected to do so in accordance with the decisions of the General Chapters which were held each year at Cîteaux. The General Chapters oversaw discipline and the revision of the customs of the order. The multiplying houses of subsequent decades endeavoured to conform, and revisions were gathered into an up-to-date *Carta Caritatis* between 1152 and 1165.[15] So throughout his life as a monk, Bernard was held secure within a system whose parameters were well understood, with the Rule of St. Benedict as a point of reference. As we shall see, he was always conscious of the presence of the Rule as his standard of monastic life.

The Formation of the Abbot

In 1115 the Cistercian houses of Morimond and Clairvaux were founded as the Order expanded, and Bernard, although only in his mid-twenties, became abbot of Clairvaux. This proved a not uncontroversial choice. He was very young. He was over-conscientious, and that could seem oppressive to others, as well as make it difficult for him sometimes to see the wood for the trees. He was well aware of that difficulty. It is striking how often he warns others of the importance of keeping an eye on the important things of the religious life.

On Consideration, the book he wrote for Pope Eugenius III, was inspired by that concern, and in it, as we shall see, he tried to save Eugenius from the sorts of mistake he himself had made. He was subject to inner conflicts, which sometimes come to the surface in his letters. Letter 7 to the monk Adam wrestles with the sometimes conflicting duties of obedience, as we shall see more fully later; Letter 1 to Robert is full of hurt pride. Bernard's temper could be violent. He could be touchy and domineering. Letter 70 reports his extreme anger against Bartholomew, one of his natural brothers. Letter 2 to Fulk of Aigrement reproaches Fulk for betraying his vocation to the life of the regular canons, to which he had been professed, and joining the secular clergy, under pressure, it seems, from his uncle, who was a canon of Aigremont.

Bernard was not the only Cisterican to find the responsibilities of the abbot's office more onerous than he could easily bear, for the extreme spirit of early Cisterican life generated great pressures. In 1131, Raynaud, the founder-abbot of Foigny, asked to be released and allowed to return to Clairvaux.

It would not be fair to suggest that Bernard did not see that there was a problem and was not aware of some at least of his own failings. For Bernard, there was not only the strain of seeking to live his vocation to an exceptionally high standard. There was almost certainly already a problem to which he was to return throughout his life in numerous asides and direct reflections: that of maintaining a satisfactory contemplative life when there are constant interruptions from persons in spiritual need themselves or with practical problems requiring solutions, to which their abbot has to be ready to attend. Bernard comments in one of his sermons on the Song of Songs upon the difficulty he has in getting an hour to himself. (It is tempting to draw a parallel with the description in Books VIII–IX of the *Confessions* of Augustine's attempts to get a moment with Ambrose of Milan.) Those are interruptions to which Bernard would probably have felt it his duty to give an ear even if he had not been abbot. When he was abbot, there could be no question where his duty lay.

Bernard is tempted to see people's willingness to interrupt him as a breach of the duty of respect they owe to their seniors. Monks ought to hesitate to bother their abbot. On the other hand, he fears that timid supplicants will conceal their needs and suffer unnecessarily if their abbot makes himself too hard to reach. He tries to balance accessibility and authority and concludes: I shall not exploit my authority; others may use *me* as they please, if that helps them to attain salvation. They will, he says, paradoxically, spare him by not sparing him.[16]

But these are the thoughts of the mature Bernard, a Bernard who is capable of reflecting upon the duties of an abbot who remains himself a monk, not of the young man who became abbot at the age of twenty-four in a house of a dozen monks, many of whom were his kinsfolk. In a sense he was already 'father' to his 'brothers' because he could claim to have 'begotten them in Christ' by firing their vocations.[17] But he had not been the choice Stephen Harding would have recommended as abbot for Pontigny or for Morimond,[18] and it seems clear that he was promoted too high and to an excess of responsibility too soon.

The strain of the life and the shouldering of burdens of office at such an early age, when Bernard was not yet himself formed in the religious life, made him ill. Book I of the *Vita Prima* describes a long period of near breakdown early in his abbacy, as a result of his excessive austerity. The situation and Bernard's stability were rescued by William, later abbot of St. Thierry and one of Bernard's biographers, who was then a Benedictine monk of Reims. William came and lived alongside Bernard in retreat in a humble dwelling outside the cloister and showed him that a life of moderation was more appropriate to a religious than a life of extreme self-denial.

As he recovered and got into his stride as abbot, Bernard faced a new problem. The Cistercians were too successful. A series of Cistercian houses was being founded: Trois Fontaines, Foigny, Bellevaux (from Morimond), Fontenay (by Clairvaux). William of Champeaux, bishop of Châlons, who had been a founder of the house of St. Victor and a protector of Clairvaux since Bernard turned to him for episcopal blessing when he was made abbot of Clairvaux, died, and in 1120–21 several canons of St. Victor entered Clairvaux. There was a stream of conversions, some, controversially, from Cluniac houses. During the 1120s, William of St. Thierry asked to enter Clairvaux himself, and Bernard would not allow him to do so. All this caused resentment on the part of other orders, and Bernard embarked on a task of guiding those who sought to move and of defending the conduct of Cîteaux and its daughters, at which we shall be looking in the chapter on monastic theology.

Bernard and the Popes

Bernard was a high-profile figure almost from the beginning. That had consequences. Conspicuously able individuals were regularly picked out for preferment in an age where talent to fill high office was in short supply.

Lanfranc and then Anselm was made archbishop of Canterbury at the end of the eleventh century, Anselm very much against his will, for he had no wish to be anything but a monk. Bernard escaped such office, but he did not escape exposure to contemporary events. He was increasingly called upon to assist the Church in public roles. At the Council of Troyes in 1128, when the first rules of the Order of Templars were established, Bernard had at least a secretarial task. His involvement with the Templars then got Bernard further widely noticed in monastic and political circles.[19] But he faced two problems. The first was an *actual* tension between these demands and the proper focus of a monastic life. The second was a *consciousness* that he was acting in ways he would have discouraged in others, and a consequent need to justify his secular work to himself and to them.

Bernard lived under several popes. The first to hold office during his active 'political' life was Honorius II. He had been important as a negotiator in arriving at the Concordat of Worms of 1122, which brought the Investiture Contest[20] to a temporary quietus. The Investiture dispute had come to a head late in the eleventh century when the precarious Church-state balance of power of previous centuries had begun to shift. Pope Gregory VII had asserted a papal supremacy that went a long way towards the doctrine of papal plenitude of power which Bernard himself came to embrace.[21] But on the ground there were local questions. A king or emperor would have preferences in the choice of bishops in his territories. He would have, as a feudal lord, to 'invest' a new bishop with the lands attaching to his see. He could not consecrate a bishop, but he could do everything else which went into making one. There was a danger of the line between the secular, or temporal, and the sacramental act being overstepped, and sometimes it was, as when a king gave the new bishop his ring (symbol of his 'marriage' to the Church and therefore to his faithful people) and his pastoral staff (symbol of his shepherd's role). That had happened to Anselm of Canterbury when he was consecrated archbishop in 1093, and even he had not understood at the time why this was a crossing of the essential dividing line between the spiritual part of the making of a bishop and the temporal part. Several decades of dispute, involving the mutual ritual humiliation of popes and emperors brought the dispute to the uneasy peace of Worms, where it was agreed that the Church should confine itself to the spiritualities and the state to the temporalities in the joint act of making someone a bishop in a given diocese.

Honorius II's election reflects the fierceness, even savagery, of contemporary politics, which were nowhere more heated than among the factions striving for control of Rome. After the death of Callistus, Honorius II emerged as pope from a chaotic scramble for control of the papacy between the Frangipani family and the Pierleoni family and their candidates, with the installation of the would-be Celestine II interrupted by armed men. Both families had to be squared before Honorius could be elected and enthroned.

It was clear to all parties that there was now a new phase of development. With the Investiture Contest to all intents and purposes settled and Church and State in a new if uneasy balance, the papacy needed to renegotiate and establish its position in relation to the Church and state alike. Honorius began by supporting Lothar III as candidate for emperor and anathematizing his rival, Conrad, and Conrad's supporter Anselm, the archbishop of Milan, who had already crowned Conrad 'King of the Lombards.' In France Honorius played a waiting game, which encouraged King Louis VI to resolve his conflicts with the ecclesiastical hierarchy. England was coaxed into allowing in papal legates after 1125. The Normans were more resistant to his diplomatic devices, but Honorius was able to obtain an oath of fealty from Roger II of Sicily in return for papal recognition in 1128. Honorius's chancellor was Aimeric, and it was Aimeric who had been largely instrumental in ensuring Honorius's election. The two worked systematically for reform in the Church. They gave support and sanction to the newly active orders of canons, especially the Premonstratensians.

In 1130, on the death of Pope Honorius II, there was a papal schism, and it was in the handling of this schism that Bernard began to come into his own as diplomat and even statesman. It was now that the challenge to his sense of priorities became sharp, for his time was taken up a good deal with travelling and advocacy of Innocent's cause.

On the night Honorius II died, the election and enthronement of Innocent II were carried out in great haste by a minority of the cardinals led by Aimeric, the chancellor. The majority of the cardinals objected when they learned what had happened, and they chose Pietro Pierleoni, who had been with Innocent as legate in France, as Anacletus II. On 23 February both 'pope' and 'antipope' were consecrated. Eight years of schism followed. In backing Innocent II against Anacletus II, Bernard supported the side which he though best represented the spirit of the reforms of the period of Gregory VII.

Anacletus could call on an alliance with Roger II of Sicily, whom he bribed with the crown of Sicily, with Apulia and Calabria. It was his claim which was most widely recognised throughout Europe. This was partly because the canons regular were able to influence opinion in many countries. Norbert, the founder of the Premonstratensians, was now archbishop of Magdeburg, and in that capacity he won over the German bishops and King Lothar III.

Bernard persuaded the English and French kings to give their voices to Innocent. At the Diet of Würzburg of 1130, the German clergy and King Lothar pronounced themselves in favour of Innocent II. Bernard and eleven cardinals travelled with Innocent on itinerary in the early month of 1131, receiving the homage of King Lothar of Germany at Liège, where Lothar was accompanied by twenty-five bishops and archbishops and fifty-three abbots. In 1131, Bernard attended a council at Étampes which had been called by Louis VI so that the French Church could 'take a position' on which was the legitimate pope. A visit to Clairvaux impressed Innocent with the fervour and simplicity of life of the monks; he was struck quite differently by the opulence and royal entertainment he received when he visited Cluny in 1132, which, even if it was a courtesy to him, was a reflection of something very far from poverty. When Innocent stayed at Cluny, he received homage there from Abbot Suger of St. Denis, who was sent for the purpose by the king. Innocent later stayed at Chartres, where he received the homage of Henry I, king of England.

Innocent held a synod at Rheims to anathematize Anacletus, and in the spring of 1133 Lothar marched on Rome as he had promised to do. He was not able to evict the Anacletus party from St. Peter's, so the papal coronation Innocent had promised him in return for his support had to be conducted in the Lateran. Lothar was still pressing for concessions about investiture, and Innocent gave him the right to receive the homage of bishops and abbots before they took possession of the temporalities at the hands of the emperor.

Bernard and Innocent entered Rome in 1133, the year of the founding of Rielvaux. Rome proved too hard to hold, and after Lothar's return to Germany, Innocent was forced to move to Pisa, but there he held a synod at which he excommunicated Anacletus and Roger II of Sicily. Bernard of Clairvaux again proved helpful, winning Milan for Innocent in 1136. Lothar returned to Italy in the same year, but the expedition was largely abortive, and Lothar died on his way back to Germany in 1137.

Meanwhile, Innocent and those who were supporting him were trying to persuade Roger of Sicily to change allegiance. In 1138, on 25 January, Anacletus died, and although his supporters immediately elected a successor in Victor IV, he did not stay the course, resigning on 29 May. The Pierleoni capitulated and made their submission to Innocent.

In 1139 Innocent held a Second Lateran Council. Its main task was to tidy up the confusion of decisions and actions which had arisen during the schism by annulling everything Anacletus had done and all his ordinations. More positively, it consolidated recent reform legislation by republishing it.

The remaining years of Innocent's pontificate saw more conflict. In July 1139, Roger II captured him and made Innocent acknowledge him as king of Sicily. There was a serious rift with the French king in 1141, and in 1143 there was rioting in Rome. Bernard's advocacy and support led to his being taken up by the pope as an adviser. So when Innocent won through to Rome, Bernard was made at a stroke a senior and established figure in Church affairs. While Innocent was in office, he frequently used Bernard as a travelling representative.

Innocent II was succeeded by Celestine II, whose pontificate was brief. Guido of Città di Castello in Umbria was a former pupil of Peter Abelard and perhaps one of the first academic importations into the papal service. Such head-hunting was to become a regular thing by the time of Innocent III. The pope would ask about promising young men in the schools and attract them into his civil service. Callistus II adopted Guido in that way, and in 1127 Guido was made cardinal deacon of Sta Maria in Via Lata by Honorius II. In 1131 and 1132, he was a papal legate in Cologne and in 1139 and 1140 in France. He was an active supporter of Innocent II's claims. Only in the matter of Peter Abelard did Guido seriously disagree with Innocent's policy and that earned him a reproving letter from Bernard of Clairvaux.

Guido's election as Celestine II followed hard on the death of Innocent II; he was the cardinals' unanimous choice from the five Innocent had named as possibilities he would himself favour. He lifted the interdict on Louis VII of France which Innocent had imposed in 1141, and he did not ratify the treaty made at Migniano in July 1139, at which Innocent had, under duress, recognised the sovereignty of Roger II in Sicily and southern Italy.

Gherardo Caccianemici, Lucius II, was a pope with a less intimate link with Bernard, though he was friendly with Bernard and with Peter the Venerable of Cluny. He had served Honorius II as legate in Germany and was instrumental in the 1125 election of Lothar III as king. It was he who ensured the choice of Norbert, the Premonstratensians' founder, as archbishop of Magdeberg. In 1130 he worked with Aimeric to support Innocent

II against Lothar when they were in dispute over Monte Cassino. Innocent II made him chancellor when Aimeric died in 1141. His own accession to the papacy was relatively uncontroversial, at least by the standards of recent elections, although he faced controversy in Rome.

The succession now moved to a candidate in whom Bernard had a strong 'domestic' interest, Eugenius III. Eugenius had been a Cistercian monk. Bernard regarded his election with some alarm, because he did not consider Eugenius to possess the acumen and forcefulness to carry the high responsibilities of his office well, let alone the spiritual focus to get his priorities right.

Eugenius had to begin his pontificate outside Rome; by Christmas of 1145 he was briefly in Rome, but early 1146 saw him in retreat again in Viterbo. Meanwhile, there was trouble in the 'crusading kingdoms'. These had been set up in the Holy Land under various Christian knights, after the First Crusade had succeeded in capturing the Holy Places for Christians. The new arrangements were, however, inherently unstable. The Christian kingdoms were an 'outpost of Empire' and could not have the resources to enable them to stand against determined attack.

The Turks captured Edessa from its Christian masters in 1145, and a group of Armenian bishops came to Eugenius to ask for his help for themselves against the emperor of Byzantium. This was the natural thing to do. The First Crusade had been 'called' in the 1090s by Pope Urban II. He had promised plenary indulgences to all who reached Jerusalem or died on Crusade. That meant a complete remission of any penances which had been imposed upon them, and it effectively promised direct entry into heaven. So it was a powerful enticement, and one only the pope could offer—though there were undoubtedly other inducements in the form of the prospect of lands and position and of sheer adventure.

Eugenius travelled to France to make the call for a new Crusade in person. He proclaimed this Second Crusade in 1145 by sending a bull to Louis VII of France.

The bull was renewed on 4 March 1146 with a commission to Bernard of Clairvaux to 'preach the Crusade.' Bernard's involvement was slowly won. At first Bernard was reluctant, taking the view that Christian energies should be concentrated upon the needs of the flock at home and not upon problems at the interface with Islam. But he became convinced despite himself that it was his duty to support the venture and a committed Bernard never did things by halves. Eugenius had not intended the German emperor to become involved because he was in need of the emperor's assistance with the familiar papal problems of the insurgency of Rome and relations with Roger of Sicily. But Bernard won the emperor for the Crusade. There are stories of how, when he preached and people were moved and came forward to 'take the Cross,' the cloth symbol of being a crusader which they were to wear on the campaign, supplies rapidly ran out and clothing had to be torn up in a hurry to make more.

Yet the Second Crusade failed; the crusading kingdoms were not successfully reestablished. That created difficulties for Eugenius. The first was the loss of face. The second book of Bernard's *De Consideratione* was directed at that area of embarrassment. Bernard had rather the same problem as had faced Augustine in *The City of God*, when he had to explain how God could allow a Christian Roman Empire to fall to barbarian invaders. The only answer was to see a lesson in it, and Bernard argued that God had meant to teach Christian Western Europe that it was not yet spiritually worthy to succeed in a holy war.

The second result of the failure of the Second Crusade was to compound the problem about Byzantium. Byzantium was the capital of the eastern half of the old Roman Empire and in some respects a trading rival. And since 1054 the Greek and Latin Churches had been in schism, as much for political as for theological reasons. To judge from such accounts as that of Anna Comnena, a member of the imperial family, at the time of the First Crusade, the Greeks tended to regard the Latins with disdain, as crude primitives, useful only in an emergency, for military support against the 'infidel' incursions from farther east. The Latins found Byzantium in some respects 'in their way' politically. Roger of Sicily and Louis VII of France pressed for a crusade against Byzantium itself, and Bernard supported them. But Eugenius did not commit himself to this project. Eugenius's interests in rapprochement with the Eastern Church led him in another direction— to urge Burgundio of Pisa to produce Latin translations of some of John Chrysostom's homilies and John of Damascus's *De Fide Orthodoxa*. These formed significant additions to the tiny store of Greek patristic material then available in the West.

Eugenius's period in office coincided with significant developments in the struggle of the mid-twelfth-century Church to deal with heresy, particularly academic heresy. This was something new, in that there were now schools of a new sort, proto-universities in which issues of academic freedom of speech were beginning to arise. Among the free speakers was Gilbert of Poitiers, who was tried for his teachings on the Trinity at Reims in 1148,[22] with Bernard of Clairvaux acting as prosecutor on behalf of the Church. Hildegard of Bingen, the abbess who had been publishing her *Scivias* ('visions'),[23] was also scrutinised at this synod.

In June 1148, Eugenius excommunicated the dissident Arnold of Brescia. Here the thrust of his displeasure was practical, as well as to do with the need to discourage the anti-establishment opinions Arnold was feared to be spreading. Bernard wrote to the bishop of Constance about Arnold, who had been a pupil of Peter Abelard.[24] He had apparently been teaching that bishops and priests could not hold property, and that all property belonged to the secular authorities. He had been condemned to silence and banished from Italy, but he returned on the death of Innocent II in 1143. Arnold had been pardoned in 1146, but he had formed an alliance with the Roman commune and was speaking of the pope as 'the man of blood'. He continued to stir up trouble until 1155, when the emperor Frederick Barbarossa condemned him to death. The synod of Reims was called by means of an invitation in which Eugenius took seriously Bernard's encouragement to take a strong line on the powers of the papacy. Eugenius now explicitly claimed for the papacy a supreme authority in things temporal as well as things spiritual. Rheims was not Eugenius's only reforming synod. He had held others at Paris (April–June 1147) and at Trier (1147–48).

In Ireland, Eugenius set up four metropolitan sees. In English affairs, Eugenius was an interventionist pope. He was supportive of Archbishop Theobald of Canterbury in his disputes with the king and he deposed William Fitzherbert from the See of York. The Roman commune was making overtures to Germany's Conrad III, who was to come to Rome for his coronation in 1152. But he died before he could arrive, and Eugenius entered into negotiations with his successor, Frederick I Barbarossa, who sent news of his election and promised the pope his protection. He did not ask for Eugenius's approval of his election, but Eugenius prudently gave it.

It was agreed at the Diet of Würzburg in October 1152 that Frederick should make an expedition to Italy. This proved useful, in that Rome's commune was persuaded by Frederick to allow the pope to instal himself in the city. In March 1153 Eugenius made the Treaty of Constance with Frederick. This was in part a mature version of the Concordat of Worms. Each sovereign power undertook to protect the other's sovereignty, or 'honour'. The pope promised to crown Frederick emperor, and in return Frederick promised not to make peace with the Roman commune or the Normans without agreement with the pope. The two stood solidly together on the subject of not making concessions of territory to the Eastern Empire.

During the pontificate of Eugenius III, the power base of Bernard's influence shifted. At its start, he had a natural 'moral' authority over Eugenius, deriving from Eugenius's period as one of his monks and their mutual consciousness of Eugenius's shortcomings. At its end he was partly discredited by the failure of the Second Crusade, and partly outmanoeuvred by a party among the cardinals which was hostile to him.[25] It was always, for Bernard, a problem that he remained an outsider to the Curia. When he wanted to exert an influence, he had to do it by letter writing and cajoling; and effective as that could be, it was no way to do business with the factions and coteries of Rome.

The last pope of Bernard's lifetime, Anastasius IV, was a Roman by birth. During the period of the schism he was a supporter of Innocent II, lingering in Rome during the periods of Innocent's absence in exile. In the years 1147–49 and 1150–52 he acted as Eugenius's vicar.

His election as pope took place on the day Eugenius died, and he was enthroned in the Lateran on 12 July. Rome allowed him to stay, which bespeaks the good relationship he had established over the years with the people of the city. He proved himself a peacemaker in other ways, too, mending relations with Frederick I Barbarossa over the appointment to the See of Magdeburg and repairing the damage done by the extended dispute over the election to the See of York. He sent Nicholas Breakspear, who was to be the next pope, as legate to Scandinavia, and as a result the payment of dues to the papacy by Norway and Sweden was achieved.

Bernard wrote to all kinds of people in connection with these public events and with the more 'domestic' happenings of the monastic world. He wrote letters of pivotal importance for the history of his age and also for the history of monasticism and spirituality. He did not always write every word of them himself, just as it is likely that his sermons were not actually preached in the polished literary form in which they survive. He repeatedly edited and revised his work,[26] and there is a body of material which survives only in the form of sayings.

Some of Bernard's secretaries are known to us, and we have already met one or two of them as authors of his contemporary biography.[27] One is William of Rievaulx, to whom Bernard dictated his first letter. The second is Geoffrey of Auxerre, who subsequently wrote two books of the *Vita Prima*,

sharing the authorship of the whole with William of St. Thierry and Arnaud
de Bonneval. He joined Bernard's side during the period of his confronta-
tion with Abelard, whose student he had formerly been. In 1145 Geoffrey
was already Bernard's *notarius*. He himself became an abbot, first of Igny
and then of Clairvaux itself. A third 'secretary' is Nicholas of Clairvaux, who
entered Clairvaux in the years 1145–46 after going as emissary for Bernard
to carry letters about Abelard to Rome. His career there came to an untimely
end when he left it in 1151–52. We also know of secretarial assistance from
Gérard de Péronne, Baldwin of Pisa, Raynaud de Foigny.

It was usual in medieval letter-writing for the writer to send an oral
message with his text, and indeed the main burden of the letter often lay in
the verbal accompaniment. So messengers needed skills of a high order.
There was also the possibility of secretarial help and amendment which went
far beyond the mere taking down of dictation.[28] The surviving words of a
letter may not be all authentically the letter as it left the mind of the author.
This was the age of the burgeoning *ars dictaminis*, or 'art of letter writing',
in which salutation formulas were devised and a proper order of exposition
for letters set out, on the model of a classical orator's speech.[29] Increasingly,
secretaries knew their job. Bernard undoubtedly dictated. Possibly sometimes he dictated only an outline. Secretaries familiar with his mind and style
might be able to do a creditable job of filling in the gaps. (A similar question
hangs over the later letters of Anselm of Canterbury.) Compositional econo-
mies were practised, sometimes perhaps by Bernard himself. The text of the
De Diligendo Deo draws on Letter 11 perhaps ten years after its composition.[30] There is an extract from Letter 73 in Letter 74.[31]

Bernard is perhaps likely to have read the end result when it had been
written out, much as a modern letter-writer who uses a secretary will read
and sign letters at the end of the day, sending some back for correction.[32]
But even with that possible safeguard, Bernard complains of the failures of
secretaries to transmit the messages he has left with them, and of their stylistic infelicities at times.[33]

That is important because it makes the task of close analysis of his writings difficult. A turn of phrase can bear only so heavy a load of interpretation as it exactly reflects the author's thought.

These were the events against the background of which Bernard led
the side of his life which was active rather than contemplative; and wherever the Church intervened or became caught up in politics, he was liable
to find himself involved. Yet Bernard's was a life in which the struggle to

balance the demands of his monastic profession and the call of the world was perpetual.

Malachy, bishop of Armagh, stopped at Clairvaux on his way to Rome in 1139 and was profoundly impressed by the life he found there. He wanted to stay, but Bernard would not allow him to. He stopped again on the way back and left four Irishmen for Bernard to train as monks, so that a Cisterican foundation might be set up in Ireland.

On Malachy's death, Bernard wrote an account of the bishop's life in which he unfolds what we may call the theology of example. The taking of experiences from the world and using them as teaching aids in this way was one of his principal methods of linking and balancing the active with the contemplative life. The contemplative was never an entirely private matter for Bernard. He *taught* contemplation, in almost everything he wrote. That made him a theologian who thought a great deal about the relationship between the active and the contemplative life, and this study will return again and again to the ground-rules of this balancing act.

Should we censure Bernard for allowing himself to be drawn into politics when he preached a very different set of priorities for others? Perhaps. It took time and energy from other things, and his best work was the writing which sprang from his conviction that the spiritual life was what ultimately mattered. We might have had more of that, and it might have gone deeper, if he had not been distracted by the affairs of popes and by the passing excitements of contemporary politics.

MONASTIC THEOLOGY

'Where shall I turn, so that I may turn to thee, my Lord God? If I ascend into the heaven, you are there. If I descend into hell, you are there too' (Psalm 138.8). Am I to turn up or down, to left or right? Bernard's answer to himself in this dilemma is that he must turn *into* a different person. He must change himself into a 'little one,' so as to learn from him who is meek and lowly of heart.[1]

The text Bernard is discussing is Joel 2.12–13: *Convertimini ad me in toto corde vestro*, 'turn to me with all your heart.' If the Lord had said only 'turn' and added nothing more, it would be different, argues Bernard. But the additional words require us to take a long-term view. We are to turn to God. That kind of conversion is not achieved in a day; it takes a lifetime. A merely bodily and therefore outward conversion is a form and not the truth (*forma . . . non veritas*). We are told to deny our bodies their sensual pleasures, but that is not enough. Wretched is the man who deals only outwardly and does not understand his inner self. But at the same time, it is not enough to be converted only in spirit. The whole person must turn to God.[2]

If this is the making of a person, we need to ask what a person is in Bernard's view. This is not a straightforward question, for the concept of personhood Bernard was familiar with lacked many of the associations which would be natural today. The word *persona* was used theologically for the Persons of the Trinity. Otherwise, it continued to have something of its clas-

sical colouration, where it meant a character in a play; it remained some-
what two-dimensional. *Persona* could be used for a given individual. 'Know
that I have no complaint about your person' (*de persona tua querelam*),
Bernard reassures one correspondent.[3] One may speak of 'the person of an
abbot' (*persona Odonis abbatis*),[4] and it is possible to defame a person.[5] But
persona largely lacked the notion of individuality as a defining characteristic of identity, which it carries with it in the late-twentieth-century West.

Similarly, 'humanity' was still being used most typically for 'human
nature' (*humanitas* in opposition to *divinitas*), and it did not yet carry the associations of the modern 'humane'. To be 'human' was to have a certain type
of created nature, not to 'be oneself' as an example of one's kind.

There is talk of the 'acceptance of persons' as something Scripture does
not approve of: 'With God there is no acceptance of persons.'[6] Bernard speaks
with approval of the Templars because they do not make such distinctions,
and they revere those who are more virtuous, not those who are more nobly
born: *defertur meliori, non nobiliori*.[7]

The thrust of Bernard's thinking about the full realisation of human
potential is one we shall meet again and again in these pages. Man's standard is God. Men and women are made in the image and likeness of God,
and they have fallen away from that image and likeness through sin. It is
their life's task to seek to be restored. To that end they must be always journeying back, always striving to know God so as to know what they ought
to be, always aware of their smallness and fallen state. 'I am a small and
unworthy person,' explains Bernard (*vilis exiguaque persona*); a mere *homun-
cio*.[8] The finding of oneself, one's 'development' as a person, depends upon
the realisation of that ideal. It does not mean being oneself as unique and
different but, paradoxically, being as close as possible to the ideal, which is
God himself. The differentiation sanctioned by Scripture is that of a variety
of gifts of the Spirit, not that which values idiosyncrasy and distinctiveness
as a *human* good.

A Higher Calling

'Conversion' in Bernard's day normatively meant making the decision to
enter the religious life.[9] 'Profession' as a monk is seen almost as a second
baptism, if that were not a contradiction in terms.[10] This *conversio* did not
necessarily involve a *metanoia*; still less was it likely to be a conversion from

no faith at all to faith in Christ, or from another faith to the Christian faith. Yet there was, as is clear from Bernard's Lenten sermon just quoted, an expectation that there would be an intensification of the religious commitment.[11] Bernard looks for an emotional component, a heightening of experience, too. He makes great efforts to stir up such feeling in his monks and his correspondents alike. But first and foremost, it was a decision to take an existing faith seriously, to make a sacrificial commitment by leaving the world and its goods and taking vows of poverty, chastity, and obedience.

Conversion is illumination of the dark places of the soul, enabling a person to see God more clearly than the sinner could manage unaided by grace. Bernard, like Augustine, takes it for granted that to see God is to desire him strongly. This is of course a very ancient Christian theme, yet Bernard uses it equally naturally in his own day.[12] God's voice is a beam of light which shows people their sins, he explains.[13] It makes for awareness.

This consciousness of a need for 'conversion' was occurring with a new frequency and even perhaps a heightened perception of social implications at this period because of a trend towards adult entry to the monastic life. The child oblate had long been the norm. But in his autobiography, the *De Vita Sua*, Bernard's contemporary Guibert of Nogent describes adult converts he knows of, such as Evrard of Breteuil, Theobald of Champagne, Simon of Valois, often senior nobles who have been knights and raised families and in late middle age wish to turn to the religious life.[14] A mature man who comes to the monastic life knows what he is doing and makes a major change in his life.

A monk undertakes several things in his profession under the Benedictine Rule. He vows to live a certain kind of life, which has outward observances, but observances designed to reflect the denial of self. One of these is silence (Chapter 6 of the Rule), which discourages those sins which can come from the loose use of language. Another is humility (Chapter 7), which works to discourage pride.

A monk binds himself to a way of life. He must say the Hours. Worship, the prayer of the community, is the central activity of his daily life, his real work, the *opus Dei*, or 'work of God'. There is also solitary contemplation, *lectio divina*, or 'holy reading.' And there is manual labour.

This life of a monk ought to be inwardly rich, that is, rich in interior spiritual and affective experience.[15] Bernard is not afraid of emotion and actively encourages it in his monks. It provides a forum within which the first definitive moment of conversion can open up into a process of change which can be called, in the full sense, a growth in holiness, a sanctification.[16] Bernard makes use of the key texts in the New Testament which speak of sanctification—texts in 1 Thessalonians 4.3, *haec est enim voluntas dei sanctificatio vestra*, and in I Corinthians 1.30, *et iustitia et sanctificatio et redemptio*.

Bernard takes it for granted that such 'sanctification' goes beyond the defining moment Reformation scholars would call 'justification'. That is clear in a sermon on the Vigil of the Nativity, where he speaks of sanctification as *interna ablutio . . . munditia spiritualis*, an inward washing which is a spiritual cleansing.[17] There are some in whom Christ is not yet 'born'; some in whom he has not yet suffered; some in whom he has still not risen; some in whom he has not ascended; some in whom he has not sent the Holy Spirit.[18] All these acts of Christ in the human person are needful.

If that is what Bernard understands conversion to be, he would appear to be making a startling claim at the beginning of his book *On Conversion*. He says that there is no true life, no other means of entering into eternal life, except by conversion.[19] But he certainly does not mean that only monks and nuns will enter heaven. He believes that variety of life is legitimate, which must imply that there is not only one way to heaven. In Bernard's *Sermo ad Abbates*, the theme of the three ways of life is explored. In a familiar topos,[20] Noah, Daniel, and Job are taken respectively to represent the life-styles of priests and bishops, the *rectores ecclesiae* (Noah), religious (Daniel), and married people or laymen (Job). All three have to cross the sea of this world. Noah crosses in a ship, but that is an uncertain and unsafe way to travel because the ship can be tossed among the waves. Job crosses on foot; although he legitimately possesses the things he has, that is the hardest way, for his possessions are a great danger to him. Daniel has chosen the best way, for a bridge is the shortest and safest route across. The bridge is narrow, but narrow is the way which leads to life. Indeed, to be in a monastery is already to be in heaven. *Tabernaculum, Clarevallis domum non manufactam intelligo*; Clairvaux is a tabernacle not made by human hands.[21]

The individual may choose his way to salvation, but God will have a hand in his making that choice. Bernard sees God as active in the conversion of souls, the hound of heaven.[22] He 'calls'. So the monk has been *chosen* by God for this better way. Bernard's God is huge and present and compelling, and he ought to be the focus of the most gigantic of human passions; that is what he demands and what he rewards. At the same time, he is gentle and tender and woos a love from his 'bride', the soul, which is freely given and infinitely pleasurable.

The *Right* Monastic Life

It was a burning question in Bernard's day which *form* of monastic life it was best to choose if one felt such a vocation. As we have already seen, there was a widening choice of Order, no longer only the Benedictine, or the 'reformed Benedictine' of Cluny; but the Cistercians, who also followed the Rule of St. Benedict, on yet another and still more ascetic understanding of its spirit; and Orders of Canons, such as those of St. Victor in Paris, following variations of the Augustinian Rule, some of them working as priests in the world in cathedral chapters or parishes.[23] The sharpness of the choice was heightened by the fact that there was rivalry between houses and Orders, with monks professed in one leaving to go to another.

Bernard wrote to a number of monks in difficulties with their vocations, particularly to those moving or seeking to move between Cluniac and Cistercian houses. With one monk, who had been vowed by his parents to a Cluniac house as a child and now wanted to be a Cistercian, he explores the question which has the most force—the vow a father makes on behalf of his son or the vow a son makes on his own behalf, especially when what the son wants to do is something better than his father had promised on his behalf. This question is about personal responsibility for one's salvation. The son's choice was no whim of a rebellious adolescent. He *begged* to enter Cîteaux; he wanted it very badly, and the abbey made him wait two years because he was too young.[24]

There is also the question which is more 'in order'. A vow made on behalf of a child too young to know what is being done must be outweighed in Bernard's view by a vow made by someone old enough to know that he is doing. (Although it was not a matter of concern to Bernard's age, a parallel can be drawn here with the practice of baptizing infants before they are old enough to make a profession of faith.)[25]

But for many contemporaries involved in these often highly visible debates, the issues were less elevated. There were high sensitivities over any appearance of 'poaching'.

The key points in the 'dialogue' between Cluny and Cîteaux were the assertions that Cluniac life lacked the simplicity and faithfulness to the spirit of the Rule for which Cistercians strove. In MS Dijon 114 (82) there survives the *Instituta Generalis Capituli apud Cistercium*, which gives an indication of the persistence of this attitude in about 1150. It insists that the Cistercian monastery is still to be a *coenobium in deserto*, a secluded place for the soul to grow. Cistercian manual labour must not make a profit; its purpose is to allow the monk to earn his daily bread. There are to be no fur clothes or linen undergarments. There is to be no living outside the cloister, for in that lie dangers to souls (*pericula animarum*). There are to be no special terms (for example, dispensation from the novitiate) for rich men who build abbeys for the Order out of their own resources and then wish to come and live in them. There is to be no dispensation, either, for the monk of the order who subsequently becomes a bishop. He is to go on living according to the Rule and to say the Hours. There is to be simplicity in the externals of worship. [26] All is to be strict and plain. From such principles derive a 'monastic theology' with which Bernard was able to identify himself.

The Benedictine houses had typically taken in infants and children given as 'oblates'. Late in the eleventh century the fashion for entry in late middle age that Guilbert of Nogent describes had partly altered that practice. The Cistercians were consistent from the beginning: Cistercian practice was to refuse entry to those under a certain age. Schools are to be kept only for those who are already professed or novices; there are to be no schools for boys, whether inside or outside the cloister (perhaps to ensure that vocations were adult vocations). And no one under fifteen may be admitted as a novice. So Cistercian education is adult education, and the formation of a Cistercian monk a very different business from the formation of a 'child oblate' at Cluny or elsewhere.

Part of the difficulty was that the Cistercian way was new. The inspiration of the Cluniac reforms had been entirely different even in its day, and it had travelled some distance down the road of pragmatism and compromise in the century since it began. [27] Like was not being compared with like. The sense of newness of vision was all on the Cistercian side. So when a young man—or even an established monk—opted for Cîteaux, his preference turned not merely on the question where his prior obedience lay, but on the different vision Cîteaux set before him.

Monasticism and Mission

Because he sincerely believed the monastic life, and especially the Cistercian life, offered the best hope of heaven, Bernard was expansionist. He saw his monastic vocation as also a missionary vocation, to a degree perhaps not envisaged in Benedict's Rule. Bernard entered the religious life with a com-

panion crowd of thirty kinsfolk he had persuaded to join him. He continued
to exhort others to join him in the religious life, or to persevere where they
were if they had already taken vows; he saw the very setting of an example
as a missionary activity. William of St. Thierry depicts Bernard as such a
seductive preacher that people hid their loved ones at his approach.[28] His
letters of business appear sometimes to have been written with an idea that
a wife may persuade her husband to Bernard's view.[29]

Bernard's missionary purpose included both sexes. Bernard did not write
much to contemporary Benedictine nuns, but Letter 114 is to a nun and is
of the type favoured by Jerome when he wrote to his Roman ladies, giving
them a programme for life and lauding virginity (or celibacy, for the married and widowed).[30] Bernard's two dozen letters to women are mostly
letters of business.[31] In writing to male correspondents Bernard speaks
comparatively infrequently of women.[32] His interest was not in any conception of a special role or task in the spiritual life for women, but in the common tasks of all human souls. Bernard's imagery of biblical women takes its
force from their symbolism, not their femininity. Dinah, Jacob's daughter
(Genesis 34.1–5), is *curiositas*, the traditional symbol of light-mindedness.
Martha and Mary, and above all the Blessed Virgin Mary, are ideas as much
as people. So for all practical purposes Bernard's concern for salvation embraced both sexes indifferently.

Stability and Pilgrimage: The Paradox

A Benedictine monk was under a duty of stability. Formally, stability was
not a matter of vow at all, although Bernard speaks of it in those terms, as a
stabilitatis votum.[33] He was capable of construing stability widely, so as to get
round the awkwardness of the appearance that his own life-style was in
breach of that duty. There are indications that he was sensitive on that point.[34]
He took stability to mean not merely—as in its strict sense—remaining in
the house of one's profession, but doing so in a manner which preserved the
bond of peace: *unanimitatis . . . vinculum; pacis firmamentum*.[35] Yet Bernard
often seems as much concerned with mere travel, which is not in itself an
infringement of stability, as with change of house or Order.

Stability and obedience to the abbot ought to go hand in hand, and indeed Bernard sets them side by side as the *duo praecipua . . . observanda*, the
two principal things to be observed in the monastic life, taking it that

stability so completely implies obedience to the abbot that it scarcely needs a mention.[36]

Bernard's ruling is that stability is the higher duty. The monk vowed stability directly for himself. It is not in the abbot's power to vary the terms of the vow.[37] The voluntary character of the monk's profession was of immense importance to Bernard's view of the bindingness of the duties he has taken upon himself. A priest is of God's calling; a monk is a monk of his own choice: *nempe monachum facit professio, praelatum necessitas*.[38] Even a child oblate must take upon *himself* the 'promise' his parents implicity made on his behalf when they gave him to be a monk, the *professio* standing upon the *oblatio*, which is not thus *exinanita sed cumulata*, not made of no account by it but completed or added to.[39] The monk agreed to the terms of his profession, but once he had done so, he became bound to obedience to the abbot, for that was one of the terms.

The Benedictine Rule speaks of the *gyrovagi*, those who are 'always wandering and never stable, following their own desires': *semper vagi et numquam stabiles, . . . propriis voluntatibus . . . servientes*.[40] Monastic wandering is a *scandalum* in Bernard's view. His early letters are much preoccupied with it. Yet he recognised that to wander was not always damaging. Spiritual journeying could and did arise out of physical journeying in Bernard's experience, and it could be a *peregrinatio*. Philip, a young canon from Lincoln, had been on his way to Jerusalem and had slept at Clairvaux on the way and been given hospitality there. He asked to stay. Bernard wrote to his bishop, Alexander, who objected to Philip's staying, to say that Philip had merely taken a shortcut on his way to Jerusalem, for at Clairvaux he was in Jerusalem. Those at Clairvaux were living the life of Jerusalem in spirit already.[41]

So stability is good for you, but not essential, says Bernard (*sed . . . ita magis expediret*).[42] There may be circumstances in which one should not be bound by it. He had felt that on his own pulses. For Bernard was in a difficult position personally, as he travelled about Europe, to insist upon the stability of others. And he found himself doing a good deal of travelling away from Clairvaux. He declares it was his own wish never to leave his monastery except on the orders of his bishop or a legate of the Apostolic See.[43]

He was professed at Cîteaux but 'sent' to live elsewhere. A great crisis has drawn us from our cloister into public life, says Bernard in a letter to Pope Honorius.[44] For it was consistently his argument that *others* should stay where they had been professed in the religious life. He argues that his own peripatetic style of life is acceptable because the move from the cloister was

made without scandal and discord.[45] He also holds travel to be justified if
the reason for it is very important.

For those not under a duty to stay put, *peregrinatio* might be positively
beneficial, for then it became pilgrimage. Between 1128 and 1136, Bernard
wrote a treatise for the Knights Templar, which takes the form of a tour
of the Holy Places. At each one he stops and gives a short talk. After the
Temple, Bethlehem, Nazareth, Mount Olivet, the Vale of Joshaphat, Jordan,
and Calvary, the pilgrims arrive at the Holy Sepulchre. Among the Holy
Places, this one holds pride of place.

That does not make all wandering a good thing, however, says Bernard,
even for those not under a vow which imposes upon them an obligation of
stability. There has to be a holy purpose to a journey for it to be spiritually
beneficial. Arnold of Brescia is a fugitive and a wanderer, who carries
on being as dangerous among strangers as he formerly was before he was
exiled.[46]

The theme of exile is closely linked to that of the desirable aspects of true
pilgrimage in the mindset of Bernard's day. It is a strong pastoral theme in
contemporary preaching, that the life of man on earth is itself an exile, from
which the task of a lifetime is to seek to return to the presence of God. In
the sermons on the Song of Songs, Bernard speaks of the body as a 'little
dwelling place' (*habitaculum*) which is not the mansion of a citizen nor the
house of a poor man, but rather the tent of a soldier or the resting place of
a person on a journey.[47] In a sermon for Quadrigesima he speaks of the
peregrinus who walks the 'royal road' (*via regia*), turning neither to right nor
to left.[48] In one of the sermons on the Psalm *Qui Habitat*, he describes how
a person walks the ways of mercy and truth, which are the Lord's ways, the
ways of life, and how he gains the fruit of his journey in salvation.[49]

Salvation is to arrive home, in that huge homeland (*ingens patria*) and
realm beyond imagining (*regio inaestimabilis*) of heaven.[50] The whole ecclesial
community is making that journey, for the Church itself is a pilgrim Church
(*peregrinante adhuc Ecclesia*).[51] So travel and wandering are not always signs
of being a lost soul. They may be the state of a soul, or souls in company, on
the way back to God. That sense of a common endeavour is shared in a salutation formula which Bernard uses in his letters.[52] Bernard explains that to
go back to one's own country is to leave the homeland of the body and go
into the region of the spirit: *repatriasse erit hoc, exisse de patria corporum in
regione spiritum*.[53] The soul is unsatisfied while it must hunger and thirst after
a righteousness it can know only in heaven.[54]

The flesh holds the spirit back, dirty with sin and not worthy to be admitted to heaven.[55] There is an echo here of the hermetic tradition,[56] which passed into the Middle Ages chiefly in the form of the notion that man is placed between God and beast and grows more like whichever he imitates in his behaviour. William of St. Thierry has a sense of it too in his Exposition on the Song of Songs. He explains that no one can come to the enjoyment of God by contemplation unless he grows like him, and the degree of enjoyment will depend on the degree of likeness. 'Love makes us like those we love.' Love is thus purposeful and transformative, and when it is taken to have a purpose purely of enjoyment it is a lesser thing than when it is seen as beneficial to the growth of the soul towards God.[57]

Within the same tradition of thought, Bernard speaks of bending down to earth or stretching up to heaven, falling sick with fleshly desire or recovering through spiritual growth.[58] Bernard emphasises that God is spirit. He is the greatest Spirit (*maximus spiritus*), who is also truth, wisdom, virtue, eternity, the Highest Good. At the same time, he is the resting place (*mansio*) of blessed spirits. Now we remain in the vale of tears outside that resting place, where *sensualitas* rules and the bodily sense (*sensus corporeus*), and the spiritual eye is dark.[59]

Bernard expected chastity of both sexes equally. His position is straightforward. Angels do not marry,[60] and it is better for human beings not to do so either. To be chaste in this life is to anticipate a condition of the heavenly life. Chastity represents the condition (*status*) of immortal glory in this time and place.[61] The frail vessel of our present body carries chastity precariously, like a precious ointment.[62] So chastity is linked by Bernard with incorruptibility. But for all its importance, it is, for him, far less important than humility, for humility contains chastity, and much else besides.[63]

Continence and chastity are not identical in Bernard's mind. He links continence with the other virtues of self-denial—vigils, fasting, works of mercy[64]—and it is, for him, perhaps in that self-denial that its virtue consists. It involves custody of all the senses—hearing, sight, smell, taste, and touch.[65] Chastity is, of its essence, a virtue which hides itself away, not seeking glory from human approval but only from that of God.[66] It fosters renewal (*constat interiorem hostrum hominem renovari de die in diem*).[67]

It is also a fortification, a very wall to the soul.[68] Continence is like innocence in repelling the contrary vices.[69]

Bernard thus persuades his brothers to keep in mind always that they are pilgrims far from their homeland, indeed cast out from their heritage.[70] He stresses that salvation is not to be found in this life (*in via*) but in heaven (*in patria*). It is important to Bernard's conception that his definitions have context. Continence is of no value to the sinner unless it is coupled with penitence, he says.[71] Bodily continence, mental effort (*cordis industria*), and uprightness of will (*voluntatis rectitudo*) spring from the same source.[72] Chastity without charity is valueless.[73] Chastity belongs with sobriety and voluntary poverty.[74]

Bernard recognises several 'realms of exile', *regiones dissimilitudinis*, understood as spiritual 'places' or states distant from God. The first is the present life, *praesens vita*, for those who are too attached to it are sent far from God: *quam quidam nimium amantes, longe dissimiles Deo facti sint*. They go down to hell: *descenderunt usque ad locum mortis*. There are three more 'geographically conceived' *regiones*, not all of exile, for one of them is the heavenly Jerusalem (*regio supercaelestis*), which is the *home* to which the exiles from God's presence seek to return. There is purgatory (*regio expiationis*),[75] a place not known to man but to God, in which the souls of those who are to be saved suffer for as long as it pleases the Supreme Judge, and as their sins require. Bernard emphasises that this is for the benefit, not the harm (*ad profectum, non ad detrimentum*), of the souls which suffer thus. Then there is the *regio gehennalis*, hell itself.[76] But Bernard knows of another realm, the *regio australis*, or the cloister.[77] This is spiritually no exile but a place where for a time the soul may dwell, on the way to becoming more perfect.

Obedience and Conscience: Spirit and Letter in the Observance of the Rule

Because of the purity of his vision of its purpose, Bernard displayed a certain radicalism in the monastic life. He took his principal vows at their root meaning, where they cohere as a single act of denial of self-will. Simplicity of life seemed to him of the essence of the observance of voluntary poverty.[78] For him, poverty and chastity belong together, for both involve doing without things desirable and desired by the natural man. Both poverty and chastity are subsumed in the vow of obedience, which goes to the very renunciation of will itself.

Of the requirements of the religious life, obedience has commonly been found to be the hardest. That is the case partly because human beings are creatures whose wills are not incidental but integral to their humanity. Having freedom of choice is constitutive for their being, as rational creatures of high dignity; but it is also the attribute which brought about their fall, and in their fallen state they can no longer use their wills for good as readily as for evil.

Several theological themes were brought to the surface for Bernard by the dilemmas of the monastic life. These arose largely out of the fundamental principles of the Rule. In his *Apologia ad Guillelmum Abbatem*, Bernard comments that 'if you think the Rule is to be kept to the letter, in such a way as to admit of no dispensation, I dare to say that you are not keeping the Rule'.[79] He recognised that in the affairs of men there can be variations of circumstance such as make it impossible for rules or laws to be applied wholly even-handedly. Some rules have more force than others, imposing an imperative. But it can also be the case that some rules bite harder because they are inherently more difficult to obey.[80] Or sometimes rules or laws may vary in their bindingness according to innate differences in their force or imperative character, which derive from God's wishes.

The duty to obey is not, then, all of a piece, and indeed, as Bernard was keenly aware, it may sometimes pull in opposite directions, so that it can be difficult to know which way to go. In his treatise *On Precept and Dispensation*, Bernard responds to an enquiry first made by two Benedictine monks of Chartres who had written to ask him questions about priorities in the matter of obedience. Bernard promised to reply to the abbot of Coulombs. The abbot in his turn asked for a developed study which could be widely circulated.

The first principle of Bernard's considered account is that in the monastic life, the duty of obedience derives from the act of consent. Those who accept the Rule and promise to keep it will progress in the Christian life if they keep it faithfully. But not *accepting* it does not stand in the way of getting to heaven.[81]

The next set of questions concerns the Rule of Benedict. Is everything it says a precept? If so, is anyone who breaks it condemned to eternal damnation? Or is everything in the Rule merely advice and guidance? If that is the case, would the consequences of breaking it be less serious? Or are some rules obligatory within the Rule and others merely intended to be helpful advice? This set of questions is a practical one, for it will clearly have pastoral consequences in terms of the seriousness with which monks take their duty to obey the Rule.

Bernard sees the problem in terms of shadings and grades of the duty of obedience: *de oboedientia, quibus gradibus distinguatur*.[82] His starting point is the fact that although anyone may accept the Rule, it is imposed on no one against his will: *omni homini proponitur, imponitur nulli*.[83] Any sanction imposed for disobedience derives from the original consent to obey.

Some things in the Rule are clearly not 'negotiable' from the human side, because they are underlying principles with a divine warrant. Bernard is clear that there is a higher duty under the Rule than that of obedience to it. Obedience must first be to the law of God. That law comprises the fundamentals on which all else is built: charity, humility, gentleness—*caritas, humilitas, mansuetudo*.[84] Without these no one can live the Christian life at all, and thus no one can live in obedience to the Rule without them. Even God cannot change these rules; to be more exact, he *will* never do so, because they reflect his divine nature.

Other rules may also be looked on as non-negotiable (*inviolabilia*) in the sense that there are no circumstances in which it is permissible to break them unless God defines those circumstances. Examples are the commandments not to kill and not to steal. But God can vary even these requirements. In war he can countenance killing. He can also countenance theft: when the Egyptians were despoiled by the Hebrews, that was at God's wish (Exodus 3.21–22).[85]

Even where there is no emergency, no extraordinary dispensation, not all disobedience is equally perilous. To disobey the commandment 'Thou shalt not kill' in self-defence is not as bad as to kill in the course of a robbery.[86]

Obeying a Person and Obeying Conscience

But it is not all about rules. A duty of obedience assumes a relationship of persons. So within the Benedictine life obedience is owed to a person, that of the abbot. (There is no continuing duty of obedience to the wishes of an abbot now dead, especially if his command was wrong.)[87] If it is certain that a superior's orders will not be displeasing to God, they must be obeyed.[88] The abbot is God's vicar, and obedience to him is obedience to the will of God.[89]

The level of obedience required is high. Obedience is due at once and without question from a monk to his abbot.[90] That adds the possibility that an abbot may *interpret* the Rule or give orders not included in the Rule, on his abbatial authority. This in turn has the implication that though the monk may have to ask himself whether what he has been told is right, he may have to conclude that it is not. If he has to obey immediately, there will be no time for reflection as to whether what is ordered is right, or whether it is in conflict with the divine law.

Bernard discusses conscience a good deal in *De Consideratione*. But it also occurs as a topic in his letters. Bernard takes sincerity to be a baseline in matters of conscience. 'Let the good and faithful servant keep faith, with a pure heart and a good conscience, not a pretended love,'[91] *Potest tamen et alio modo lota facies, conscientia pura et unctum caput intelligi mens devota*,[92] he says in his letter on the duties of bishops. Conscience ought to be steady, settled, a *secura . . . conscientia*.[93]

Conscience ought to be fierce with us if we go against it. 'I believe their conscience has been gnawing them,' comments Bernard.[94] Conscience can nag, as well as gnaw: *quod conscientiam nescit remordere vel remordentem nequit homo sentire*.[95] Its promptings should be respected.[96]

Beyond this point Bernard does not seem to have gone in exploring the question whether conscience is an innate monitor, a part of the person, or simply the voice of God speaking within. Much of what he says would bear any of these interpretations.[97] Hold a conversation with your conscience, and it will tell you why you are leaving your Order, your brothers, your place of profession: *tua tibi conscientia respondeat cur abieris, cur ordinem tuum, cur fratres, cur locum, cur me, . . . deseruis*.[98]

Bernard is sure that each individual has a conscience.[99] It bears witness to us about our behaviour, and that suggests that it has some independence of the mind in which it works and can see its conduct clearly and critically.[100] As Peter the Venerable puts it, conscience holds us back.[101] Bernard believes that conscience tells us things. 'To whom does his conscience not speak?'[102] Bernard sees it as its own 'place'. Something may lie on one's conscience.[103]

Conscience gnaws at us within, like a worm.[104] We should not be distressed to feel it, for it is better to be eaten up inwardly now, while it can do us good, than to be so gnawed for an eternity without hope.[105] A bad conscience is full of the fear of hell.[106] If we behave rightly, conscience is silent,[107] as when we patiently accept penance. In a *pura conscientia* is a sense of safety.[108] An unshaken conscience does not fall to the beseiging of temptation.[109]

An abbot may require a monk to do something his conscience tells him God would not wish him to do. Should a monk obey his abbot, if his abbot is leading him astray?[110] Bernard says several times that no one has a duty of obedience if that means doing wrong. There is no obligation to obey the commands of a superior if they are contrary to the will of God.[111] It is better to obey God than man.[112] No prohibition is valid if it seeks to forbid what God commands; no order is valid, however high the authority, if it seeks to require what God forbids.[113] It would be a perverse understanding of the meaning of obedience if a higher duty (to do right) was disregarded for the sake of a lower (the duty to obey one's abbot).[114] The abbot is not above the Rule, for he himself is a professed monk before he is an abbot.[115] So despite his strong insistence on the special duty of obedience a professed monk takes upon himself, Bernard would appear to place obedience to conscience even above obedience under the Rule. He does this by some blind sense of priority, for he lacks the materials, and the terminology, to advance far along the road of the discussion of synderesis of the thirteenth century.

Obedience and Circumstances

However, Bernard does not explore very far the implication that a person may set his own 'conscience' above that of his superior. Instead he comes back to the issue of the intrinsic force of rules and looks at another question: whether it is possible to say objectively whether any given course of action is good or bad, so as to make the judgement where one's duty lies with reference to the act, rather than to one's superior. He points out that the law of obedience is not concerned with virtues or vices.

Some things are indubitably good, others certainly bad, but other things fall between in a category neither wholly good nor wholly evil.[116] These 'middling things', argues Bernard, derive their goodness or badness from circumstances of manner, place, and time.[117] When that is the case, we have a duty to obey our superior's wishes. That makes the superior's wish in itself a defining circumstance.

Some things *intrinsically* indifferent can *become* wholly good or wholly evil. Marriage is in itself a thing indifferent because it is neither enjoined nor forbidden. But once a marriage has been entered into, it cannot be dissolved. Holding property is a thing indifferent in itself, but once one becomes a monk, one is forbidden to hold property.[118] Circumstances have moved a middling thing into a settled thing.[119]

The duty of 'instant' obedience is qualified by Bernard as he thinks it through. Obedience should not be instant or unquestioning. The Bible says,

'Prove all things; hold fast to that which is good,' and that means taking thought for what one's conscience says. So it is with the duty of absolute obedience. There are thus limits to obedience; it has a measure, Bernard acknowledges. Its measure is the tenor of the profession itself, and it cannot go beyond that.[120]

One can go 'less' or 'more' in the direction of obedience but not against one's duty.[121] Yet the orders of a superior do not move the boundaries set by the monk's profession. The monk cannot be required to do more than he promised,[122] or what is impossible.[123]

On the other hand, and conversely, perfect obedience knows no bounds. The truly obedient desire to obey more and more: perfect obedience.[124] It can even be asked whether obedience is co-terminous with virtue: *et his suis terminis virtutem eamdem circumcludi*?[125]

Does it follow that the gravity of disobedience is in proportion to the duty of obedience to a given rule or person? The virtue of obedience was present to a supreme degree in Abraham: *Summae et admirabilis oboedientiae virtus in Abraham*.[126] Abraham is also the 'father' of all believers, *pater omnium credentium*.[127] Did Abraham deserve praise (*laus*) and grace (*gratia*) in proportion to his obedience?[128] The Rule contains both precepts which protect the monk[129] from sinning and remedies for disobedience.

The motivation of obedience, the sheer willingness for self-abnegation, is thus an important circumstance. The Rule sees it (Chapter 71) as mutual, as eager, for the monk wants to obey his abbot (Chapter 5). It becomes part of a monk's way of life, the stuff of his dealings with his brethren (*conversatio*), that he is obedient, and that applies even if he is promoted to a position of authority such as that of prior.[130] It is good to obey for fear of hell; it is better to obey in order to keep a promise; it is best to obey from love of God.[131] Wherever there is culpable negligence, there is a 'contempt' for these things which is damning. (*Ubique enim et culpabilis neglectus, et contemptus damnabilis est*.) The negligence is caused by languor, the contempt by pride.[132]

Humility and Pride

In his early letters, Anselm of Canterbury gives many indications of the character of monastic friendship as understood in Benedictine houses. It is passionate in expression, but coolly interchangeable between individuals. For example, he writes to two of the monks who had left Bec to go to Canterbury with Lanfranc, formerly head of the school at Bec, and he ends each apparently intimate letter with the instruction that it is to be exchanged with the other, so that both monks may read both letters, for what applies to one applies to the other.[133] The letters to Gundulf, who was noted for his capacity to water the seeds of Anselm's teaching with his tears, abruptly cease to be intimate when Gundulf becomes bishop of Rochester, and Anselm moves very properly from *tu* to *vos* in his mode of addressing him.[134] The feeling is controlled, purposeful; its purpose is edification. The friendship is a friendship of monks who have given themselves up to God and whose liking for one another depends upon that commitment.

Ailred of Rievaulx wrote a Cistercian treatise on spiritual friendship in which he begins with the contrast between this sort of friendship and the ordinary kind naturally enjoyed in the world. 'I used to enjoy the company of my friends at school,' he says. 'I liked nothing better than to love and be loved. But I did not understand the true nature of friendship. I was enticed hither and thither.'[135] Then he read the Bible and the Fathers. He learned that in Christian friendship, Christ always makes the third.[136]

Ailred gives a picture of the lively intercourse of a Cistercian house. He describes a recent occasion when he was sitting in a crowd of the brothers, who were jostling one another to come up to him and ask a question or dispute a point, one from Scripture, another about behaviour (*de moribus*), another about the vices, another about the virtues. Ivo alone was silent. He made several attempts to ask his question, but he was not able to get a word in. Ailred approves of him for not joining in this confusion of trivial and time-wasting questions (*vana et otiosa*), but fixing his attention steadily upon something which it would be profitable to know (*utile*) and waiting his opportunity to ask about it.[137] It is, Ailred comments, the monk's task to learn humbly. He should be ready to listen and not anxious to make his own contribution.[138] So Ailred comes to a definition of friendship which begins with Cicero's concept of it as a bond of mutual agreement about things human and divine, loving and kind: *rerum humanarum et divinarum cum benevolentia et caritate consensio*.[139] He thinks it should include this agreement, and that it should also be mutually courteous and spiritually purposeful. At the heart of it, he places the presence of Christ.

For Bernard, too, there is in his concept of Christian friendship a necessary sense of a companionship which will extend into the bliss of heaven. He speaks of a friend as one who is his fellow servant, his companion on the journey, and his co-heir of heaven in the life to come.[140] We should keep each other company with prayer and fasting, he exhorts his brethren.[141]

Bernard's first substantial work was a book on the steps of humility and pride, which he wrote at the request of Godfrey, one of his kinsmen who had joined him in entering Cîteaux and then gone on with him to Clairvaux. Closely linked with Bernard's 'monastic theology' of obedience is his teaching on humility and pride as they are lived and experienced in the monastic community of 'companions in the spiritual life'.

Bernard is aware of the irony of his presumption in writing on humility as though he were an expert. He tells Godfrey that he has thought about that point and decided that charity obliges him to do it, unworthy though he is.[142] Bernard defines humility as a virtue by which a person thinks little of himself *because he knows himself well*; he knows what he really is. That view implies that it would not be true humility to speak of oneself as less than one knew oneself to be.[143] Bernard can point to various ladders and sets of steps: Benedict's Rule with its twelve steps to truth, the ten commandments; Jacob's ladder.[144] He approaches the subject of the steps of humility with a twist: he takes the reader down the steps of pride. The ladder climbed by those who go up is the same as the ladder descended by those who go down.[145]

Bernard's first step of pride is curiosity. This is a term which had a technical and to modern eyes a suprisingly pejorative sense, at least since Augustine. Curiosity is the urge to know things one should not wish to know.[146] The reason one should not want to know them is that they will lead one astray from concentration upon the things of God, from God himself. A monk begins to become distracted. He is always listening and looking, to discover things which are not his business and which take his mind away from its concentration on God. The only proper lifting up of the eyes to look about one is the lifting of the eyes to heaven.[147] A humble monk practises *custody* of eyes and mind alike.

The second step of pride is levity of mind. The mind which is frequently distracted from God by trivial and unworthy things gradually comes to enjoy them. That enjoyment runs counter to the qualities of gravity and restraint which are exemplified in the humble.[148]

The monk descending the ladder of pride moves on to a third step, where he is always self-satisfied with his achievements in the spiritual life. If he has done something wrong, it slips from his mind; but he is keen to point out others' faults. He is empty-headed and giggling.[149]

The fourth step down takes the proud monk to boasting. He boasts of his virtues, telling others how to be virtuous like him.[150] That leads to the fifth step, which is showing off. It is not enough for the monk now to assert his greater virtue. He needs to be seen to outdo others in good works. Whatever the Rule requires, he does it more or better, for example, eating less than his brothers when he is fasting. He would rather starve his body than his pride, says Bernard shrewdly.[151]

The sixth step is to receive others' compliments complacently. The monk's test is now not his own motivation but the good opinion of others.[152] Once he is convinced of his own superiority, it seems natural to the proud man to expect to be put in the highest place at meetings, to be heard first. He expects to be promoted, and if he is not he says that the abbot is jealous of him.[153]

If this paragon makes a mistake and is called to account for it, he will not admit it. He will deny that he has done it. Or he will admit that he has done it and say that he was nevertheless right to do so. If that is impossible, he may try to pretend that the sin was not as bad as it looked. If that is impossible, he will say he meant well. All these run counter to the duty a monk has under Benedict's Rule to admit his sins humbly and to express contrition.[154]

But our proud man may appear to do that. He may confess, but hypocritically, not believing inwardly that he has done anything wrong. He may confess very loudly, beating his breast and making a great matter of it. The test to which a perceptive abbot will submit him is to impose a heavy penance. A truly contrite sinner will embrace penance willingly. Not so the proud man; he will grumble.[155]

If there is an attempt to call him to account by requiring him to submit to the judgement of the whole community, he may take the tenth step of pride, which is open revolt. Now he is indeed on the road to hell. He feels free to sin, not yet quite free, since his conscience still sometimes checks him. But with the twelfth step he moves into habitual sin and becomes malevolent.[156] His will for good is corrupted.[157] Disobedience consists not in not acquiescing, but in refusing to acquiesce (*nolle acquiescere*).[158]

Bernard summarises the steps of pride by grouping them: the first six show contempt for the proud man's fellows, the second group for his superior, the last two for God himself.[159]

Now this is all practical, pastoral theology. *Purposeful* following of the Rule is not a necessary consequence of the monk's profession. That is to say, it does not happen automatically. Cluny seduced Robert of Châtillon. It allowed sloth and called it 'contemplation'. It commended feasting and condemned fasting; it told this young monk that God did not mean us to suffer; that he gave us food so that we might enjoy eating it.[160] Everyone at Cluny flattered him, so as to encourage him to stay.[161]

Bernard's consistent argument is that that will not do. A monastic theology is a theology of effort and self-discipline, of persistence of purpose.

ACADEMIC THEOLOGY

Bernard and a Different Sort of Learning

We have been describing a monastic theology in which the realities are spiritual. That does not, to a twelfth-century reader, make them the less intellectual.[1] When Anselm, in the ontological argument of his *Proslogion* (II–IV), made the leap from the notion that the God who is 'that-than-which-nothing-greater-can-be-thought' exists in the mind to the assertion that he must also exist in reality,[2] he was speaking not merely philosophically, but in the terms of a world of thought in which reality has a spiritual and even a devotional dimension. *Animus* is not *anima*; mind is not soul; however, and increasingly, in the world of the school and in the understanding of scholars in Bernard's lifetime, the cultivation of the former was taking place in some kinds of school in a forum not primarily concerned with the growth of the latter.

Was conflict between school and cloister a real issue to Bernard?[3] One must not push the perception of a 'trend' too far. It is open to question whether there was a sufficiently developed 'school' tradition at this date for it to be possible to conceive of such an opposition other than at the level of personalities with a preference for one approach rather than another, where it was certainly sometimes actively expressed. Nevertheless, a certain amount of ground can be laid. It is uncontroversial that Bernard was not 'academically' trained in the way Abelard and Gilbert of Poitiers were. He never had that kind of schooling. Bernard was never a student himself in one of the new schools growing up around such masters. He never gave the time they did to the study of the texts they exploited to such innovative effect. He never experienced at first-hand the temptations of the excitement, the challenge, the incipient adversariality, the scope for making one's name. He never sharpened his wits by challenging his master in a lecture on logic.

How well then did Bernard really understand any difference we might now point to between the 'academic' and the 'monastic' theology of the day? He had ample opportunity to hear *reports* of what was being taught in the schools, through his correspondence with Hugh of St. Victor and with William of St. Thierry, who had been reading Abelard, and through his travels in northern France, preaching in Paris and elsewhere and talking to students and masters. No doubt Geoffrey of Auxerre, who became his secretary in 1145, was able to help him with an account of more recent work. But such reportage is not the same as reading intensively and extensively for oneself. And these individuals had their axes to grind and will have given him a slanted view. That certainly happened in the process of persuading Bernard to take up the cudgels against Peter Abelard, as we shall see in a later chapter.[4]

Knowledge is a talent to be used, says Bernard. He replies to Bruno, archbishop-elect of Cologne, who had written to ask whether he should accept the bishopric. 'You are afraid, and with justification, for I fear it myself, that you might do wrong if you did not put the talent of knowledge which has been committed to you to use.'[5] So Bernard did not think the possession of knowledge unimportant, or that duties did not attach to having and using it.

And he was far from being a bigoted opponent of the use of secular studies, including grammar, logic, rhetoric, the quadrivium of arithmetic, music, geometry, and astronomy, or of any other technical assistance which might prove illuminating. He would not want to be seen altogether to condemn the liberal arts. It is not the skill but the mode and purpose of the use of the skill which disturbs him. Indeed, in a sermon on the Song of Songs, he emphasises that he does not want to prohibit the study of the *artes* or to give the impression that he thinks them of little account.[6] He takes a sensible, moderate view of several of the vexing questions of the day concerning their use.

Reasoning may be formal, logical, and then Bernard will be suspicious of it, unless it is conducted in the loving spirit of a seeker after truth whose eyes are fixed on God.[7] Bernard was impatient with verbal subtleties of a type different from his own. He describes Abelard's reasoning as a war of words (*pugnae verborum*) marred by novelties of expression (*novitates vocum*).[8]

The scholar striving for exactitude, as Abelard and Gilbert were, trying to enlarge technical language so that it could encompass and express ideas not put into words before, pushing at the boundaries of the subject, is ridiculed by someone who is, ironically, himself skilled with words, but in a quite different way.[9]

Gilbert of Poitiers, says the commentator and diarist John of Salisbury from firsthand knowledge, was able to draw on a wider range of patristic sources than was Bernard, although he did not know the Bible so well. His especial skill was in bringing together knowledge from different disciplines and applying them one to another, but with the strictest regard for the proprieties governing each.[10] He could be obscure.[11] Gilbert of Poitiers was slow to be roused, but once stirred to vigorous debate he became a great deal more comprehensible.[12] John of Salisbury clearly recognises that Bernard had a different sort of learning from Gilbert of Poitiers. He speaks of their prominence *in dissimilibus studiis*. He identified Bernard's skills as they appeared to a worldly observer. John says that Bernard was outstanding in the elegance of his style (*singulariter eleganti pollebat stilo*). He was steeped *in litteris divinis*, so that he could 'fittingly expound' the whole of Scripture: *decentissime explicaret*. Bernard had mastered the words; indeed, he had made them his own to such a degree that he could hardly write except in the words of Scripture.[13] That is visibly true in the texts which survive.

John of Salisbury acknowledges that Abelard gave as good as he got in response to Bernard's campaign of vilification against him after Sens. Abelard denounced Bernard, in return, as a seeker after vainglory and someone who disapproved of everyone who disagreed with him.[14] That is more than sour grapes; it gives us a glimpse of a Bernard who could be active in instigating attacks upon academic theology.

It is in the context of this clash, both of personalities and of areas of relevant expertise, that we must set any attempt to characterise the contrast of cloister and school in Bernard's mind.

Making Sure: Opinion, Faith, and Certainty

William of St. Thierry was alert to the problem that faith seems something essentially uncertain, a mere *aestimatio* of things unseen. Can that mean that our common faith is no more than an *aestimatio*, and that everyone can believe what he likes? Clearly that cannot be right. All Christians must hold the same faith.[15] As an apologist for the faith and a defender of the simple among the faithful, Bernard had one sure and important ground for disquiet about academe. Academic study can offer no certainties. Scholars are always changing their minds. John of Salisbury, who studied in the schools while Abelard and Gilbert of Poitiers were teaching in them, speaks of an *academicum fere ad omnia fluctuantem*.[16] Bernard thought certainty important to the welfare of the faithful. The need to protect souls from having their confidence overturned was uppermost in his mind in all his theologising. Although it seems he thought the unity of Christianity could not ultimately be broken, truth itself can be endangered by a heretic, Bernard claims.[17] It can even be set at risk by the wrong kind of intellectual enquiry. Bernard says in a letter to a Cardinal that academics are not interested in the truth, only in fables.[18]

He contributes something in this context to a debate of the period about the place faith occupies in the conspectus of 'opinion', 'faith', and 'certainty'. Paradoxically, in view of his worries about logic being taken too far, he explains that understanding depends on 'reason' and to that degree it can be secure. What stands to reason will *ipso facto* be reasonable. There lies certainty: *Certissima . . . probatio et indubitabile argumentum*.[19] So Bernard was not hostile to reason. That would have run counter to the belief Bernard shares with all his Christian contemporaries that it is in his capacity for rationality that man most closely resembles the Creator. Augustine took that for granted, and Bernard had no quarrel with Augustine. A rational being will see that it ought to love God because that is where its happiness lies. It will wish to conform its will with that of God because it will see the reasonableness of God's wishes.[20]

Here, Bernard begins from the faculty of reason, reason understood as a power of the soul. There is always some slippage between *anima* and *animus* here. It is the soul with which Bernard naturally has the highest concern, for souls, not minds, are what have to be saved.[21] The conversion[22] and care ('cure') of souls comes before everything else.[23] But in this epistemological context, the soul is treated as the seat and faculty of knowledge.

Keeping within the Augustinian tradition, Bernard says that the soul is nothing but reason, memory, and will.[24] In the sinner, this faculty of reason cannot work properly. It is blind, because it cannot visualise the situation in which it finds itself; it is too ill to function properly; it perceives the dirt and mess within but cannot see what to do about it.[25] Memory and will are similarly impeded from discharging their function.

One of the things reasoning may do is *prove*. *Probatio, probare* have various senses in Bernard's writings. Perhaps the leading theme is that of a 'testing' (*probare fidem*).[26] The shedding of blood for Christ may seem a proof of someone's faith, but it is a proof man, not God, needs to see, for God already knows who the true believers are.[27] There is also a notion of 'proving' by experience.[28]

The converse of proving is disproving.[29] There is the possibility of showing something to be not so, as well as of showing it to be so. There is an idea that proof may be discriminating, that is, that it may press for exactitude.[30] But the main idea is of making certain. 'It is required of you that you prove not by word or tongue, but by work and by truth, that I was not deceived and that you were not a liar': *a vobis exigitur, non verbo aut lingua, sed opere et veritate probare, nec me fuisse fallacem, nec vos mendacem*.[31] Not to make something certain may be to threaten someone's faith. Here *probatio* is contrasted with *reprobatio*.[32]

Between 'proof' giving some degree of certainty, and disproof taking it away, is opinion. Opinion rests on what *appears* to be true, but which it is recognised may prove not to be so when more evidence or conflicting reasons appear. Bernard's concern is that, when the holder does not recognise the provisional character of his grounds for thinking as he does, there is the risk of what is mere opinion being mistaken for certainty.[33]

Faith has a security which cannot in the end depend on reasoning, for it rests on authority. It has a 'certainty' where 'opinion' does not; but the basis of that certainty may remain obscure in the sense that it cannot necessarily be demonstrated. There remains an element of trust. It is of the essence of faith that it is trusting. It makes its commitment in reliance upon a person. Certainty depends on the locus of the trust, and if the trust is lodged in Christ it is secure indeed.[34]

That view may expose faith to the risk of seeming no more than 'opinion', for certainty can point confidently to its reasons. It should be realised that faith has its own certainty, and that it is a certainty of a different order from anything which can be demonstrated, perhaps, paradoxically, because it involves trust in things not seen.

Faith may, however, still be deemed 'reasonable'. It is reasonable when it thinks at all points as it should about Christ, so that it cannot be diverted from the purity of the Church's teaching by any mere appearance of truth, or by any heretical or devilish devices.[35] Bernard sees the abuse of reasoning (to weave complex and misleading arguments which go over people's heads) as a threat to a simplicity of faith, which must of its nature be characterised by this proper and necessary trust. Faith does not argue; it accepts.

But an attitude of patient acceptance is potentially dangerous. There must be grounds for confidence that the trust will not be misplaced. Bernard lived before the debates of the sixteenth century about Scripture's special, indeed unique, place as authority in matters of faith. He accorded it that place naturally. But he saw no contradiction between that position and the confidence that the Church would teach the faith reliably. The *fidelitas* which is an expression of obedience to superiors in the monastic life is also appropriate, in his view, in the submissive attitude of the faithful soul to the teaching of the Church.

We shall come back to this theme later. Its relevance here is that Bernard sees a danger when reasoning is used to *challenge* the faith and thus make it seem *unreasonable*. Bernard claims that Abelard's fault is to think that all matters of faith are susceptible of analysis by reasoning.[36] Indeed, Bernard contends that Abelard thinks nothing ought to be believed until it has been established by reasoning, and moreover a reasoning which is inherently disputatious.[37]

So Bernard is mistrustful, not of reason but of some of its uses, not of 'reason' but of 'reasoning'; not of 'reasoning' *per se* but of misdirected reasoning. This may take various forms. His strictures on the need for vigilance about overconfidence are matched with a warning about enquiring inappropriately into what is *supra nos*. Bernard would consider that an enquirer was doing that if he tried to press with reason alone beyond the boundaries of the mysteries of faith. That is why he dislikes Abelard's aggressive and arrogant style, for Abelard seems presumptuously to think reason can do more than in fact it can.

Anselm is clear about the inability of reasoning to penetrate deep mysteries, but he thinks reason ought to go as far as it can.[38] Bernard says the same sort of thing, though he believes that there are ways in which we should seek to get above ourselves by an upward spiritual striving. For both men, it is important that a 'Christian' philosophy know its place. Its researches do not go beyond the bounds of what is appropriate to it to explore.[39] There are things which are on a level with us as human beings, things below, and things above.[40] A Christian philosophy is consequently characterised by a proper humility and marked by a tendency to bear fruit in hope and charity, and, paradoxically, also by a gigantic ambition. 'We desire wholeheartedly to go above ourselves [*supra nos*] in knowledge of him, and we are snatched away to him in rapture with all the force of our spirit.[41]

A Christian Philosophy

It is hard to say how Bernard would have defined the scope of the academic discipline we now call 'theology'. *Theologia* was still not at this date the natural term to use for the study of the Christian belief system.[42] *Studium sacrae scripturae* would be more usual. Bernard does not use the term *theologia* except in the context of his debate with Peter Abelard.[43] There it was forced upon him by Abelard's choice of title for his own book on the subject. So Bernard uses the word *theologia* only pejoratively, pairing it with *stultilogia*, 'foolish talk': *in primo limine Theologiae, vel potius Stultilogiae suae*.[44]

Philosophia was the word for precisely the secular-minded questioning researches which Bernard observed to be so unstable in their orientation and their outcomes. *Philosophia* had a respectable history as a word used to describe the intellectual researches of Christians into their faith.[45] Augustine was happy to employ it in that way. Bernard understood in almost Augustinian[46] terms that there exists a *Christian philosophia*, a love of a wisdom spiritual as well as intellectual. He uses the term 'philosopher' approvingly in his sermon for the Feast of St. Clement when he calls Clement ' a philosopher of that day': *illius temporis philosophus*.[47] The right kind of 'philosopher' is exemplified by St. Paul; his philosophy is better than the philosophy of this world.[48] Preaching for the Feast of Saints Peter and Paul, Bernard calls both 'our teachers'. But, he says, 'they do not teach us to read Plato or to become entangled in nets'; nor to be 'always learning and never come to the knowledge of the truth.'[49] For secular 'philosophy' can be a trap that trammels the pursuer: *quid tamen? Si te philosophiae huic totum repente devoveris.*[50] In Abelard's *Dialogue of Christian, Philosopher, Jew*, the Philosopher argues against, not for, the faith.

Philosophy could, then, within carefully defined limits, be a study perfectly proper to Christians. It is that with which we must begin, in trying to get a sense of what it was that made Bernard uneasy about the academic study of theology.

When he wrote his book *On Loving God*, Bernard himself spoke modestly of his poor expertise in this area. Nevertheless he puts a sting in the tail of his disclaimer—he will say something regardless, in case his silence is taken to suggest that he is a 'philosopher' of the wrong kind: *accipite de mea paupertate quod habeo, ne tacendo philosophus puter.*[51]

Both learned and unlearned may aspire to a properly Christian 'love of wisdom'. Yet Bernard recognised and respected expertise. He speaks of the specialist knowledge of a physician: *medicus aliquis et physicae peritus intellectum etiam habet.*[52] He notes the expertise of the lawyer. It is not disturbing to those expert in the law if we go on in the manner of those who know little, as the law of love requires.[53]

What, in Bernard's view, is the place of the study of the classics and other secular writings in a Christian's reading? One answer is that they have a place alongside the Bible and the Fathers. To Gilbert the Universal, bishop of London from 1128 to 1135, Bernard says, 'Undoubtedly you are a wise man, taking your pleasure in all the books and studies of the wise men of the world, and studying the divine Scriptures so as to give life to their meaning and apply it to the present day.'[54]

But 'alongside' is not the same as 'on equal terms'. The ancient philosophers may simply get it wrong.

Bernard censures the classical philosopher—here Plato in the *Timaeus*—for looking for a material cause. The wrong kind of philosopher asks the wrong kind of question. God does not need matter, he says; he makes his own. *Frustra philosophi materiam quaerant: non eguit materia Deus.*[55]

The classical philosophers are, moreover, characterized by a love of the vain and the trivial. The 'philosophers of the gentiles' are mentioned in Scripture. By a misplaced faith they are given up to the pursuit of vain things.[56] Although they knew God, they did not recognise him to be God. They did not glorify him as God.[57] Everything under the sun is vanity, cries Bernard in this vein, in a sermon for the Feast of St. John the Baptist.[58] By that he means that knowledge sought in this wrong and unbelieving spirit is 'empty'. Not only faith but truth itself excludes vanity. For where truth is in full occupation, there is no 'room' for vanity's emptiness: *Non enim est quo vanitas intret, ubi veritas iam totum occupavit.*[59]

Bernard's basic intellectual distinction is thus between a true wisdom and a vain curiosity.[60] A good deal of the *De Gradibus Humilitatis* is about the dangers of *curiositas*. *Curiositas* is trivial and irresponsible and unworthy enquiry. Bernard knows this to be pursuit of a knowledge which does not lead to salvation. It is, paradoxically, the *more* seductive as it is the more vain. He is so concerned about it that he gives nearly as much of the treatise to this stage of pride as he does to the other eleven *gradus* together.

In a series of 'Sentences', Bernard links 'knowledge for its own sake' with *curiositas*. Knowledge acquired so as to show off he connects with vanity; knowledge obtained so as to edify a brother he conjoins with love. By contrast, knowledge sought for the love of God and to build up life he classifies with wisdom.[61] Some seek knowledge for the sake of knowing, and that is vanity; some get knowledge so as to sell it, and that is a simoniacal wickedness (*simoniaca pravitas*). Again by contrast, some 'know' so that they may build up others and themselves, and that is holy love (*pia caritas*).[62]

'This wisdom of this world is folly in the sight of God.' The foolishness through which it pleased him to save the world, so that he might confound the wisdom of the world, indeed confounded the wise.[63] *Sapientia mundi, quae stultitia est apud deum.*[64] God chooses the foolish things of this world to confound the wise. *Elegit Deu . . . stulta mundi, ut confundat sapientes.*[65] What God regards as wisdom and what God regards as foolishness are the reverse of what the reader may expect.

Much of this is common ground in Christian apologetics. But in Bernard a further, unexpected, feature of the true, Christian philosophy, is its practicality. For, on the face of it, philosophy is essentially abstract. Peter and Paul, says Bernard, 'have taught me to live. Do you think it is a small thing to know how to live?'[66]

In the *De Consideratione*, Bernard suggests a grand plan for what is to follow. The best way for Pope Eugenius III to obtain the fruits of the investigation upon which consideration will take him is, Bernard says, for him to look systematically at himself, and then successively at what is below, around, and above him.[67] The integrity of the person, his orderly conformity with what he ought to be, is important. If the highest place is filled by a person of the lowest character, that is an enormity, says Bernard. The best defence against that is for the individual who occupies that office to know his own faults and seek to remedy them.[68] That involves some applied philosophising.

So the first section of what follows constitutes Bernard's treatise on knowing one's place, his equivalent perhaps of Abelard's *Scito seipsum*. Bernard preached a sermon on this theme.[69] His argument is that honest self-appraisal will teach the pope—and by extension every Christian—two things above all: that he is unworthy, and that he is nevertheless made in the image of God. Without this double realisation, no one can know anything else, for he will not be able to approach the task of knowing with the wisdom Christian philosophy requires.

And one should not lose sight of what one has been and known, for all that should form part of the process of learning more. It is especially important, in Bernard's view, that Eugenius should never forget that he was a monk, for it remains Bernard's firm conviction that in the monastic life lies the best possibility of achieving perfection in this world, better than that which is in prospect for a pope who is not a monk at heart.

These notions cast further light on Bernard's conception of the relationship between 'knowledge' and 'wisdom'. To know with *wisdom* is to know with a kind of wholeness, and in a way which readily applies what has been learned to the individual's own situation. The model is the Father's sending of his Son, the Word. He sends out the Word, but the Word does not leave him; he is always with him. Your closest brother is your mother's only son, your very self, he tells Eugenius.[70] The lesson is that one should not spend time on any getting of knowledge which is not conducive to salvation. By definition, a 'Christian' philosophy is concerned with salvation, for Bernard's categorical imperative is salvation.[71]

Those, then, are Bernard's position markers. They include no real surprises except his confidence in the application of Christian philosophy to the living of a good Christian life.

An Intellectual Spirituality

If we are to argue the centrality of *consideratio* to Bernard's system of thought, it has to be asked why Bernard discusses speculative theology so extensively *only* in this last book of the *De Consideratione*. It has been suggested that the reason is that he had only just discovered Boethius or perhaps Plato's *Timaeus*.[72] But there is no need for such a postulate. The fifth book is a natural outworking of the theory he has been exploring in the first four. He needs to be able to explain to the pope not only what he is authoritative over, but also what is authoritative over him. To that end, he needs to set out for the pope his place in the spiritual and intellectual as well as the ecclesiastical and political hierarchy.

It would be surprising if Bernard did not touch from time to time on classical philosophical themes, stock points of interest to antiquity which recur
in twelfth-century discussions. But they are strikingly few. And for the most
part, they, too, are commonplaces.[73] There is reference to Aristotle's *Categories*, though Bernard could have acquired that through reading the discussions of Augustine and Boethius on the problems raised by the *Categories*
in Trinitarian theology.[74] Bernard's theory of knowledge and his view on
the role of body and senses is explored in one of the sermons on the Song of
Songs.[75] In the sermon for the Feast of All Saints, Bernard explains that
the *sapientes mundi* make a division of the soul into rational, irascible, con-
cupiscible. Concupiscence has its positive and its negative, too, in desire and
contempt. Irascibility also has two opposing faces, in 'good humour' and
'anger'. Bernard asks whether this worldly philosophy corresponds with
everyday experience. Knowledge and ignorance, he suggests, are like the
having and the not-having of the same thing (*habitus* and *privatio*). This is
also an Aristotelian idea which was transmitted by Boethius. There is a reference to the Aristotelian substance and quality of the *Categories* in a Sermon
on the Assumption: *virtutis enim species, et non veritas, quasi qualitas est, non
substantia*. But this is once more such a commonplace of Augustinian and
medieval discussion that it can hardly be taken as significant evidence in
itself of an awareness of the philosophical categories as an area of expertise
in their own right.[76]

What, then, does Bernard have to offer as a philosopher that is new or
distinctive? It is fair to say that there is not a great deal He speaks of a chaste
and holy love, which to possess is to become like God. *O amor sanctus et castus
. . . Sic affici, deificari est*.[77] For Bernard 'love' is thus an instrument of deifi-
cation,[78] a means of returning from the 'realm of unlikeness' to God to a
region of 'likeness'. It is the approach to a right relationship with God. But
it is an intellectual as well as an affective exercise, and here perhaps is something more Bernardine than Augustinian. Augustine's is an intellectual spirituality. Bernard's is an intellectual affect. Nevertheless, the main source of
Bernard's seeing things this way is likely to have been Augustine. Augustine
envisaged the heavenly encounter of the soul and God in eternity as a
'mutual gazing' of the understanding.[79] For Bernard, it is intense in feeling
as well as in concentration.

The vocabulary of this discussion is by no means settled, though it is possible to see trends within it. Chalcidius, commenting on Plato's *Timaeus*,
defines 'consideration' in rather this way as contemplation, as something

primarily directed towards the divine: *consideratio . . . ob assiduam contemplationem rerum divinarum et immortalium nominata*.[80] There is therefore a conjoining of the metaphysical with the physical. That is the axis in classical philosophy. The content of a Christian spirituality of divine love is not yet present. Boethius—in whom we may postulate a different understanding if he was indeed a Christian, and even if he was not, since he had access to Christian writing—has a developed view. He explains that there are as many kinds and branches of speculative philosophy as there are proper subjects of consideration.[81] *Visio* and *contemplatio* were used by Augustine as ways of describing *speculatio*.[82] Augustine also has the idea that speculation is 'seeing a *long* way' (*longe videre*).[83] Jerome links *speculatio* and *intuitus dei*.[84] Gregory the Great mentions that various Hebrew words mean *speculatio*: Maspha, Bethel, Sion. Cassiodorus adopts the stock idea that in Scripture 'Sion' means *speculatio* and also the Church.[85] Cassiodorus also describes *speculatio* as that through which God is gazed upon in the hearts of the faithful: *per quam deus fidelium corde prospicitur*.[86] Cassiodorus links in his usage of *speculatio* the Augustinian idea of a 'gazing into the eyes of God' and the idea that the 'place' where we do it is both the soul and the Church. It is, in short, an activity within that marriage which the soul makes individually with Christ and which the Church as a whole 'enjoys with Christ', both of which are celebrated in the Song of Songs.

For Bernard, consideration is *active* thinking, giving life to any sensible images it produces, but essentially independent of such images for getting its results. To gaze on God without the assistance of images drawn from the senses is an indication of a purity truly angelic. Human virtue is marked by a freedom from enslavement to bodily desires and an ability to think without bodily assistance. The creature goes out of itself and transcends itself. Then the eyes of the mind 'see' internally, not prompted by outward things. Bernard does not use the phrase *oculus mentis*. He does, however, use *oculus cordis*, which equally refers to the 'eyes of the mind'. He takes for granted Augustine's view that sin has the effect of clouding the mind and making it impossible to think straight.[87] Because of sin, there can be a confusion of the eye of the mind to be cleared.[88] The vision of the eye of the mind is sharpened by doing works of mercy.[89] Similarly, the inner 'hearing' does not depend upon the ears. It is a sense which attends to an inner voice, just as the eyes of the mind see images within.[90]

Bernard outlines a theory of the way in which 'understanding' may be gained that is strongly geared to the 'linear progression' notions of 'return from exile', of 'pilgrimage', and of 'ladder climbing'—which are such consistent leading ideas in his thought. Consideration is exploratory. It is trying to find out that which it does not yet know for sure.[91] The Christian, he argues, has a well-marked 'path' to such knowledge. By reading Scripture he can contemplate invisible things directly. He does not have to climb a ladder through the impressions of the senses, forming images for the understanding to grasp, in the way outlined by Augustine and others.[92]

Three kinds of *consideratio* can be identified in Bernard,[93] for there are, he suggests, three modes of attaining knowledge. The first is practical, employing the evidence of the senses in the endeavour to behave well in the sight of God; the second is scientific, knowledge oriented, that is, attained by diligent study of all the evidence so as to find God; the third is speculative, involving a direct intellectual apperception of the truth, which becomes possible to the soaring spirit when it throws itself in trust upon divine assistance.[94]

The three modes of consideration in Bernard's thought can thus be summarised in this way:

1. *Dispensativa*, which uses the sense and sensible realities for the common good (*socialiter*).[95] That means examining how they can be applied.
2. Exploratory (*ad vestigandum*). This kind of consideration climbs steps, *gradus*, by philosophical methods (*philosophando*); it is a reflective *aestimatio*, investigating and weighing (*scrutans et ponderans*).[96] So again, it involves 'considered' intellectual effort, calmly inquiring and weighing.
3. Speculative consideration is *se in se colligens*,[97] *consideratio* at its highest. Here, 'philosophy' is done in such a way as to bring the mind to a just estimate of itself. This is an internal process.

Bernard takes it for granted that the way to knowledge of God is upwards, that the spiritual is above the material.[98] Like others of his period, he makes no difficulty about carrying inferences across the boundary between natural and supernatural, although that does not mean that he blurs the distinction. The *excessus* of rapture goes outside the mind (*excessus mentis*),[99] and there is a journey into a new dimension of being.[100] It is, Bernard insists, a *raptus*, a snatching away, rather than an ascent.[101]

All this places intellectual endeavour, and especially intellectual inquiry, properly and squarely in the arena of an affective spirituality for the Bernardine Christian philosopher. What is the mode or methodology of this intelligent and enquiring spirituality, in which love and thought are conjoined? One answer Bernard gives is in terms of the kisses of the Song of Songs. Bernard is reticent about his own knowledge of the state or condition of rapture, but there are strong hints that he had some experience of it. Bernard speaks of a 'mutual knowing' of Bridegroom and Bride, which makes it possible for the Bride to become familiar with Christ. There is *agnitio*, in which there is love and intimacy, frequent converse, and kisses.[102]

The Bride's sleep in the Song of Songs (2.7) is taken by Bernard to be a figure of this rapture or *ecstasis* or *excessus*. This passage of the Song of Songs seems to him supremely to exemplify this, and indeed to take matters beyond speculation to a higher state, close to the true mystical union of heaven in eternity.

Bernard begins his exegesis from the Bridegroom's holding the Bride in his arms to protect her from being disturbed. God did not disdain to bend down to protect our weakness in this way in a sweet and familiar companionship, he says. He *came* to the soul, in her exile.[103]

Yet the sleep of the Bride is not the peaceful repose of the body, nor is it like death in the normal sense.[104] It is like a death only in this, that in this sleep the soul is drawn out and flies away from the mind, so that it is able to 'think' in a way which is not possible by normal rational processes. The soul in ecstasy is cut off from consciousness of the world around it. It is as though it were a dove flying away to be at rest (Psalm 54.7).

Paradoxically, an escape from sense is an escape from death, for sensual desires are deadening. This is a death which does not take away life but enhances it. The body does not perish, but the soul is lifted up. Bernard would like to go further and to be like the angels in the corresponding 'death' of ecstasy that is possible to their nature. The angels, he thinks, are not only without the distractions of sense, but the very images of corporeal things pass away for them, and they become able to enter a converse with the pure likeness of God.[105]

This is what contemplation really means, says Bernard. This is its apotheosis. *Agnitio* carries the colouration of 'recognition' and 'knowing well' of *agnoscere*; for Bernard it is a knowledge which is the consummation of love,[106] a fullness of knowledge.[107]

Bernard is thus here in a region which is as much epistemological as spiritual and affective. He is saying both that the only kind of knowledge which is without distractions is that which knows directly, and without the assistance of images and comparisons; and that that is the highest and most accurate mode of knowledge *because* it is direct, using no intermediary aids.[108]

That does not mean that where there is no distraction there can be no interruption. Bernard implies that he knows rapture to be a state in which sinful human beings cannot remain for long. Rapture is only to be enjoyed for a moment in this life. Bernard returns to the gazelles of the fields (Song of Songs 2.7). The sleeping Bride is to be protected from their intrusion. Who are they? Bernard identifies them both with the souls of those who have already died and are thus for the moment freed of their bodies and with the angels who dwell in the presence of God. Bernard sees the experience of ecstasy as involving a concentration so absolute that even fellow souls in the same ecstasy ought to hesitate before they interrupt it. The Bride alone shall judge when she is ready to enjoy their companionship in her most intense experience of God.[109]

Rapture is not achieved without effort and determination. The Bride enters the King's chambers. Her handmaids cannot follow. They are too weak to run with the same passionate devotion as the Bride. They arrive after her, and that makes them too late to obtain entry.[110]

So Bernard can perhaps be said to offer an alternative to academic theology that fleshes it out, enlarges it, and offers a complementary system as a correction to what he perceives as its excesses. He does so without rejecting all it had to offer in his own day, but with a concern for its dangers sharply in his mind. What he thought those dangers were, we shall come to more fully in a later chapter on 'negative' theology.[111]

EXEGESIS AND THEOLOGY

Bernard's Knowledge of the Bible

'Your Word goes out from you irrevocably, Lord, and it will not come back to you empty, but it will do that which you sent it to do.'[1] Bernard is speaking of Christ here, but the Bible, too, is God's Word, and he is confident that the advice in the Bible is salvific: *scriptura salubriter monet*.[2] What, then, does Scripture do? Scripture is a 'witness',[3] testifying to God's will. Bernard commonly uses *scriptura* as shorthand for *scriptura sacra*. The terms *divina Scriptura* and *divina pagina* are also to be found in his writings. The key ideas, never far separated and communicated by *sacra* and *divina* in this context, are the holiness and divine inspiration of this special text. Scripture, for Bernard, is the Word of salvation (*verbum salutis*),[4] and, for him, the Bible was consequently the most important thing he read.

There was, to William of St. Thierry's mind, a hierarchy of importance. The 'songs' of the ancient patriarchs and prophets seem to excel in their treatment of Christ and the rational soul.[5] Bernard might not have put it so strongly, but he would have been familiar with and sympathetic to the general tendency of contemporary exegesis to give special prominence and attention to some books of the Bible.

The pattern of 'continuing education' under the Benedictine Rule was largely one of self-teaching. The Benedictine or Cistercian monk engaged

regularly in *lectio divina*, holy reading, by the method of patient, slow, reflective mental mastication of the text, 'chewing' and 'ruminating' until every
vestige of flavour and meaning had been extracted from it. William of
St. Thierry, again, speaks of 'revolving' and 'peering' at the text with a passionate love inspired by the Holy Spirit.[6] Bernard's later writing shows the
marks of this training in his complete familiarity with Scripture, to the point
where he can scarcely write a sentence without echoing a biblical text. Indeed, Bernard cites and echoes Scripture even where he is not quoting it and
commenting directly upon it, and arguably that is itself a mode of exegesis.

Bernard's use of the text of the Bible is not uniform. He makes limited
use of the Pentateuch, Joshua, Judges, Chronicles, Esdras. He had his preferred books, chiefly those which were everyone's favourite at this time—
the Psalms, the Wisdom books, the Gospels, the Pauline Epistles. He had
his especial favourites, such as the psalm *Qui Habitat* (Psalm 190).[7] For a given
purpose he would do research. He was asked a question about the celebration of a feast for the Maccabees and looked assiduously into the matter before replying.[8]

The development of the standard gloss on the Bible, the *Glossa Ordinaria*,
which was going on apace in his lifetime,[9] may partly have passed Bernard
by. The first collection of glosses which can be linked with the period
of Bernard's abbacy (possibly derived from the scriptorium of St. Victor)
arrived with Prince Henry, brother of Louis VII, far too late to have influ-
enced Bernard's intellectual formation. That does not mean he lacked
exegetical models or access to patristic comment.

The influences of Augustine, Gregory the Great, and other Fathers are
visible in his work. The contents of the library at Clairvaux at this early date
are not known, though there is an *a priori* likelihood that the profile of its
holdings resembled that of other monastic houses of the period. By the end
of the twelfth century there were copies of the Latin Fathers, homilies of
Origen, a homiletic collection going under the name of Chrysostom, letters
and treatises of Cyprian, letters and sermons of Leo, and works of Isidore,
Bede, Rabanus Maurus, Paschasius Radbertus, and Florus of Lyons.[10] There
are indications that the abbey acquired large, handsome volumes of the
Fathers. In 1147–48, Philip, prior of Clairvaux, told the abbot of Liessies that
several works of Augustine he had requested could not be sent because they
were bound with others in big books. He asks the house to send a copyist to
Clairvaux with parchments, so that he may make copies.[11]

These are not merely bibliographical questions. They underline not only the type of thing Bernard may have read, but also the limitations of his reading when it is compared with that of opponents of his later life, such as Peter Abelard and Gilbert of Poitiers, who were familiar with another literature, on which they founded a method of criticism and analysis in which Bernard's education gave him no opportunity to gain an equal facility.

Bernard was, moreover, an extremely practical exegete. He liked to emphasize the way the teaching of the Bible chimes with the ordinary experience of life,[12] perceiving that coherence is an exegetical activity in its own right. So theology can be drawn from exegesis taken with observation of daily life. The sequence of Christ's life shows that someone who has been circumcised still needs to be baptised, although, Bernard contends, there is no need for a baptised person to be circumcised.[13] It ought to be asked why Christ himself was circumcised. It would have seemed scandalous to contemporaries if he had not, says Bernard, just as today the Church would be scandalised if an infant was not baptised. So Christ submitted out of humility, not necessity.[14]

There was one further dimension of Bernard's exegesis,[15] which was his idea that Scripture should be used for the winning of infidels and heretics to, or back to, the faith. This was common ground with his contemporaries. William of St. Thierry says in his preface to his commentary on Paul's Epistle to the Romans that Romans is full of complications. He does not intend to seek to unravel them all, certainly not by himself. He is going to gather together the views of the Fathers; no more. His readers can expect not the presumption of novelty and vanity but the solid authority of the Fathers. That will dress his little bird up in sufficiently bright feathers. The purpose of the whole is to provide something substantial by way of argumentative ammunition against the Jews and against heretics. A similar consciousness is visible in Peter the Venerable.[16]

Interpretation

It was a well-established principle that the text of Scripture was capable of interpretation. That could mean merely unfolding, *expositio*. Bernard speaks of the 'exposition of the preceding part' (*expositio praecedentis partis*)[17] of one of Gilbert of Poitiers's 'dubious interpretations' (*suspecta expositio*).[18]

But *interpretatio* could mean more than one thing. The *interpres* was a 'translator'. Jerome so described himself, and it was his conviction that his translation was not in itself divinely inspired. That has the implication that he understood that in rendering the text of Scripture in another language, he was also placing a particular construction on its sense. Bernard uses *interpres* and *interpretatio* in the sense of 'translator' with reference to Jerome. 'Our interpreter bears witness that that is a common word in Hebrew': *Testatur autem interpres noster in hebraeo verbum esse commune*.[19] On the other hand, Bernard sometimes also seems to take *interpretatio* to refer to interpretation in the wider sense. 'Those armies which are called "Cherubim," if that interpretation [or translation] is allowable': *Illi tamen agmina, quae Cherubim nuncupatur, si eis sui vocabuli servetur interpretatio*.[20]

It was well understood that *translatio* may take place within a single language. It involves a movement from a given signification to another, often a metaphorical one.[21] But here, as in the use made of Jerome's translation into Latin and despite Jerome's warning, it was universally assumed in Bernard's day that the text would support any amount of scrutiny for the purposes of interpretation because it was itself as much the inspired Word as the *verba* uttered by God in the ears of the authors of Scripture had been. The iconography encouraged that view, with its pictures of the Holy Spirit as a dove with its beak in the ears of the Evangelists.

The Meanings of the Text

On Titus 3.4, which says that the kindness and humanity of our Saviour was apparent at the Epiphany: *Apparuit benignitas et humanitas Salvatoris nostri*, Bernard comments: 'We have heard in the Gospel how the Magi entered and found the boy with his mother, Mary. It is obvious that they found exactly that, for Jesus took real flesh. But his second epiphany was at his baptism and then the Father bore witness to him, the heavens opened and the Holy Spirit descended like a dove and the Father said "This is my beloved Son".'[22] There are things which 'appear' only in a further investigation of the text.

No one in Bernard's day thought the text of Scripture had only one meaning. Everyone took it for granted not only that there are several significations to be attached to given passages, but that some of them had to be searched for, because they would not be immediately apparent on the surface. It was an important assumption for the monastic scholar that this search took care and thoroughness. To find these additional spiritual senses requires hard work—not merely 'study' but the living of a virtuous life in obedience to the commandments of God. 'Not the letter but the spirit; not learning but the following of the Lord's commandments': *Non littera, sed spiritus; non eruditio, sed exercitatio in mandatis Domini*.[23]

Intus and *Foris*

In Acts (9.3) it says that suddenly light shone round about Paul. This was an outward light, explains Bernard, for hitherto Paul had been unable to perceive by the inward light (*intus adhuc luminis incapacem; qui necdum infundi poterat*). Now he was drenched in a divine illumination: *divina saltem circumfunditur claritate*. So that Paul should no longer be unable to take in what God wanted to tell him, the testimony entered by his eyes and his ears alike, for he also heard a voice.[24]

Clarity is a good thing, a *desideratum*, in teaching about God.[25] But it may not always be God's way. When Christ ascended on the appointed day, he went into the clouds. He was then not fully visible (*plane lucida*), but covered and overshadowed: *sed subobscura et obnubilata*.[26] So it is not inappropriate that his Word should also sometimes be full of secrets. The inner senses of Scripture are 'hidden'. Such a meaning is *reconditum*. The theme is repeated in myriad ways. The sense is within, the sound outside: *intus sensus, foris vox*. The sense is on the page, yet not on the page: *habet in codicibus, sed non in codicibus*.[27]

Yet *intus* is not always better than *foris*. There may be mere phantom appearances of truths. Those who are 'outwardly' seeking 'the splendour of righteousness' may be hypocrites and 'inwardly' only pretending: *Extra petentes nitorem iustitiae, intus habentes phantasmata simulationis*.[28] But broadly speaking, the presumption in Bernard's exegesis is that excavating the inner meaning is a profitable intellectual and spiritual exercise, and always the right thing for the exegete to do. 'When you listen to the Word of God, attend much more to what God is saying inwardly than to what man is saying outwardly, for that living and efficacious Word is the very voice of God, converting souls.'[29]

The literal sense is therefore incomplete, if only for the reason that it does not get the full spiritual benefit out of the text. The literal interpretation should certainly not be allowed to get in the way of that further exploration and prejudge the spiritual, warns Bernard: *Dummodo sane spiritualibus non praeiudicet sensibus litteralis interpretatio*.[30] What it says could sometimes be told more plainly only with another interpretation.[31] It is as though a full vessel were held in the hands and the holder would not open it so that its contents might be used for anointing. *Foris haeret in littera, contrectat manibus vas plenum et clausum, nec aperit ut ungatur*.[32]

One of the values of having the spiritual senses at the exegete's disposal is that they make it possible to get around the difficulty that the literal sense is sometimes very opaque indeed, and that is one reason why it is inclined to dominate the spiritual with its crude obviousness. The literal sense can even be repugnant. Augustine found it so as a young man, as he admits in the *Confessions*.[33]

The danger is worse even than that, for it lies—as the Bible itself acknowledges—in the risk that the letter may kill.[34] Bernard daringly classifies the literal sense with the teaching of secular wisdom and the philosophers in this respect. He claims that both can be called 'the letter which kills, according to the Apostle'.[35]

The presence of a spiritual sense rescues the text from its death-dealing capacity. When the spiritual sense is taken together with the literal as a salt or a spice, the poison finds its antidote: *Alioquin littera occidit, si abseque spiritus condimento glutieris*.[36] Another way of putting it is that the spiritual sense sugars the literal. A text may sound strict or severe according to the letter, but with spiritual interpretation it may taste sweet: *Et iuxta litteram quidem durum sonat; secundum spiritualem autem intelligentiam dulce sapit*.[37] A text may be hard on the outside but very sweet within: *Durus in cortice, sed suavissimus in medulla*.[38] The example Bernard is considering is from Matthew 4.3: 'If you are the Son of God, tell these stones to become bread.'

The spiritual sense thus has power to *transform* the literal. It is not merely an additional sense or senses. Even if the literal sense is itself beautiful, the spiritual may be more important or significant, *consequentius*, and clearer to the understanding and more useful to the conscience: *planius proper intelligentiam, utilius ad conscientiam*.[39]

Bernard speaks of the 'spiritual sense' here in a collective, generalising way, but in fact he, like his contemporaries, recognised three such senses, making four in all, with the literal or 'historical' sense. In some respects, this part of the exegetical heritage was, by Bernard's day, relatively straightforward.[40] Augustine had worked, with reluctant admiration, with the system of the Donatist Tichonius. Tichonius's was the method which under-lies Augustine's *De Doctrina Christiana*. The reluctance Augustine felt de-rived not from any dissatisfaction with the system but from the fact that Tichonius was a schismatic. When Augustine wrote, and in the West, it was still unclear how many spiritual senses there were and how they were to be identified. But Gregory the Great established four: the literal or historical, the tropological (or moral), the allegorical, and the anagogical (or prophetic). The term 'allegorical' was also used comprehensively for the three spiritual senses. The literal sense simply told the story it appeared to tell on a straight-forward reading. Moses was exposed on the waters by Pharaoh's daughter. That is historically true.[41] The allegorical pointed to a divine truth. The moral taught the Christian how to live. The anagogical promised him heaven.

Figurativeness

Durus est hic sermo, 'This is a hard saying,'[42] says Bernard, exploring 'Go, accursed ones, into eternal fire' (Matthew 25.41). 'The Lord was speaking of repentance, but in a *figure*, as to those to whom it was not given to know the mystery of the Kingdom of God.'[43] To say that there is a figurative mean-ing is different from claiming that there is a spiritual sense, for it bears on the technical differences in the ways in which the words signify. By a 'trans-ference' of their usual signification (*translatio*), words may mean not what they appear to mean but something else. Bernard refers a good deal in his exegesis to the questions of 'modes of signification' which were so highly interesting to contemporaries. He shows some awareness of what was afoot here in the contemporary academic world.

The leading idea was that a sound has to be attached to something, made to 'signify' it by some act of 'imposition', before it becomes a word or a name. (*Nomen* serves for both 'noun' and 'name' in the Latin.) One of Bernard's preferred terms is *designari*: *non incongrue designatur*.[44] 'For I believe this is not incongruously designated'; *Credo enim non incongrue . . . designari*.[45] Adversity is usually 'designated' by night in Scripture: *solet in divinis Scripturis adversitas designari per noctem*.[46]

Bernard speaks explicitly of 'imposition' in the Sermon for the Circum-cision of Christ when he is discussing the naming of Jesus. Up to that day, the angels could say they knew a heavenly secret. Jesus was 'named' before he was conceived in the womb. [47] He did not need an angel to name him. *Innatum ei hoc nomen, non inditum ab humana vel angelica creatura*.[48] Yet Jesus was 'named' by the angel (Luke 2.21). And *on* that day his name was 'imposed': *sed ego nunc primum ei fiducialiter salutis nomen impono*.[49] Bernard stresses that he was only so 'called' in that way (*vocatum*). The angel did not 'give' him the name in the way that Adam gave the animals names in Genesis but merely used it openly for the first time.

Jesus had many names according to the Prophet, who called him 'Wonderful', 'Counsellor', 'the Mighty God', and so on (Isaiah 9.6). The prophet did not mention this one name which was foretold by the angel, the one to which the Evangelist testifies when he says *'vocatum est nomen eius.'*[50] 'Where [in this list] is the name which is above all other names, the name of Jesus, at which every knee shall bow?' Perhaps, suggests Bernard, that one name is somehow to be found in all the others, *sed expressum quodammodo et effusum*.[51] All these appellations are comprised in the name 'Jesus', Bernard suggests, and perhaps they are spelt out so as to ensure that no one fails to be aware of them.[52]

Whichever way we look at it, the naming of Jesus and all language about God raises special problems, of which Bernard was highly conscious. It is against that background that the technical discussion of the day has to be set.

God's unity means that he has no parts, no number. He is simple in his nature and immutable. He is what he is (Exodus 3.14). So the bodily imagery of left hand and right hand used in the Song of Songs (2.6) would not readily seem to fit him. Nevertheless, Bernard argues, the Fathers teach us, and the usage of Scriptures shows, that it is appropriate to draw analogies from familiar created things in trying to understand divine mysteries. 'Adversity' and 'prosperity' are usually spoken of in terms of left hand and right hand. So it seems fitting to interpret these terms in the Song of Songs as meaning, on the one hand (the left) Christ's threat of punishment and on the other hand (the right), his promise of the reward of heaven.[53]

A word could have a straightforward or primary link with the thing signified, or it could have a link involving some 'transfer' of usage, as in a metaphor. The first might be described as 'proper', the second as 'improper'. In Bernard's day there were those who thought the reverse: that any sense attaching a word to God ought *ipso facto* to be considered the 'proper' sense, even though it seemed clearly figurative. When God is called the 'Father of mercies', who can fail to see that the Son is being referred to by his own name: *quis non videat vel proprio nomine Filium designari*.[54] That can arguably be held to be the 'proper' signification.

The idea that an interpretation should be 'fitting' is crucial. Fittingness is a strong idea in twelfth-century thought. It is far more than a vague belonging. It has to do with right order (*rectus ordo*). Bernard's favourite expression for this is not the Anselmian *decentia* or *convenientia*. But he does speak in terms of *aptari*: *Quibus non incongrue illud potest aptari*.[55] Bernard is especially fond of saying that a term is used *congrue* or *incongrue*. Sometimes the congruity is merely conceptual: *non incongrue dicitur*.[56] Sometimes there is some identifiable resemblance to be built on. Something may be 'not incongrously said to be freedom of choice': *non incongrue dicitur . . . liberum arbitrium*;[57] *ut non incongrue ut supra diffinivimus esse quod solet liberum arbitrium appellari*.[58] We say, not incongruously, that the angels are signified by the eyes [for they see God face to face], the patriarchs through the ears [for they heard the Lord speaking to them], the Prophets through the nostrils [for they were 'inspired' by the Holy Spirit]: *nec incongrue per oculos Angelos, per aures Patriarchas, per nares Prophetas, significari diximus*.[59] 'It is not incongruously that in this text the favour of human praise should be understood by "honey"': *potest non incongrue hoc loco mellis nomine favor humanae laudis intelligi*.[60] 'I do not think those wings are incongruously called knowledge and devotion, with which the Seraphim are born to him who is above them.'[61] The judgements of God can—not incongruously—be called 'feet'.[62] Fear itself is a temptation and so it may appropriately be said: *Quia ergo timor ipse tentatio est, congrue dictum est*.[63]

At the least, all this created a problem with equivocation, for words could clearly mean several things, even at the same level, literal or figurative. What does it mean to speak of a coming together, asks Bernard: *quid est coetum vocare?* It is to preserve unity, to favour peace, and to love the brotherhood. *Unitatem servare, diligere pacem, fraternitatem amare*.[64]

Of the many possible senses, proper and figurative and so on, Bernard picks up from Augustine and Anselm a general awareness that there exist 'usual' or 'common' usages. There is 'usual speech', *usitatus sermo*, 'common speech', *communis sermo*; 'deep speech', *profundissimus sermo*.[65]

There are also, the same sources insist, 'ways of speaking'. This is in part a matter of 'custom' in Scripture. For example, it is 'usual' there for the Holy Spirit to be designated a dove: *per columbam Spiritus Sanctus soleat designari*.[66]

A 'mode of speaking' can also be paired with the 'art of persuading', implying that some of the reasons for speaking in different ways are rhetorical:
quodam loquendi usu vel arte persuadendi.[67]

All this heightened a consciousness natural to Bernard that words should
be used with care and purposefulness to achieve defined ends, and that it
must be presumed God is well aware of that need and was better at it than
any human author when he inspired the text of Scripture. These are the
instincts of a rhetorician.

Exegesis and Rhetoric

Preaching involves interpreting and expounding the Word of God, and
therefore *enlarging* upon it. But Bernard takes delight in a contrary theme,
the notion that as an act of generosity and humility, God compresses himself into a tiny compass in order to make himself man. The *Verbum abbreviatum*, the infant Word, is still further abbreviated by circumcision, says
Bernard (Luke 2.1).[68] What is the connection between the circumcision and
the naming of Jesus? (*Circumcidit puer, et vocatur Jesus. Quid sibi vult ista
connexio?*) He suggests that Jesus was circumcised as a true child of Abraham
and 'named' Jesus as Son of God.[69] But he takes the opportunity to draw a
moral. This is the ultimate 'conversion': *Haec plane, fratres, perfecta con-
versionis est forma*. 'The Word is short but full, living and efficacious, and
worthy of all men to be received': *O verbum breve, sed plenum, sed vivum et
efficax, sed dignum omni acceptione*.[70] Again, preaching on Romans 9.28,[71]
Bernard cries out to the 'brief Word of the abbreviated Word, but filled
with heavenly sweetness': *O breve verbum de Verbo abbreviatum, sed caelesti
suavitate refertum*. Once more: the brief Word is, despite its size, living and
powerful: *O verbum abbreviatum, attamen vivum et efficax*.

It is an irony, then, that Bernard is rarely brief in his examination of a
biblical text. He never takes much of a text to examine at a time. But the
examinations are intimate, and he will draw a great deal out of each phrase.
He stays close to the text, picking it up and putting it down as he goes along.
'So that he may know how to reprove evil and choose the good': *Ut sciat . . .
reprobare malum et eligere bonum*. 'Even here you hear the good and the evil':
Etiam hic bonum et malum audis.[72] 'Hide your sayings in my heart': *In corde
meo abscondi eloquia tua* (Psalm 118.11). *Sed quomodo in corde servandi*. 'How
are they to be held in the heart? Is it enough for them to be held in the

memory?'[73] 'Now indeed, brothers, what has been said in exposition of this verse would seem sufficient, if the prophet had said. . . .': "*iam quidem, fratres, quae dicta sunt, ad expositionem versus huius viderentur posse sufficere, si dixisset propheta. . . .*" But the prophet said more than that, so we go on with the sermon for some time'.[74] 'Flowers appeared in our land': *Flores apparuerunt in terra nostra* (Song of Songs 2.12).'It is not out of keeping that Nazareth is interpreted as "flower"': *Neque hic discrepat, quod Nazareth interpretatur flos.* 'For beauty and sweetness and the hope of fruit commend flowers': *Commendat enim flores pulchritudo, suaveolentia et spes fructus.* There is a 'three-fold grace': *gratia triplex*.[75] In the manner of a classical rhetorician, Bernard uses a list of texts saying much the same thing for their cumulative effect.[76]

He is confident here of several connected things. The tiniest part is the whole Gospel, speaking the Word. The name of Jesus cannot be empty of meaning (*vacuum aut inane*). There is no shadow here, but the truth: *Non est in eo magni nominis umbra, sed veritas*. There is profundity.[77] That is not diminished by the smallness of the compass. Indeed the infant Jesus, the tiny Word (*Verbum abbreviatum*), was the full power of God. 'And the same who is in brief in the prophets can more clearly be read in the Gospel to have been made flesh': *et ipsum quod in Propheta abbreviatum, manifestius in Evangelio legitur caro factum*. 'This parable applies to us, my brothers': *Nos, fratres mei, nos respicit haec parabola*. 'For Christ did not need the testimony of the angel, nor of any human being': *Christus enim nec angelio eguit testimonio, nec humano*. 'There is a threefold witness to his saving work, to prevent us taking the name of God in vain': *triplex propriae salutis testimonium, ne forte videamus assumpsisse nomen Dei in vanum*. 'And it is necessary for us to be circumcised, brothers, and to receive the name of salvation not merely literally, but in spirit and in truth; and to be circumcised not in one member only, but in the whole body.'[78]

'After eight days were completed, that the child should be circumcised, his name was called Jesus': *Postquam consummati sunt dies octo, ut circum-cideretur Puer, vocatum est nomen eius Jesus* (Luke 2.21). From the beginning, Bernard comments, God accepted a measure. He created the world in weight and measure and number[79] and also gave a measure to man: *protinus homini modum praescripsit*.[80]

It is impossible to over-interpret, since there can be no meaning in ac-cord with the faith which God did not intend to be found when he inspired the text. If something is to be found in the Sacred Page it is truly present, not an importation, for there can be nothing God has not already thought of and put there to be found: *verum id quidem sine praeiudicio dixerim, si cui forte aliter visum fuerit, maxime si quid alius in sanctorum paginis invenitur.*[81] 'I do not doubt that this understanding is correct, and it seems to be borne out by an interpretation in another part of that letter': *non nego hunc intellectum, quin rectus sit; sed ex alio loco ipsius epistolae, superior interpretatio videtur approbari, ubi dicitur.*[82]

William of St. Thierry has a strong sense of the theatre of the Song of Songs. It is written as a drama, he says, a comedy, with characters speaking and acting.[83] It was Bernard's habit, too, to try to bring the persons in the biblical story alive, to make the episode vivid. In an advent sermon he cited Song of Songs 2.8. 'Lo he comes leaping. You see him, O beautiful one': *ecce ... veniet is salien. . . . Venientem vides, o pulchra.*[84] Preaching is a branch of the *ars rhetorica*, one of three to grow from the trunk of the 'tree' of ancient rhetoric during Bernard's lifetime. The first is the *ars dictaminis*, the art of letter writing we have already touched on;[85] the second the *ars poetriae*; the third the *ars praedicandi.*[86] Each took different principles from the ancient art. The art of letter writing concentrated upon structures and cadences and the etiquette of the salutation formula. The art of poetry concentrated upon the use of figures and ensuring that a literary composition had a beginning, a middle, and an end, though not necessarily in that order. The art of preaching was the art of persuasion, and it taught a detailed procedure for analysis and for devising a structure.

Alan of Lille wrote an *ars praedicandi*[87] later in the twelfth century which set a pattern for the thirteenth century. In Bernard's day there were no preceptive manuals except Guibert of Nogent's *Moralia in Genesim*, which imitated Gregory's *Moralia in Job* and provided a reflective preface on methods of preaching.

The normative pattern in Bernard's time was still for the homilies of Augustine and Gregory the Great to be read in monastic houses. Some abbots preached freshly upon the text of Scripture. St. Anselm was one, and his similitudes survive in a reported form. Bernard of Clairvaux was another, and for him, too, there are fragments (*sententie*) which perhaps reflect the varieties of live recollections of his speech.

Bernard has clearly before his mind the twofold sense of exegetical purpose to be found in Augustine's *De Doctrina Christiana*. He sees the need for the Christian to be able to appreciate the stylistic devices God himself has used in Scripture, in order to help human understanding. But he also sees the value of the Christian's being able to use the same sorts of devices for their persuasive force in winning others to the faith.[88]

The twelfth century was a period of considerable experimentation in genre. It was also self-conscious about style. Bernard would have known of the three styles of classical rhetoric from Augustine, if not from the *Rhetorica ad Herennium*. The idea was that the subject matter or the purpose of a piece of writing would itself require a presentation which was appropriate. A plain style might best suit a narrative or an argument; a 'high' or 'fine' style full of imagery used to move or persuade or edify, where that was the task in hand; and an intermediate style for intermediate purposes.

Bernard's practical stylistic mastery clearly owes a good deal to his solid classical formation at the hands of the canons who taught him in his boyhood.[89] But he also wrote under the stylistic influence of Scripture itself, and of Augustine. And he wrote, too, as an author of his time. In this, his best comparator is St. Anselm, in whose intellectual formation were mixed similar ingredients, and in whose letters and prayers and meditations similar games are played with figures of thought and figures of diction.

Anselm's writing could be full of conscious artistry, most noticeably in his prayers and meditations. But at the same time it was always controlled, resolved, requiring no *retractationes*, even many years later. Bernard is affective and impulsive as a writer. He thinks on his feet; his words flow along. That fluidity does not argue a lack of control; but there is 'performance' here in a way which is not so obvious in Anselm. There are oral and therefore 'rhetorical' features of the work of both men. Anselm certainly preached, but he published no sermons. He talked,[90] and what struck people were his analogies—powerful, apt, muscular, memorable.

Yet Bernard was a self-conscious stylist. His courtesies play delightful and disingenuous games with the topoi. For example, at the beginning of the *De Consideratione* he tells Eugenius III that he is quite unable to say what the rules are for writing a treatise which is at once intimate and formal.[91] There are other indications that Bernard was conscious of the difference *genre* makes. He suggests that his *On Precept and Dispensation* should be regarded as a 'book' rather than a 'letter': *Liber, si iudicetis, non epistola censeatur*.[92]

There is much sheer play in Bernard's use of words that is unavoidably lost in translation. He speaks of a peace not promised, but delivered; not broadcast, but given; not prophesied, but presented: *ecce pax non promissa, sed missa, non dilata, sed data, non prophetata, sed praesentata*.[93] There is such pattern making everywhere. We are begotten in filth, gestated in darkness, and born in pain: *in sordibus generamur, in tenebris confovemur, in doloribus parturimur*.[94] The figures of thought which survive in translation are matched in the Latin by figures of diction.

Bernard knew how to create a patterning of figures of thought with figures of diction, using the Augustinian devices which were also handily at Anselm's fingertips. In a letter to Prior Guigo of Chartres and the Carthusians on *caritas*, Bernard says, 'I read your letter, and the letters I turned over in my mouth struck sparks which I felt in my heart': *et quas volvebam in ore litteras, scintillas sentiebam in pectore*.[95] *Litteras* matches *scintillas*; *volvebam* echoes *sentiebam*; *pectore* pairs with *ore*.

Paradox is as attractive to Bernard as it had been to Augustine, and he marks it in a similar way, with patterning of word endings. 'And the world was made by him and the world knew him not' (John 1.10), he quotes. He explains that what happened was not the coming of one who had not been there before, but the appearance of one who had been hidden: *Non ergo venit qui aderat, sed apparuit qui latebat*.[96] Here again the figure of thought is matched with a figure of diction. In life, action may be passive and passivity may be active, while salvation works upon the earth.[97]

There is repetition for emphasis, here, of *consolamini*, then of *clamare*: *Domine, quid me vis facere* (Acts 9.6). *Consolamini, consolamini dicit Dominus Deus noster* (Isaiah 40.1). *Dicit hoc Emmanuel, nobiscum Deus. Clamat hoc stabulum, clamat praesepe, clamant lacimare, clamant panni*,[98] with its *clamat, clamat, clamor, clamor*.

Bernard's use of proof texts and examples is also highly 'conscious'. He knows that an example is an effective persuader and imprints itself deeply on the mind: *qua exemplum efficacius persuadet et altius imprimit animo*.[99] God loves a cheerful giver (II Corinthians 9.7), and Bernard will give examples of cheerful giving from throughout the Church: *totius Ecclesiae proponamus exempla*.[100]

The question of style is, however, merely the top level of something far deeper. Imagery is not mere decoration in Bernard. At the root of every decision to employ a metaphor or simile is a decision about what constitutes the 'proper' usage. It could be argued that all language 'properly' speaks of God, for reference to God can never be a secondary matter. It could, on the other hand, be argued that no human language can 'properly' speak of God but only his own Word, for human language must always be inadequate to express what he is. William of St. Thierry takes up this point in his *Disputatio adversus Petrum Abaelardum*: 'It should be noted that these three names, Father, Son and Holy Spirit . . . are, just like other names, improperly said of God': *de Deo improprie dicantur*.[101] In the *Sententie Divine Pagine* of the school of Anselm of Laon at the turn of the century, we find an explanation of the puzzle of this need for *translatio*, the shifting of sense from literal to figurative. God is ineffable, not because we cannot speak of him, but because we cannot speak of him fully or exactly as he is. Since we can do no better, we use our human words in a transferred way, so that we may discuss him not for his benefit but for ours.[102]

Thus we come again and again in this study to examples of the principle that behind the obvious stands a truth not perhaps at once apparent, but, once found, more profound, instructing the soul in the way it should go. That idea chimes strongly with Bernard's instinct for a mystery and allows him his mistrust of too much striving for explicitness.

POSITIVE THEOLOGY

Bernard did not want theology to be novel. He wanted it to be right, that is, true to the faith, helpful to the salvation of the faithful. He was not a 're-former' in any sense which involved seeking improved clarity and exactitude in the official formulation of statements of the faith, nor in seeking to challenge at any point what the Church had been teaching. His is the theology of 'damage limitation'; he strove to place a check on what others had done and said, which he feared would injure the confidence of the faithful, their simple trust in what the Church taught them.

Bernard's fundamental theological assumptions are entirely conventional. They are those of the Christian West of his day. At least he meant them to be so. He rocked no boats. That does not mean that his emphases are not often his own or that his work lacks sometimes spectacular insights. Yet we are not looking at a systematic theologian, but rather at a 'reactive' one, who writes about problems as they arise and are presented to him.

Bernard was often asked for his advice[1] on theological problems which had arisen in the course of someone's study of the Bible or reflection on the liturgy, or which had presented themselves in some other way. Bernard sets about resolving the questions with which his correspondents present him by asking himself what principles are involved. The underlying principles are ready in his mind. He has only to apply them, and on the whole, he does so in an unruffled way, if his questioner comes to him in a sincere spirit of enquiry.

Long before events obliged him (as he felt) to turn polemicist, he had established a reputation as a reliable authority in such matters. Hugh of St. Victor wrote to him when he was composing his *De Sacramentis Ecclesiae* to ask his opinion on baptism and incorporated much of what Bernard said, without acknowledgement, in the finished work.[2]

Bernard had also been asked why the Maccabees, 'alone of all the righteous men of the old Law', have a place in the calendar and a feast day like the Christian martyrs. Bernard delayed his answer for some time.[3] He says he had simply not been able to produce an answer straightaway. He had hoped to find something in the Fathers which had a bearing on the subject. He had failed. So he proposes to say what he thinks, on the understanding that if his correspondent can do better or finds something helpful in the Fathers, he will in his turn tell Bernard, for Bernard will wish to know.

The question is this: why do the Maccabees, alone of the 'righteous under the Law', have an annual feast and enjoy veneration alongside the Christian martyrs? They did not after all go to heaven, but to limbo.[4] Bernard discovers a distinction which is helpful to the justification of the Church's liturgical practice. The cause of death of the Maccabees and Christian martyrs was the same. It was righteousness. But the martyrs under the new Law were themselves righteous. The Maccabees merely denounced those who were not righteous, for they taught that the unrighteous would perish. The Maccabees had in one respect the same kind of martyrdom as those Christian martyrs who died because they would not sacrifice to strange Gods or forsake their God. In that sense the Maccabees can be said to have 'confessed the true faith'.[5] He makes comparison with Simeon, John the Baptist, and the Holy Innocents, all born under the old Law, for whom feasts are also celebrated.[6]

Bernard has approached the problem in the conviction that he must retrieve the credibility of the feast of the Maccabees; there can be no question of saying that the Church has been wrong to celebrate this feast. So he looks for the deep grounds of similarity between the Maccabees and Christian martyrs which may make it appropriate to treat the Maccabee martyrs as though they had been Christian martyrs.

Notable recurrences of perennial issues of theological debate created the controversies of Bernard's day. It will bear repeating that the guiding principle of all Bernard's theological problem solving was Bernard's desire to protect and preserve orthodox belief in the minds of simple men. We have seen that Bernard was not by inclination primarily an academic theologian,

if by that we mean that he was not strongly drawn to the philosophical problems raised for many of his contemporaries by the application of grammar
and logic to the study of the Bible and to the discussion of Christian
doctrine. He himself had no intellectual difficulties, and he regarded such
free-ranging intellectual curiosity as dangerous to the faith of ordinary believers. 'Is there a stumbling-block here?' is his most characteristic question.
It may be that this should be regarded as a flaw, and a serious one. The fact
that a point in dispute may be upsetting to the faithful does not mean that it
does not present a real problem, or that it can be set aside summarily. If it
is a real problem, it will recur, as Christian theologians have found century
after century.

But Bernard's reluctance to create disturbance did not mean that he did
not tackle academic questions readily enough when he was presented with
them, in situations where it had become his duty to do so in defence of the
faith. And his tendency to be a 'reactive' rather than a 'proactive' theologian
does not mean that Bernard gives no indications of what we may call his
'positive' theological position.

The range of theological topics Bernard wrote on is predominantly
Augustinian. He did not readily look for new problem areas. He would not
have expected such a search to prove helpful. Nor did he attempt anything
like a *summa*. Like Augustine, he did his theology for pastoral purposes, in
sermons and letters and occasional treatises addressed to specific needs, and
largely piecemeal. Since Bernard imposes no order or sequence upon us,
the ordering of the elements adopted in this study is after the pattern of
Thomas Aquinas. We have to wait for Peter Lombard's *Sentences*, which
were written in the generation after Bernard, for that to become the natural
sequence in which to study theology, but it is not entirely at variance with
the practice of Bernard's own period.

The Nature and Attributes of God and
the Doctrine of the Trinity

William of St. Thierry in his *Disputatio adversus Petrum Abaelardum*, written to Bernard and Geoffrey of Chartres, concentrates anxiously upon the
Trinity.[7] So it was partly because of his encounter with the stories about what
Abelard was alleged to be teaching that Bernard entered into the debates of
the day surrounding the nature and attributes of God and the questions about

which, if any, Persons of the Trinity were especially to be associated with certain attributes.

There was also an influence from another 'heretical' quarter, the teaching of Gilbert of Poitiers. Bernard touches on the heresy for which Gilbert of Poitiers was tried at the Council of Rheims.[8] It was a very technical heresy, and it is by no means certain that Gilbert's accusers understood what it was he had been trying to do. Bernard begins from the principle, clear already to Augustine and Boethius, that the Aristotelian categories break down with respect to the Godhead. The attributes of God are not variables like the attributes of creatures, but of his very essence. Creaturely beauty may grow or diminish; God is invariably beautiful, for he is Beauty itself. To argue that there was anything from which God has his existence would be to make that itself God. Now Bernard's concern is that in saying that God is God 'by his divinity' (*divinitate*), Gilbert seemed to have added a fourth to the three Persons.[9] Bernard insists that it must be possible to speak of 'three' without implying any 'multiplication' of unity, of 'one' without subtracting from the Trinity of the Persons.

He looks at various notions of unity. It may be collective, as when many stones make a single pile. It may be a unity composed of parts or members, as in the human body. In marriage, two become one flesh. There is the unity of body and soul in one human being. There is a moral unity, by which a person behaves consistently and with integrity. There is a unity born out of mutual charity, as when the members of a community have one mind and one heart. There is a unity of desire, in which the soul clings to God in the desire to be united with him. There is the unity in which the Son of God condescended to become man. But only in the Godhead is the unity that of a single substance.[10]

A defining belief of the Christian tradition is that God is both one and three, and no more than three. This was early taken to be so central that when someone's baptism was called into question in the early Church (for example, because he had been baptised outside the *catholica*),[11] the test was whether he had been baptised with water in the name of the Trinity. *Substantia una est, personae tres sunt*, as Bernard puts it.[12] The debate about the *terminology* to be used for 'substance' and 'person' took a different form and direction in the East; the language difference here was crucial.[13] The basic principles accepted in the West had been laid down within the Latin tradition by Augustine and Boethius. The problem was that the Persons of the Trinity are one God, coeternal, equal, yet in some manner differentiated into three.

Equality is not the same as identity. It is not incompatible with differentiation. It is possible for two to be so equal that there is a single 'shining' of both, just as if they are one. *Et usque adeo aequalitas, ut una sit claritas amborum, sicut ipsi unum sunt.*[14]

Yet there are other things we say of God, besides calling him 'Father', 'Son', and 'Holy Spirit', and there we do not imply that there is a differentiation. We call him good, omnipotent, and so on. What is the difference? Some might say that there was no difference. There is a divine substance or nature or essence (the Latin terms *substantia*, *natura*, *essentia* are used interchangeably by Augustine). No one doubted that that was common to all three persons. Fatherhood, sonship, proceeding, clearly belong exclusively to distinct persons.[15] There are divine attributes, such as eternity, goodness, mercy, justice, of which on the face of it it is not apparent whether they are common to all three persons or special to one. One of the issues repeatedly debated, and returned to in Bernard's day, was whether we should link specific attributes with specific Persons of the Trinity. It was suspected that some held the view that 'omnipotence', for example, belongs especially to the Father, 'wisdom' to the Son, 'love' to the Holy Spirit.[16]

One way of approaching this is to develop the notion we have just touched on, that is, to say that these divine attributes differ from the attributes of creatures in that they are substantive, not accidental. That is to say—for this was habitually put in Aristotelian terms after Augustine and Boethius had set the precedent[17]—they belong to the 'category' of the substance which cannot vary without altering what the thing is, and not to the categories of accidents such as quantity, situation, action, passion, which in creatures are changeable without altering what the creature essentially is. The only exception to this rule about the special reference of the *Categories* in the case of God is the category of relation. The Father and the Son bear an eternal relation to one another, and the Father is not the Son and the Son is not the Father. With reference to his 'substantive attributes', God is not good on some days and bad on others. He is always good. He is good*ness*. The *longitudo, latitudo, sublimitas, et profundum* of the *De Consideratione* is God himself.[18] This classical philosophical theology (as developed in contemporary exegesis) is to be found in a sermon for the Nativity. God's mercy is eternal (Psalm 102.17). But who is coeternal with the Father but the Son and the Holy Spirit? And each of them is not so much merciful as mercy itself (*et uterque quidem non tam misericors quam ipsa vere misericordia*). They are all mercy, but they are all one mercy, as they are one being, one wisdom, one divinity, one majesty. So when the Father is spoken of as the Father of mercies (*in eo tamen quod Pater misericordiarum dicitur Deus*), that must be taken to designate the Son (*quis non videat vel proprie nomine Filium designari?*). And he is well called the Father of mercies, whose nature it is to be merciful.[19]

In this way, Bernard gives the advocates of the view that there may be attributes proper to only one Person of the Trinity beyond Fatherhood, Sonship, Procession. It was not of course necessarily true that those to whom such views were attributed necessarily held them, and Peter Abelard was, as we shall see, indignant to be told that he did.[20]

In the *De Diligendo Deo* and its paired Letter 11, Bernard takes the discussion of this controversy some distance. He refers to the notion that the attributes of God are not accidents but substantive. 'No one can think "love" is here to be taken as a quality or any sort of accident' (*accipere qualitatem, vel aliquod accidens*). Otherwise I should be saying that there is in God something which is not God (*alioquin in Deo dicerem, quod absit, esse aliquid quod Deus non est*). Charity *is* the divine substance.[21]

Equally unacceptable would be to say that there could be anything uniting God (his substance) which was not itself God. This was alleged to be Gilbert of Poitiers's heresy. He was said to have taught that there is a fourth thing in God, the divine substance 'by which' God was God. Gilbert of Poitiers drew Bernard's fire in the Sermons on the Song of Songs. Gilbert teaches—as Bernard alleges[22]—that when one says 'God, God, God', that is a reference to the divine substance, yet not to what God is but to that 'by which' he is. *Cum dicitur: Deus, Deus, Deus, pertinet ad substantiam, noster commentator intulit. Non quae est, sed qua est.*[23] 'Perish the thought that there should be a substance or any kind of thing by which God is, and which is not God': *Quod absit . . . esse videlicet substantiam vel aliquam, omnino rem, qua Deus sit et quae non sit Deus*, comments Bernard.[24]

Yet there must be a common substance of the Persons of the Trinity, Bernard urges in Letter 190 on the errors of Abelard.[25] Not to agree with the Church that the Holy Spirit is *de substantia*, or one substance with the Father and the Spirit, is to deny consubstantiality (as Arius did), and by implication to preach quite openly that the Holy Spirit is a creature.[26]

The relationship of the Holy Spirit to the Father and the Son had become a controversial question in its own right, since the division of the Greek from the Latin Church in 1054.[27] The schism was not in the first instance primarily about that, nor indeed perhaps really about the theological questions at all; but the theology had entered into it as it had hardened. There had been a difference on the subject between East and West since Carolingian times, when the *filioque* clause been added to the Nicene Creed in the West, and with it an explicit statement by Latin Christians that the Holy Spirit proceeds from the Son as well as from the Father. Anselm of Laon and his school were taking an interest in this problem at the turn of the century, discussing the disagreement between the Eastern and the Western Churches, that is, the Greek and 'our own': *dissentio inter orientalem et occidentalem ecclesiam, id est grecam et nostram.*[28] Anselm of Canterbury had addressed the Greeks at the Council of Bari of 1098 on the subject of the Procession of the Holy Spirit, at the invitation of Urban II. That address grew four years later into a treatise, *De Processione Spiritus Sancti*. He had later written the letters on the sacraments, because there was also disagreement over the use of leavened or unleavened bread in the eucharist. Anselm of Havelberg had talks with Greek Christians on the theological issues in Bernard's own day.[29]

Bernard does not see how, if anyone tries to divide the Persons from the substance or the properties from the Persons, he can call himself a worshipper of the Trinity, for in either way one would exceed the permitted numbers of one and three: *qui in tantam rerum numerositatem excesserit.*[30] The Persons are 'not other than the one God, the one divine substance, the one divine nature, the one divine and supreme majesty. That is what the Church believes (*catholica confitetur*).[31] On the other hand, there must be differentiating properties of the Persons, by which they differ without ceasing to be a unity.

Bernard is especially concerned over the 'errors' of Peter Abelard—and here we must anticipate the subject matter of the next chapter . Abelard had apparently tried to provide an analogy from logic to help his students grasp the doctrine of the Trinity (though it is by no means clear exactly what he had taught). He had said that the Son is to the Father rather as species is to genus, or as a seal made of brass is to the brass from which it is made. Abelard appears to have been reaching for a way of describing a relationship in which, although one derives from and is reciprocal with the other, there is no subordination.

Bernard's own Trinitarian theology is written largely in reaction against this kind of talk. He accuses Abelard of subordinationism, of trying to 'grade' the Persons of the Trinity. Abelard, he says, is saying that the Father is full power, the Son some power, the Holy Spirit no power at all.[32] This is worse than Arius! he cries. It is not to be borne! 'For he says that the Holy Spirit proceeds from the Father and the Son, but that he is not of the same sub-stance' (*sed minime de Patris esse Filii ve substantia*), he alleges.[33] If Abelard is arguing that the Holy Spirit proceeds from the Father and the Son but not from the substance of the Father and the Son, he seems to be saying that the Holy Spirit comes from nothing, for even created things come from God (Romans 11.36).

Bernard is therefore visibly engaged with the debated issues of the day in this area of Trinitarian theology. But it is equally apparent that he is not seeking to say anything new. On the contrary, he is trying to hold a middle course, in line with what he believes to be the Church's orthodoxy.

This is a theological policy, a 'reductionism to the status quo', which is important for the very possibility of Bernard's breaking new ground in his thinking. His 'newness' consists not in innovation but in freshness, in put-ting something in a new and striking way, which enhances or intensifies the faith of the believer.

Creation and Fall

We see this pattern repeated in Bernard's treatment of a theological theme which lends itself especially to this refreshing and reviving emphasis on an affective spirituality. God created the world for its good and not for his own. He had no need of our help in order to create, as Bernard points out.[34] More-over, he can have made nothing which was not good, true, beautiful, in short, like himself, except that the things he made must have been less in the de-gree of their realisation of these perfections because they were creatures. Bernard takes for granted here the Augustinian principle that *being* is itself a good, that by bringing creatures into being God is automatically making them good.

So God *made* his creation without a burden of guilt upon it, and without a penalty due from it, for it owed God no reparation.[35] The rational creation had a choice. It could remain good, or it could turn away from the good. In the event, some angels and all mankind preferred (of their own volition) to fall, rather than to exercise their free choice in the direction of remaining faithful to the purpose for which they were created by grace.[36]

Therefore a threefold divine task, indeed a Trinitarian work (*Trinitatis operatio*), came to be needed, to bring about the fulfilment of God's original and indefectible purpose for what he had made. For there was never any question that Bernard would allow his purpose to be frustrated. Bernard describes this 'work' in different ways in different writings. In the treatise on grace and free choice he lists *creatio, reformatio, consummatio*.[37] Elsewhere he speaks of *creatio, reconcilatio, confirmatio*.[38] But the principle is the same. God must act to restore creation before it can be perfected according to his intention. (Perfection typically has to do with 'completion', 'fulfilment', or 'consummation' in twelfth-century usage.)

God's intention must include the conformity of the creature to the Creator, insofar as that is possible for any creature. For comparison to be made and restoration to a resemblance to God to be possible, there has to be likeness. One cannot match like with unlike: *quid sibi ergo vult ista inter tam dispares comparatio?*[39] The image and likeness of man to his Creator consists in a threefold freedom, says Bernard. In freedom of choice lies man's image of God. Freedom of counsel and freedom of pleasure denote man's likeness to God.[40] Yet the divine likeness is above all a likeness to God's wisdom and power.

The highest in the hierarchy of angels enjoyed the highest degree of this likeness before they fell. The good angels had a power to persevere without sin or sorrow. Adam had a degree of likeness just below that of the angels. Adam was created able to to be without sin and sorrow, but not to remain so in perseverance. The fallen angels who are now the devils have no perseverance, and they are in sin and sorrow, even in hell, for in hell they rebel against their just punishment and so they suffer.[41] The devils have now no degree of likeness to God at all.

In the case of the angels (and here Bernard agrees with Anselm), no restoration was appropriate. Bernard certainly takes the fall of the angels seriously. He speaks, as Anselm does, of the fact that the angels cannot be restored: *sciebat enim nullam angelis patere redeundi viam*.[42] Some good angels remain unfallen, so God's purpose for this class of creature is fulfilled in them. But the fall of mankind is a matter far more pressingly a human concern.

Bernard concentrates upon the image of God and its restoration in man. There was no true image of God in the world after the fall of Adam. In Christ, the woman of the Gospel (Luke 15.8) lit her lamp and swept the house of the vices, seeking her lost coin, the image of God, which was buried in the dust, its lustre lost. She wiped it, took it out of the 'region of unlikeness', and restored it to its earlier beauty.[43]

In the case of humanity, there is a possibility of the 're-formation' of human nature, so that what was de-formed by Adam may be con-formed again to the originally intended *forma*. *Naturae reformatio, ut, per Adam deformatus, conformaretur.* To bring about the restoration of the image of God in man, so that mankind would be able to enter again into the threefold freedom he was designed for, the Incarnation was needed.

Christ came as the 'form' (Philippians 2.6) to which human nature had to be re-conformed. For in order that the image of God might regain its original form, it had to be re-formed out of that from which it had originally been formed. Wisdom is that form, and conformation to it means that the image is present.

Bernard further sees this 'form' as order. It orders the universe, stretching with quiet purpose from one end of it to the other.[44]

That is the framework within which Bernard sets his account of what had to be achieved by the Incarnation.

Cur Deus Homo: Why God Became Man

Among the texts which survive from the School of Anselm of Laon are discussions of the reasons why man fell and God rescued him. Various suggestions were being canvassed. Perhaps man was puffed up (*habet quandam elationem in se*). Perhaps it was just that he was tempted by the serpent—that would set man apart from the angels, who could not be retrieved when they fell because no one had pushed them into error; in the case of mankind, there was some excuse.

When God set about retrieving mankind, he could have done it by a word of forgiveness. Why did he not do so? It was more fitting that he should perform some act for which we should love him and be grateful. And the Devil would have complained if there had been no recognition of his rights.[45] Bernard moved away in part from Abelard's emphasis, in his commentary on Romans, upon the setting of an example to the exclusion of all the other reasons.

There was also Anselm of Canterbury's signal account of the matter in his *Cur Deus Homo*. Bernard's contribution to the contemporary debate on why God became man (*Cur Deus Homo*) was to shift the focus from Anselm of Canterbury's idea that the key thing was paying a debt.

Why did God become man, living a human life on earth, and dying like any mortal? Bernard's discussion of the question *Cur Deus homo?* in his sermons and treatises reflects a detailed knowledge of this contemporary literature, not only from Anselm and Abelard but also from the scholars associated with the cathedral school at Laon, at which we have glanced already. Again, it is not, except in certain points of emphasis, an original view, but it makes a considerable contribution in its attempt to reconcile views which seemed to many contemporaries contradictory, or, at best, alternatives. Above all, for our immediate purposes, it enables us to compare, outside the arena of the trial itself, the theological ground on which Bernard and Abelard stood when they met at Sens in 1140.

Someone had asked Bernard a question which Anselm of Canterbury had already considered.[46] Why could God not repair the damage done to his creation by Adam's sin without going to such lengths as to send his Son to die? He could (*valuit*), says Bernard, but he preferred (*maluit*) to follow the course he did.[47] He does not attempt any revision or endorsement or exploration of an alternative to Anselm's hypothesis. There is none of Abelard's brisk run-through of the options, striking out those which do not apply.[48]

Like Anselm, although he gives different reasons, Bernard is concerned to emphasize the hugeness of Adam's offence. He draws a striking contrast between the six days in which God created the whole world and everything in it, and the thirty years during which 'he worked your salvation upon the earth'.[49] That took longer because it was much more important. He has in mind throughout the importance of sin, the hugeness of Adam's offence; this simple but powerful governing principle informs everything he says. In one of the sermons for Advent, further aspects of the theology of incarnation and redemption are discussed (again, questions raised by Anselm of Canterbury and, again, with Bernard's own distinctive answers). Why did the Son become man and not the Father or the Holy Spirit? If we think about the cause of our exile, Bernard suggests, we can see, at least in part, how appropriate it was that the Son should be our principal liberator. The offence was a lie, for Satan thought himself equal with God and seduced man into a pride like his own. The Son is Truth, so he was able to counterbalance the lie. Once more, a principle is implicit in Bernard's argument, and once more it is the notion of appropriateness or fittingness.[50]

Bernard wanted to drive home as forcefully as possible the hugeness of what was done by Christ, and the great need in which man stood, and he did it by creating the most powerful effect he could. 'Who can doubt that there was some great cause that such majesty should deign to descend from so far, and into so lowly a place?' he asks. 'It was out of necessity', is his answer. The theme of 'necessity' is repeated.[51] This was no empty nativity or fruitless demeaning of himself on God's part.[52] Three things in particular compelled the Lord Jesus Christ, he says, to undergo the Cross and the ignominy of death; a pure filial obedience, a *compassibilis et communis miseria*, and the certain victory over the Devil.[53]

But Bernard had also said that God *could* have done things another way. That assertion is not incompatible with the one about necessity. To God, all things are possible, but he will always go the best way. William of St. Thierry similarly wants to hold to a theory of 'necessity', for to suggest that it was not necessary for Christ to come into the world at all might seem an assault upon the mystery of our common salvation, the *sacramentum communis salutis*.[54]

Since Anselm of Laon and his brother Ralph had explored the problem in their lectures, and Anselm of Canterbury had written his *Cur Deus Homo* in the 1090s, the topic had been attracting a new interest. A number of ideas had gained currency, and one question in particular had been hotly debated. When Adam and Eve consented to sin, they did so at the instigation of the serpent. They gave themselves up to him. Did it therefore follow that the Devil had rights over man for which he was entitled to compensation if he lost them? To say that he did made it easy to explain why God became man. It would be unjust of God simply to take back man for himself from the Devil, who was rightly man's master, but if he paid the Devil a ransom he could justly make man his own again. This hypothesis removed the difficulty of explaining why an omnipotent God did not simply put right what had gone wrong by an act of will and make all as it had been before.[55]

Anselm of Canterbury found this explanation unsatisfactory because he could not accept that the Devil could be rightful lord over those whom he had tricked into his service. He was a thief, and a thief has no right to the property he has stolen.[56] The litigants in this case are not as Hugh of St. Victor thought, God, man, and the Devil,[57] but only God and man.

Bernard does not agree with Anselm about the Devil's rights, but it is Abelard he attacks on the subject. He rails against him. He tries reason: if we agree that the world is the Devil's 'house' (John 14.30; Luke 11.21), and man his 'goods' (Matthew 12.29), we cannot, surely, say that the Devil has no power over man? The Devil may have usurped his power, but God permitted him to keep it.[58] Man was lawfully delivered up to the Devil and mercifully set free in such a way that justice was manifested even in his liberation.[59]

Bernard believes in an active Devil. He writes to the abbot of St. John of Chartres about the way in which Satan's messenger, disguised as an angel of light, is trying to drip into the 'mouth' of the thirsty soul the illusory sweetness of his waters. He argues that no one but Satan would be stirring up dissension and troubling unity and peace.[60] That would have been Satan's way from the time of his own fall and his approach to Adam and Eve in the garden. Bernard thus keeps this third party in play between man and God in the equation whose conclusion is the necessity of the Incarnation, in a way Anselm was strongly disinclined to do. But his main interest is in the internal economy of the divine actions, which must have reference within the Trinity itself.

In Letter 190 and in the treatise he wrote for the Templars, Bernard goes on to explore the question of the Redemption in terms which show how close his concerns were to Anselm's in the *Cur Deus Homo*, except for this significant difference over the Devil's rights. It was fitting, he says, for man's recovery to be brought about by an act of mercy on the part of his liberator, and for justice rather than power to be exerted against man's enemy.[61]

In Anselm's view, an offence has been committed against God by man, and the debt to be paid is due from man alone, and to God alone. God cannot simply forget the offence to his honour, or he would remain dishonoured, a thing unthinkable with God. Man cannot repay the debt himself; he is too weak and sinful. God cannot send an angel to repay it, for two reasons. The angel would be man's saviour and would therefore deserve man's grateful service forever; that service must be restored to God. But an angel would in any case not be able to pay the debt because he has no part in human nature; he would not, in effect, 'stand for' man. Only God himself can pay the debt if man is to become his grateful servant. Only man himself can pay the debt if it is to be duly wiped out. The only solution which presents itself is the one which was in fact adopted. God became man and was able to pay the debt on behalf of the debtor.[62]

In both the fall of man and the fall of the angels, Bernard puts the emphasis upon disobedience to a person. He encourages his listener to put himself in God's place. In his first Sermon for Advent, he describes the scene for us. Adam and Eve offended specifically against the Son in their disobedience (*quod Filii Dei est . . . surripere tentaret*). God the Father took the offence seriously because he loved the Son, and it was for this reason that he punished man severely. This is a view quite different from that of Anselm, who thought the offence to God's honour was certainly not to the Son in particular, but to the Godhead as one. It takes us at a stroke out of the region of the philosophical issues Bernard was considering when he looked at the nature and attributes of God and at Trinitarian theology. The Son redeemed mankind for love of the Father because the Father has lost so much for his sake.

'What,' asks Bernard, 'does the Son do', seeing the Father's zeal for him and how he is refusing to spare the offenders, and indeed how the whole of creation is being affected? 'See', he says, 'the Father is casting off his creatures for my sake.' It was out of love for the Father that the Son entered upon his work of redemption. 'On my account he has lost many angels and all mankind', the Son continues, as he resolves, for love of the Father, to put things right. The divine act of redemption is therefore an expression of the love of God for the Trinity.

Bernard gives a glimpse of the inward conversation of the Godhead. He paints a picture of the scene at the heavenly Council where the method of redemption was decided upon. 'A Council was assembled in the secret places of heaven, for the restoration of lost man.' To the Council came Mercy and Truth, to meet each other, for if mercy cannot meet truth it is not mercy but misery, and if truth does not come to meet mercy it is not truth but severity. As a result of their discussion, justice embraces peace, and the plan is made.[63]

What Bernard was trying to achieve in this singular reconstruction was perhaps to present the facts in a way which would enable his simpler listeners to understand the force of the Son's desire to redeem the world.

Where Anselm thought in terms of God's having raised the humanity in Christ to one with his divinity, Bernard was speaking for his own contemporaries in talking of the 'descent' and humiliation involved. He insists that so startling an act, so extreme a departure from immutability into mutability as God's becoming man, could only be accounted for by a compelling necessity. The discussions Christians and Jews had been holding in recent decades had brought sharply into focus the astonishing nature of what had been done in order to save mankind. It was a great stumbling block to Jewish converts, as it had been to the philosophers of a Platonist persuasion in the late antique world, that they were obliged to accept that God descended from his height above creation and became man. Gilbert Crispin's Jew of Mainz made much of that.[64] Anselm of Canterbury placed the 'necessity' involved in the overriding importance of bringing the universe back to its right order (*rectus ordo*). Only when God's honour was restored and man was made again a being fit for heaven, could God's plan be carried out.

Abelard, says Bernard, answers the question 'Why did God redeem the world by so laborious a method, when a word from him or an act of his will would have done?' by distinguishing between 'need', 'necessity', and 'reason'. The 'need' was man's and the angels', too, and also God's. The angels needed perfected men to make up their depleted ranks and fill the spaces left by the fallen angels. God himself needed to take action to fulfil the purpose of his will. The 'necessity', however, is man's, not God's.[65] It is we men, not God himself, who were sitting in darkness. The 'reason' for the Incarnation was simply the pleasure of the good doer of the deed.[66]

Anselm's explanation is elegant, but it gives a single, narrow reason for the Incarnation. It does not touch on the birth of Christ as an infant, his growing up in the world, his life and ministry. Although he had certainly read the *Cur Deus Homo*, Brnard saw this example of a perfect human life which Christ set as of sufficient importance to be put *beside* his redemptive death as a reason for the Incarnation.

Peter Abelard seems to have been the chief advocate of the more extreme view that the example Christ set was to be regarded not only as of equal importance with the act of redemption, but also as constituting the real reason why God became man instead of redeeming man by a direct exercise of naked power. This view was set out in one of the 'sentences' or *quaestiones* with which Abelard's *Commentary on Romans* is interspersed. Abelard is discussing Romans 3.25. What does the Apostle Paul mean by saying that we are justified by Christ's blood? 'First we must ask by what necessity God became man so as to redeem us by dying in the flesh, and from whom he redeemed us, who it was, in other words, who held us captive by right and by his power (*iustitia vel potestate*), and by what right he freed us from his power (*et qua iustitia nos ab eius potestate liberavit*).[67] These were the parts of the question in its contemporary form.

Abelard works his way systematically through all the points of view that have been advanced in the debate on the subject. Firstly, it is said by some that Christ redeemed us from the power of the Devil, who has had rights over us since Adam sinned and obeyed the Devil of his own free will. No lord can take another's servant legitimately without his lord's consent. There can be no Devil's rights in the matter. Man sinned against God when he disobeyed him.[68] Thus far Abelard is with Anselm. Abelard now insists that God could simply have forgiven man's sin, as he forgave many individual men before the crucifixion. He cites a number of Scriptural texts to demonstrate that this is so.[69] The only reason Abelard can conceive why God became man and suffered as he did was to show man how to live as he ought. If he had come solely to be crucified, surely God would have had a greater reason to be angry with man forever because he had so brutally crucified his Son, than because he had eaten a single apple while he was in paradise?[70] We are made more righteous, *iustiores*, by Christ's death than we were before, because of the example Christ set us, kindling in us by his grace and generosity a zeal to imitate him.[71]

When William of St. Thierry drew Bernard's attention to Abelard's arguments, Bernard was stirred to anger. In Letter 190 to Innocent II, he says that he has searched Abelard's 'book of sentences'[72] and his commentary on Romans and found him thus attacking the mystery of our Redemption. He recounts Abelard's teaching and points to what he regards as the principal offence there: Abelard is saying that it was not to free man that God became man, but for some other reason.

Bernard would not rule out the setting of an example, although he does not make it the main reason for the Incarnation. It is hard to know, says Bernard, whether we ought to feel more deeply when we contemplate the place where Jesus lay in death, or when we think of his life.[73] Both his life and his death were necessary for the good of man, and equally necessary.[74] By living, Christ taught us to live, and by dying, he made it safe for us to die.[75] More, by wiping out the effect of the original sin which prevented us from living as we should, he made it possible for us to follow his example of life.[76] Bernard thus sets side by side, equal in importance, the two reasons for God's becoming man which were being debated in the schools of the day. His life sets us an example for living; his death redeems us from death.[77]

Even though Bernard did not attempt to compose a treatise on the theology of the Redemption, his teaching on Incarnation and Redemption, piecemeal though it is, is both consistent and comprehensive. Characteristically, he preferred to diffuse his views in his preaching, trying to bring his listeners to a vivid apprehension of certain aspects of the matter. He showed them the importance of what was at stake, the greatness of what had been done, the divine generosity which combined so many benefits in a single act of redemptive love

A Doctrine of Man and
the Process of Salvation

A theology of incarnation and redemption always presupposes a doctrine of man, and we have already glimpsed some of Bernard's ideas about 'humanity' and the human person. But there is more to say in this context. Bernard discusses the make-up of human beings in another way, in his attempt to answer the question how the saving work of Christ is applied to the individual, so as to bring him personally back into conformity with God's purpose in creating him.

For all is manifestly not well as yet. In this present life, all is sorrow and suffering. Even joy has its sorrows, if it is bodily joy. To eat when one is not hungry gives no pleasure. Without the goad of needing them, food and drink and shade from the sun cease to be desirable.[78]

Sense perception is, says Bernard, a living movement outward of the body. It is driven by natural appetite or desire. It is governed by the will, which consents or does not consent to the movement of the desire. The will itself is directed by reason, although not always and not reliably.[79] Animals have sense perception and appetite, but they do not have rational will, and so they can be neither just nor unjust and neither happy nor unhappy, blessed nor unblessed.[80]

The will, says Bernard (squarely in the Augustinian tradition), is that which makes a human being blameworthy or not; mere dullness of mind, failure of memory, bluntness of sensibility, are not culpable.[81]

The will can be compelled by no force or necessity to oppose its own wishes or to will any particular thing in preference to another.[82]

Bernard distinguishes freedom from sin, freedom from sorrow, freedom from necessity. The first is a freedom which ought to be ours by nature. We were created free from the necessity to sin and able to continue freely in that freedom. We are restored to that freedom by grace through the work of Christ. We are to be 'raised' to a glory which is freedom from sorrow in the world to come.[83] The first gives us superiority over other living creatures; the second makes us masters of the flesh; the third enables us to overcome death itself.[84]

For Augustine, one of the crucial questions was whether the wills of fallen men and women can strictly be called free when they can will the good only with the aid of grace, and their only truly free remaining choice appears to be in favour of evil. Bernard argues that freedom from necessity belongs alike to God and all rational creatures, whether angelic or human and whether good or bad. It is not greater in the just man than in the sinner and it is not greater in the angel than in the human being.[85] The consent of the will to good he deems still free, even though it has to be directed that way by grace; it is free because it is voluntary; it remains an act of the will.[86]

Freedom of the will continues to exist even in a captive mind, a mind enslaved to evil.[87] When someone says he wishes he could have a good will but it is beyond him, that is no argument for his lacking freedom of the will. He is testifying to his lack of the freedom which is called freedom from sin. Whoever wants to have a good will proves that he has a will for good.[88] Bernard is thus defining freedom of choice as that freedom by which the will is free to judge itself to be good if it has consented to the good, and bad if it has consented to do wrong.[89]

Choice Bernard considers to be an act of judgement. It is judgement's task to distinguish between what is lawful and what is expedient; it belongs to counsel to examine what is expedient and what is not expedient; it belongs to pleasure to recognise pleasure and its absence.[90] He notices that these things can operate separately. We can see that something ought to be done and then do the opposite. Not all that we see to be right is identified as giving us pleasure; on the contrary, often we can find it hard to endure doing the right.[91]

Memory, like reason, is not a *mere* faculty of the soul for Bernard, but the soul itself; the soul is thus both observer and observed.[92] It is capable of self-knowledge. Only the spirit of a man, which is within him, knows the person, he says. Look inside yourself and you will yourself be able to see if there are vices hidden there. Sin leaves dirty marks on the memory.[93] Your inner judge is your best judge.[94] One way in which God assists this process in those he loves is by an illuminating act of grace. The illumination God sheds enables the soul to see itself more clearly; it *brings* the soul to self-knowledge. It opens the book of conscience in which the soul can read its wretched past and see it for what it is.[95]

God's grace does not compel. It merely makes plain to the reason how the will ought to respond. Bernard describes the stages by which, once man begins to cooperate willingly with grace, God is able to bring him to the state he intends for him, complete his redemption, and make him at last free of the necessity to sin.

'The Most Famous Question'

But that takes us in turn to Bernard's treatment of the *famossisima quaestio*[96] of grace, divine foreknowledge, and predestination and their relationship to human freedom of choice, considered in the 'Anselmian' terms of the interplay of what appear on the face of it to be conflicting imperatives. The *De Gratia et Libero Arbitrio* of the 1120s was sent to William of St. Thierry for comment before it was copied for distribution, and William, if not Bernard's sternest critic, was certainly the living theologian who had the most positive influence upon him. Arguably, William was a better theologian than Bernard. He had, in abstract reasoning, a longer reach and crisper phrasing. And Bernard was not nervous of him as an 'academic' whose mindset and assumptions might be suspect and whose logic remorseless with spiritually precious things.

In the text as it comes down to us, Bernard distinguishes creating grace from saving grace. Creating grace made the will; saving grace enables the will to will the good, so that the will has no merit in doing so. But when the will wills evil, it is to blame for its own act, and no operation of grace is involved.[97] Perfect conversion is conversion to good, so that only fitting or permissible things will be found pleasing by the will thus altered by grace.[98]

Free choice ought to try to govern its body in the same way as God rules the created world, steadily commanding each sense and each member, so as to prevent sin from having control.[99]

Neither grace enabling good choices nor temptation leading to bad ones, takes away from freedom of choice, Bernard argues. In a reciprocal and assisting gesture, God's grace helps those he recognises to want salvation. He does not force the unwilling; he makes them willing and then helps them to will rightly. That does not take away their freedom; it merely helps move it in the right direction. This is an area where it is notoriously difficult to 'place' God's contribution on a scale at one end of which he does everything and at the other end of which the human will does it all.

Bernard deals here with a number of Scriptural texts which appear to suggest that temptation may constrain the freedom of choice of the will. Paul, for example, speaks of the war in his members which makes him captive to the law of sin (Romans 7.23). But, as Bernard points out, Paul also says that he delights in the law of God in his innermost self (Romans 7.22).[100]

What is to be made of apostates? Some are forced to abjure their faith by fear of death or a threatened penalty. It might be argued that a purely verbal denial in which the speaker did not believe was not truly apostasy; it might be argued that the will could not be forced into guilt if the apostasy was against the person's will. Peter is a case in point. He denied the truth, but for fear of death (Matthew 26.79). If we ask what he wanted, we should have to answer that he wanted to be Christ's disciple. That desire never changed. What he actually said was that he did not know Christ, and he only said that because he wanted to escape death.[101] That was in itself an innocent will, for there is nothing wrong with not wanting to die. The will to be a Christian was also innocent. It was indeed reprehensible that he lied, for he was more anxious to save his body than his soul. His sin was not to hate Christ but to love himself. Peter was under no compulsion but consented to betray Christ only so far and insofar as he feared death.[102] Bernard is able to tease out of this a distinction between a compulsion in which we are passive, allowing something to happen which is against our will but doing nothing to prevent it, and an active compulsion of the will.[103]

The gift of grace is not an unmixed blessing. We should be very fearful when we receive grace. 'Be fearful when grace smiles on you; be fearful when it departs; be fearful when it returns,' says Bernard. The first fear is appropriate because there is no certainty that grace will remain. God is a free agent. If your actions are unworthy of grace, it will gently withdraw. It is not a gift to be neglected or taken for granted. It will certainly not put up with becoming a subject of pride to him who has it. But if grace departs, there is still more cause to fear. And if it returns, there is again the fear that it will go away again.[104]

God works for salvation through creatures in three ways: without their consent, against their consent, and with their consent. For example, he can use an insensible or irrational creature as a means of salvation, thus employing a being which cannot give its consent because it has no will; he can use the wicked for the salvation of others, to which they certainly do not give their consent; and he can use the good and good angels, whose consent is given.[105]

Bernard takes Augustine's view that no one can know whether or not he is saved; to be 'in the net' of the Church is not to be sure of heaven.[106] It is a mystery hidden throughout the ages, and the predestined who are to be blessed will emerge, as it were, from the abyss of eternity (though one may make a guess as to who will be among them).[107] No soul can know whether it is worthy of the bridegroom's love or of his hatred: *quis scit si dignus est amore an odio*.[108] There are many *cubicula* in the king's palace. Each soul can enjoy its own secret place of assignation with the Bridegroom. The Bride-groom decides the places, and by a merit apparent only to God, they are allo-cated to queen, concubine, handmaid.[109]

There is a pastoral problem about a doctrine of hidden predestination. The Christian who believes that all is settled and nothing he can do can make any difference may be idle or arrogant in the matter of good works. If grace has his future in hand, it seems he need not trouble himself to do good works. Song of Songs 2.5 speaks of flowers and apples. The Bride is full of love; she sees the Bridegroom; she hears him talk to her at length; he feeds her; she rests in his shadow. She is given to drink but she thirsts for more. The withdrawal of the Bridegroom after these delights leaves her pining. She begs to be comforted with the scents of flowers and with fruits until he returns.[110]

If the Bride is taken here to be the Church, the flowers and fruits are Christian souls. The flowers are the beginners in the faith, still fresh and tender; the fruits are those who are mature in the faith. Surrounded by these, the Church, a pregnant and fruitful mother, waits the more patiently.[111] But also within the pattern of this imagery lies an assurance that the flowers and the apples are faith and works.[112]

Bernard sees will and necessity as inevitably opposed, for if I must do something, I can have no choice about it. He says so again and again. 'Either necessity presses or a benefit beckons': *Vel necessitas urgeat, vel utilitas moneat*[113] 'Where there is necessity, there is no choice': *Ubi quippe necessitas, iam non voluntas* .[114] 'Where there is necessity, there is no freedom': *Porro ubi necessitas est, libertas non est*.[115] 'The necessity of many is the virtue of few'; *Necessitas multorum est, virtus paucorum*.[116]

But there is another loading of 'necessity' which makes for a tension, such as that between the need in which mankind stands and the divine rescue. Jesus acted with fittingness and to meet a need, *convenientia et necessitate*, for the reconciliation of the human race, *in reconciliatione humani generis*.[117] *Necessitas* may be the 'need' of a friend: *sed in hanc importunitatem urget me Christi caritas et amicorum necessitas*.[118] Or it may be an 'emergency' of the kind which takes Bernard away from his monastic home.[119] Here necessity is set over against the response to that necessity. The owner of the will makes a choice thus to respond, rather than being *constrained* by the necessity to do so.

But this element of willing response must raise the issue of 'merit'. Merit is not the contentious issue for the twelfth century which it was to be for the sixteenth. Generally speaking, twelfth-century thinkers were content with the doublethink involved in holding, on the one hand, that we can do nothing good without the aid of grace, and on the other, that what we do that is good may have merit in God's eyes. When Bernard speaks of the threefold work of grace—*creatio, reformatio, consummatio*—he is clear that by grace we give our free consent (*propter consensum voluntarium nostrum*), and it is counted as merit to us (*in merita nobis reputabitur nostrum*).[120]

God gave people both merits and rewards (Ephesians 4.8; Psalm 68.18). The merits were for now; the rewards were for the eternal future. It is this to which Paul referred when he said that we who have the first fruits of the Spirit groan inwardly as we wait for adoption as sons.[121]

Human merits are gifts of God, says Bernard. The free choices of human beings are either justly condemned by God, for their sinfulness is the fault of the individual making the choice, or they are mercifully rescued and turned into good choices. That is to God's credit, not the individual's, for the individual could not succeed by himself in choosing the right.[122]

The sole merit of free choice lies in the consent it involves. Even though we may not be able to give our consent to the good without the help of grace—and Bernard is sure that we cannot—paradoxically, the merit still lies in that consent. For God involves us in it.[123]

Of these, only the reformation can be counted to us as merit, and the truly righteous man knows that his only contribution is to give some measure of consent to the work of grace in him and on his behalf. He thus consents by fasting, vigil, continence, works of mercy, and virtuous practices of various sorts. These activities assist the righteous actually to become better. There is inward renewal.[124] And the crown which is the just man's reward is not his own but God's.[125]

Bernard is, in a similar way, uncontroversially conscious of the notion of justification. He brackets vocation with justification, for those God calls he also justifies (Romans 8.2.28ff.).[126] Someone called through fear and justified by love presumes himself to be of the number of the blessed, being well aware of that promise.

It has already been hinted that Bernard has a clear grasp of the doctrine of sanctification.[127] Those who are 'self-righteous' do not know God's righteousness directly because they think their righteousness comes from themselves and not from God. The truly righteous see the work of grace in their righteousness. They know themselves to have been created by grace, reformed by grace, and brought to perfection by grace. They are created in

Christ (Ephesians 2.10), with freedom of will. They are reformed through Christ into the spirit of freedom (II Corinthians 3.17). Their perfecting by grace will take them to heaven.[128]

Bernard's Doctrine of the Church:
The *Catholica*

All this working out of the process of salvation for the individual takes place, Bernard assumes, in the context of his or her membership of the Church. He would not seek to make the sixteenth-century reformers' distinction between that membership and the relationship of the soul to God. He is broadly of the Augustinian view that there is no salvation outside the Church. But he accepts, like Augustine, that because God knows who are his own, it is not possible to know who exactly make up the Church. He recognises that it is possible to see when someone 'leaves': *quando exierunt aliqui de Ecclesia*.[129]

When Bernard thinks about the Church, he looks in the first instance to the qualities of its leaders. Already in his earliest treatise, the *De Gradibus Humilitatis*, Bernard was writing about the example Christ had set by his death, the necessity which brought it about, the example of a perfect human life he had given as a model.[130] He and his readers were entirely familiar with the notion that the good lead lives which are exemplary, that a saint's life serves the purpose of showing others the way to live, now that Christ himself is no longer visibly present among men. Saints, like Christ, are still alive among us even when they are dead.[131]

At the beginning of his treatise on the life of St. Malachy, Bernard gives the value of the *example* they set as the traditional reason for recording the lives of the saints.[132] They are mirrors in which others may see what they themselves ought to be. The lives of saints are a teaching aid; they set up a mirror before humanity.[133] They are a salt to give flavour to the lives of people on earth (Job 7.1). Saints are flavoursome, a kind of relish for the life of people on earth.[134] Yet they are effective in this way only because they are such a rarity. For the present age is greatly lacking in such examples. Here at least Bernard is an adherent of the 'old age of the world' school of thought. It seems to him a positive indicator of the imminence of the end of the world that there should be so few good men to be seen at present.[135]

That lack of good examples is particularly shameful in the case of those who ought to be setting an example of leadership in the Church. Look about you, exhorts Bernard. You will see that these are smouldering torches, not the brightly burning lights they ought to be.[136]

He censures particularly those highly placed in the Church who do not content themselves with modest amounts of worldly goods but are conspicuous in their consumption of its luxuries. The very offices of such officeholders are demeaned when their holders seek not the salvation of souls but the luxury of riches: *Ipsa quoque ecclesiasticae dignitatis officia in turpem quaestum et tenebrarum negotia transiere, nec in his animarum salus, sed luxus quaeritur divitiarum*.[137] Here Bernard allies himself with a position deemed revolutionary in others, the satirists and critics of the establishment and especially of pomp and circumstance in bishops, whose position later in the twelfth century became associated with Waldensians.

But even those not highly placed, or not initially highly placed, could have their effect. An exemplary figure such as Malachy could be expected to show exceptional characteristics from his earliest youth. One was, in this sense, a saint by divine appointment. That is to assert that God makes a person a saint by grace. It was a commonplace of contemporary hagiography that such a saintly individual would have had a mother who recognised his qualities while she was carrying him in her womb, as Bernard's mother was reported to have done.

Bernard says that Malachy had himself recognised his vocation as a young man and had gone to see a holy man who lived locally, so as to learn from him how to live a dedicated life, a life of prayer and fasting. He became a pupil of a man who was himself lowly of heart.[138] He undertook humble and thankless tasks, such as the burial of the poor.[139] The saints are, in these ways, means of calling people back to the lives they ought to be living.

However, Bernard's idea of the Church goes far beyond this loose notion that Christians ought to set one another an example. For one thing, the Church ought to teach. Christians have to know what they should believe, and unless they are instructed they cannot have an informed faith and there is a danger that they will fall into error. That means that the Church's ministers, and above all the pope, have a magisterial responsibility. Where the Church's 'father' is Pope Innocent II, the Church herself, *sancta ecclesia catholica*, is *Mater*, Mother.[140] But (certainly from the Fourth Lateran Council of 1215) she is also teacher, *magistra*. Her ministers consequently have a teaching office, a duty to maintain the faith. The supreme duty was already held to lie with the pope. It was a natural concomitant of the idea that he had 'plenitude of power'.

The challenge which was to arise from the conciliarists in the last medieval centuries, and from the reformers in the sixteenth century, was not yet apparent. In the letter of the bishops of France to Innocent II, it is asserted that those things which are confirmed by apostolic authority are always valid (*rata semper existunt*), and they cannot be invalidated by any subsequent caviling or 'envy' (*invidia*). The bishops are therefore coming to Innocent for a ruling on Abelard.[141] When invited to reply to Abelard at the Council of Sens, one of the grounds on which Bernard first refused was that it was not an abbot's but a bishop's task to make rulings on matters of faith: *nec mea referre, sed episcoporum, quorum esset ministerii de dogmatibus iudicare*.[142]

But we have still not got to the heart of the matter, to what determines the *status ecclesiae*.[143] Faith in Christ makes the Church, but it is not merely official teaching which does so. It was uncontroversial for Bernard that catholicity was one of the 'notes' of the Church and, moreover, a substantive and constitutent feature of its very self, its *esse*. Bernard speaks of the Church as 'the *Catholica*', using the adjective as a substantive. What the Church believes, *Catholica confitetur*;[144] *ut assentiat Catholica* is what the faithful hold in consensus.[145]

There is a *catholica veritas*.[146] Unity is of the essence of the faith. The *catholica* must be one, and to return to the Church is to return to unity with it: *ad catholicam rediit unitatem*.[147] Heresy is dangerous because it fragments or infects that singleness of mind in belief: *Quomodo et ipsam Catholicam paene totam hoc virus infecit*.[148] Bernard speaks of the *catholica fides* in his Letter 190 against Abelard's errors,[149] for what Abelard has done is attack the catholic faith with his errors: *Quibus fidem catholicam impugnavit*.[150] This unity is far more profound than the Church's polity or governance.[151]

Sacraments

Necessary or Sufficient to Salvation

So much for what the Church is. But what is it *for*? One of its tasks is to be a channel through which the salvation of individuals may be completed, Christ's sacrifice applied to the needs of the Christian soul.

The theme of salvation, and of what is necessary to it, is frequent in Bernard—*Commodi ad salutem;*[152] *saluberrima requies*.[153] He speaks disparagingly of someone who thinks he can save himself: *credens ad salutem te posse sufficere tibi*.[154] 'If I do not wash you, you have no part with me' (John 13.8). In this text, says Bernard, lies hidden the truth that it is necessary to salvation that Christ should wash Peter's feet, for without that even Peter would have had no part in the Kingdom of Christ. *Aliquid igitur latet quod necessarium est ad a salutem, quando sine eo nec ipse Petrus partem haberet in regno Christi et Dei*.[155]

The will to be saved is not sufficient for salvation, but on the other hand, no one is saved who is unwilling.[156] Can faith alone be sufficient for salvation? Can it be the case that nothing else avails without faith?[157] Without love the other virtues avail nothing for salvation.[158] We are not able to abstain completely from small sins, so while we live in this body, daily repentance suffices for our salvation: *ad salutem sufficere potest paenitentia quotidiana*.[159] Bernard hopes his brothers will always be found faithful and humble, for both are necessary to salvation: *Opto enim semper cos et fideles et humiles inveniri, quo utrumque summopere sit necessarium ad salutem*.[160] Bernard therefore includes an extremely various range of possibilities in the class of those things which are necessary to salvation. He is clearly not over-anxious about points which could have been the occasion of acrimonious debate in the sixteenth century.

It was uncontentious that the sacraments were the instruments of grace for this purpose, and it is helpful to look especially closely at that area. For the questions what a sacrament is and how many there are were not controversial in Bernard's day. The categories were generously drawn. In his sermon *In Cena Domini* Bernard acknowledges that there are many sacraments. He cannot speak of them all in one sermon. So he will restrict himself to baptism, the eucharist, and the washing of feet.[161]

Above all, a sacrament was seen as a mystery throughout the theological writings of the period. The term *sacramentum* is used equivocally both for *mysterium* and for the specific sacraments of the Church. It is partly because of this idea that Bernard disapproves of Abelard's attempts to open up the mystery of the sacrament too far,[162] for Abelard is accused by Bernard of eucharistic heresy (an error *de sacramento altaris*).[163] In a sermon for All Saints' Day Bernard speaks not of the *sacramentum altaris* but of the *mysterium altaris*.[164]

In the *Vita S. Malachiae* Bernard speaks of the *usum saluberrimum confessionis*, the *sacramentum confirmationis*, the *contractum coniugiorum*, patently not intending to imply that these three are different kinds of thing in any sense which would make one technically a sacrament and the others not.[165]

There is direct reference to the *paenitentiae sacramentum*.[166] Yet it was possible to speak of the 'sacrament of circumcision' (*circumcisionis sacramentum*),[167] even though circumcision was of the Old Testament and not of the New. At the coming of the Lord, who is the mild Lamb, baptism replaced the painful bloodshed of circumcision.[168] Bernard also describes a 'sacrament of redemption'.[169]

The concept of a sacrament is not, however, altogether vague in Bernard. He understands the Augustinian definition of the outward and visible sign of an inward and spiritual grace. Above all, Bernard recognises that a sacrament is a *sacrum signum*, a sacred sign, or a holy mystery (*sacrum secretum*).[170] Many things are done for their own sake, many for the purpose of indicating something else, and those are called signs.[171] The *signa* of investiture vary according to what the investment involves. Someone is invested with a canonry by means of a book. An abbot is invested with a kiss. A bishop is invested with a kiss and a ring.[172] What is the gratia *unde per baptismum investimur*? It is the purgation of sins.[173]

Ut enim de usualibus sumamus exemplum, to take a common example, a circle may have no significance. But if it is given as a ring, to invest someone with an inheritance, then it is a sign, and the person who receives it might say, 'The ring is of no value but the inheritance is'. Thus it is with the Passion of Christ. It gives value and meaning and purpose to the signs of the sacraments. For this were all the sacraments instituted, the Eucharist, the washing of feet, and baptism: *ad hoc instituta sunt omnia sacramenta, et ad hoc eucharistiae participatio, ad hoc pedum absolution, ad hoc denique ipse baptismus*.[174]

About 1127–28 Hugh of St. Victor had asked Bernard some questions about baptism. Bernard answered him in a letter. Can anyone be saved without baptism (or martyrdom as a substitute for it)? What about someone who seeks baptism but dies before he can receive it? *Cum vera fide et contritione cordis expeteret baptism, sed praeventus mortis articulo, assequi quod cuperet non valeret*; when someone in true faith and contrition of heart seeks baptism and cannot receive it before his death, is he damned?[175] Augustine certainly thought that people could be saved by faith alone, for then they would have the desire to receive the sacrament of baptism.[176]

Bernard wrote at length on baptism in his Letter to Hugh of St. Victor, exploring the still more testing question whether it can be right for God to destroy people who are righteous, just because they do not know the Christian faith.[177] (Bernard distinguishes different kinds of ignorance of the faith.

There is culpable ignorance, proceeding from idleness or unwillingness to learn: *aut sciendi incuria, aut discendi desidia, aut verecundia inquirendi*.[178] There is ignorance which is not the fault of the ignorant. There is ignorance which is sinful.)[179]

It can also be asked when, historically speaking, baptism began, for if baptism is necessary to salvation it seems hard that some individuals born before the institution of baptism should have been denied its benefits. It was instituted by Christ, and Scripture says that no one who is not reborn of water and Spirit will enter into the kingdom of heaven (John 3.5).[180] Those born before Christ could not have had faith in Christ. Can they be saved, when they cannot have had faith?[181]

It is important for these reasons to be clear whether the sacraments are efficacious. Bernard held that the sacraments have power or force: *tanta vis est sacramentorum*.[182] But it is a curious efficaciousness if we cannot see the effect. People ask why, if baptism takes away our original sin, there remains in us so strong a desire to sin. When we fell by sinning, explains Bernard, we fell on a sharp stone and it wounded us. We can wash the cut, but we still need medicines to heal it. The wound itches.

He suggests taking the sacraments as a series. Baptism does its work, but it does not stop us sinning. So there is the sacrament of the Body and Blood of Christ to numb the pain and take away our consent to *serious* sin. A person who receives the Body and Blood does not so often become angry, nor does he become so seriously angry when he does lose his temper, because of the *virtus sacramenti*, the power of the sacrament which is working in him.[183] The Christian can nourish himself daily at the table of the Body of Christ: *Potestatem se habere quotidie in mensa sua corpus Christi et sanguinem consecrandi ad nutriendum se in corpus Christi et membra*.[184]

We should not feel despair that we are unable to be without sin. We have the further 'sacrament' of the washing of feet. Again, Christ says that if he does not wash us, we shall have no part in him (John 13.8). That means that the washing of feet must be necessary to salvation, for without it even Peter would have had no part in the Kingdom.[185]

The problem with this doctrine—and Bernard does not seem greatly alert to it—is that it can seem to detract from the uniqueness of baptism. Chromatius of Aquileia describes the washing of the feet by our Lord as an *ablutio peccatorum*.[186] Bede (who is likely to be Bernard's source here) comments in the same vein: *ubi aperte monstratur quod haec lavatio pedum spiritalem carnis et animae purificationem sine qua ad consortium Christi perveniri non potest insinuat.*[187] But Bede stresses that this is not the remission of sins (*remissio peccatorum*), which happens once and for all in baptism, but rather that to which the sinner daily turns for the cleansing of grace: *sed illam potius qua cotidiani fidelium reatus sine quibus in hac vita non vivitur cotidiana eius gratia mundantur.*[188]

The Eucharist, too, is efficacious. At the table of faith (*mensa fidei*), we eat the bread of sorrows and drink water, and the vessels are the vessels of penance. At the table of hope, we eat the bread of comfort, and the vessels are the vessels of consolation. At the table of love, we eat the bread of life and a wine which brings joyousness and all the delightful things of paradise.[189] The Eucharist is seen by Bernard as a participation in the Passion of Christ. It is also an imitation of Christ, for in it we do as he did in the flesh. That is why we speak of the *altaris sacramentum*, where we receive the Lord's Body (*ubi Dominicum corpus accipimus*), and just as it seems that the form of bread (*panis forma*) enters us (*in nos intrare*), so we know that he himself enters into us, to dwell by faith in our hearts (*ad habitandum per fidem in cordibus nostris*).[190]

Bernard appears to have accepted the theory of transubstantiation, though he nowhere goes into its ramifications in any technical detail. He was born at the height of the controversy, in which Berengar of Tours was condemned for views which went the other way, and the Church in the West took up an extreme and well-defined position on the literal changing of bread into the Body of Christ and of wine into his Blood. Transubstantiation involves a high doctrine of the Eucharist because of its insistence upon the literal presence of Christ. That carries in its turn a strict requirement of liturgical observance. Bernard identifies as an *abusio* any allowing of a deacon to undertake this royal priestly ministry (*sive quod diaconus mensae regiae deputeutur ministerio*). No mere server of the king (*regis dapifer*) should administer the mystery of the altar (*mysteriis altaris inserviat*).[191] At Easter, the celebrant ought to come *ad altaris officium* in white vestments.[192]

Antichrist and the Last Things

Bernard of Poitiers in his *Apologeticus* criticises Bernard of Clairvaux for discussing his brother's death in one of his sermons on the Song of Songs. He is bringing his dead man to the wedding party.[193] What does Bernard of Clairvaux have to say about death?

Bernard turns to a question which vexed Augustine and Gregory the Great, that is, the state of souls who have died during the period before the resurrection of the body at the Last Judgement.[194] Bernard is confident that freedom from sin and from suffering is already enjoyed by such souls. For they are in God and with Christ and the angels in heaven. Nevertheless, they cannot yet have their full glory because they still lack their spiritual bodies.[195] The state of souls after death and before resurrection is, Bernard believes, already one of bliss. They are wholly engulfed in an ocean of eternal light. Yet they desire to have their bodies back. They are not entirely happy. In a human being, the flesh is the proper partner for the soul.[196]

Another question falls under the head of the Last Things, that of the signs of the end of the world which may be seen in the present time. Dom Norbert, says Bernard, spoke to him in that way, saying that there would be a general persecution of the Church in his lifetime.[197] Bernard himself was not so alarmist, but clearly such ideas were in the air. Some, including Bernard, were using Antichrist language.[198] Peter Abelard, he claims, goes before the face of Antichrist to prepare his ways, making pronouncements on the faith, the sacraments, the Trinity, which go against orthodox teaching: *de fide, de sacramentis, de Patre et Filio et Spiritu Sancto, praeter quam accepimus, enuntians*.[199]

Nevertheless, the familiar themes—that this is the old age of the world; the end of the world is at hand; Antichrist has come—are not especially strong in Bernard.[200] He was keener to put things right in the present than to bewail a situation about to come to a dramatic and final end. He was too inveterate an interferer to be able to stand back and wait for the consummation of all things.[201]

So Bernard's 'positive theology' is traditional. That would in any case be to him his greatest virtue.

NEGATIVE THEOLOGY

Scandala: Stumbling Blocks

Offending God and 'offending' the 'little ones' by putting stumbling blocks in their way are different things. You cannot put a stumbling-block in God's way. But it is certainly possible to offend him. One of the things which offends him most is 'offending' his 'little ones'.[1] Bernard saw the ordinary faithful in this light as 'children in the faith'.[2] It is never lawful to cause scandal, or to command what would cause scandal, he insists.[3] But you only fall over a stumbling block (*scandalum*) if you cannot see it. And because they are 'little ones', the *simple* faithful cannot clearly see what is in their way, and so their faith may be damaged when they 'fall over' an idea put in their way by an irresponsible person or a heretic.

Yet Bernard reveres simplicity. It is, he emphasises, the simple, the poor in spirit, who are to enter heaven.[4] So Bernard's theory of the faithful as children is paradoxical. On the one hand it makes them, in their simplicity, spiritual giants. On the other hand it makes them vulnerable; for he is insistent that these helpless, the relative innocents who lack the education to see that they are being misled, ought especially to be protected.

One of the reasons why it matters if the faith of simple people is damaged is that such a 'taint' lingers upon them: *quo semel est imbuta recens servabit odorem testa diu*, says Bernard in a letter to Chancellor Haimeric.[5]

They do not easily shake it off, because they do not have the intellectual equipment or the expert knowledge of theology to enable them to do so.

There are certain simple and obvious stumbling blocks which can be pastorally looked for, and so do not require a developed theological explanation of an academic sort. But an explanation in terms of a simpler, more pastoral theology can be appropriate. Bernard attempts that more than once. He is much aware that the faithful find worldly things seductive. He holds up awful warnings to them. The world may seem to reward those who love her—for a time. But her rewards are unreliable, the pleasures she affords fickle.[6] The only thing certain is death. It is therefore wise to prepare for death very seriously and not allow oneself to be captivated by worldly pleasures. To that end, one cannot be too conscious of the scale of the consequences of sin, their eternal importance.[7]

It is also pastorally straightforward to emphasise that there is no such thing as *hidden* sin. The divine light will eventually fall brightly on everything the sinner has done.[8] Bernard is aware that many fear other people's opinions more than the wrath of God. They try to disguise their true selves from their neighbours. But Christ sees everything. He became a human being, and he is never unaware of the deeds of human beings. Do not dare to do in his sight what you would hesitate to do in mine, exhorts Bernard.[9]

Such things aside, there remain stumbling blocks which do need a more formal, thought-out, even academic explanation, and, as Bernard saw it, even a theology geared to dealing with these matters that seeks to rebut heresy.

What Is Negative Theology?

'Negative theology' has two meanings in Christian theology. The first belongs to Christian mysticism. This is the idea that all we can know about God is what we cannot know about God, for example that he is in-finite, in-visible. By contemplating that mystery, the spiritual enquirer hopes to glimpse something of what God is. This was an approach which had its vogue in the late antique world, especially in the writings of Ps.-Dionysius and was to be rediscovered in the later Middle Ages. It is hinted at in Anselm of Canterbury's reference at the beginning of the *Proslogion* to the 'inaccessible light' in which God dwells. But it was not in general a habit of thought of Bernard's day, except insofar as it was very clear to everyone that God is ultimately beyond human knowing, and beyond the reach of human expression, too.

The second[10] sense in which 'negative theology' can be taken is to describe the thinking required to deal with heresy and schism. This is a theology concerned with the rebuttal of unorthodox opinions, as distinct from the setting forth of a positive account of Christian truth, although of course the truth will be described in the process. Aquinas wrote not only a systematic theology (*Summa Theologiae*), but also a systematic treatment of erroneous beliefs about the Christian faith(*Summa Contra Gentiles*), in recognition that two distinctive methodologies are required for the two modes of doing theology. These two, positive and negative theology, are in some sense mirror images of one another.

Historically, a challenge to the faith has led again and again to its being set forth 'positively', more clearly, with points not explicated before being made explicit, and with fresh refinements. Arguably, that has been, on the whole, beneficial to the faith.

Was Bernard an effective campaigner against heresy? Was he competent in this 'field' or activity of negative theology? Bernard was heard to say that he doubted whether this was the kind of task for which he was best fitted (*suum hoc non esse renuntians*), but perhaps that was disingenuous.[11] Bernard was involved in two memorable trials, at which leading academics of the day were brought to account for teaching which was thought to be leading the faithful astray. Geoffrey of Auxerre gives an account of the trials of both Peter Abelard and Gilbert of Poitiers in a single chapter of Bernard's biography, the *Vita Prima*. He sees both as aspects of Bernard's work against the unbelievers who seduce the faithful. Geoffrey emphasizes Bernard's unwillingness to become involved[12] and describes how he was won round and persuaded that it was his duty to go into battle against these heretics. An important consideration in explaining Bernard's diffidence is that defending the faith (as distinct from teaching or expounding it) could seem an awesome responsibility. When, a decade before the end of the eleventh century, Anselm of Canterbury heard that Roscelin of Compiègne was saying that Anselm taught an unorthodox doctrine of the Trinity, he took up his pen in his own defence. He wrote an open letter to all faithful people, with an apology. Yet when he contemplates himself in the act of trying to strengthen and confirm the faith, he sees himself as a ridiculous figure, laden with ropes and tackle, working earnestly round the base of Mount Olympus, lashing it and pegging it so as to prevent its falling down.[13] He has made the attempt, though not because he believes the faith to be in need of his efforts; he has written to defend *himself*.[14] But faith is one thing and the minds of the faithful another. The minds of the faithful may well need fighting for. Abelard's teaching seemed to William of St. Thierry and to St. Bernard to pose no merely superficial threat to the security of orthodox faith in the minds of the faithful, but to strike at its very foundations with both subtlety and force.[15]

The Creeds of Negative Theology

Geoffrey of Auxerre explains that Abelard was a famous master of the day (*insignis*), of great learning, but teaching treachery to the faith (*sed de fide perfide dogmatizans*) and also teaching profane novelties of word and sense (*profanas novitates vocum et sensuum*).[16] Bernard did not start the attack on Abelard. But an attack was made, and it generated in reply a piece of writing which was itself a form of 'negative theology'. When Peter Abelard set about defending himself against the allegations that he was a heretic, he composed an *Apologia* for Bernard in reply to Bernard's Letter 190. It survives only in fragments. But a briefer response survives intact.[17] In both versions, Abelard refutes the allegation in nineteen 'heads of the heresies' (*Capitula haeresum* XIX) that the propositions listed are in fact all to be found in his works at all. He points out that there is no work of his called the *Sententiae*, although he has been accused of holding opinions expressed in that work.[18] 'Where,' he protests indignantly, 'did I say that the Father was full power, the Son a certain power, and the Holy Spirit no power' (*Quod Pater sit plena potentia, Filius quaedam potentia, Spiritus Sanctus nulla potentia*).[19]

Abelard, like Anselm confronted with the accusations of Roscelin at the end of the eleventh century,[20] made the mistake of trying to explain. 'I said that it was a certain power of God to be able to discern all things; . . . I said that his love tended to kindness rather than to power, so that love can be called the "will" of God rather than his "power".'[21] That was the way to court more accusations of heresy, for such explanations themselves required explanation and defence. They were saying when he was tried at Soissons that he had been teaching that there were three gods, laments Abelard.[22]

What justice was there in the accusation that Abelard's views were heretical? The nineteen heresies[23] include views which were probably really held by Abelard; others, taken out of context or qualified by Abelard, were condemned by Bernard without taking those qualifications into account or accepting Abelard's contention that the condemned opinions were not his at all. Abelard was not alone in being indignant at being accused of heretical views on the basis of words in a book he had not written. As we shall see in a moment, Gilbert of Poitiers felt the same.[24]

So one of the tasks of negative theology may fall to the *accused,* in setting out his rejoinders to the allegations made against him. He may go farther and construct his own 'positive theology' in the form of a *credo*. Abelard also wrote a 'confession of faith' for Heloise, which Berengar of Poitiers tells us about, as well as the *Confessio Fidei 'Universis'*. John Marenbon suggests that these are not in themselves polemical in tone but explanatory, even peda-gogic.[25] The *Apologia* is directly addressed to Bernard. The *Confessio Fidei Universis* is written to the Church at large. Bernard is Abelard's declared enemy, but Abelard has no enmity towards the Church. His appeal in this work is therefore to the mutual charity which ought to subsist among Christians, of which he counts himself one.

Abelard does not back down, but he declares himself to have been mis-understood. Here we have a theologian identified by many of his contemporaries as a dangerous heretic doing a highly specialised kind of 'negative theology' for himself. He is seeking to 'place' his own thinking, to declare it orthodox, and to disassociate himself from those opinions which have been attributed to him, but which he does not in fact wish to own.

A *confessio fidei* of this sort is an example of a genre which others accused of heresy attempted or were required to attempt. A confession of faith was formally required of heretics of the Waldensian persuasion before 1184.[26] Throughout the Middle Ages, where there were inquisitions into heretical sects, a similar pattern of drawing up lists of articles of wrong belief and requiring assent to articles of the true faith was repeated.

The 'Waldensian creed', if we may call it that, asserts a doctrine of the Trinity which it claims to be in accord with the Nicene, Apostolic, and Athanasian Creeds. It is careful to assert points which polemicists claim the Waldensians deny. It includes items which belong more naturally in the arena of the dualists, who differed crucially from the Waldensians in that they believed in two Principles in the universe, a power of evil opposed to the power of good, equally divine and engaged in an eternal war for supremacy. The dualists (Cathars, Albigensians, Bogomils), were not strictly Christians at all, although many of their adherents were confused peasants who also went to the local Christian church.[27]

Ermengaud, at the end of the twelfth century, says Valdès was the origi-
nator of the 'Waldensian' error, though he swore to a cardinal of the Roman
Church that he had never held such views as were attributed to him.[28] The
Waldensians appear to have been ecclesiologically unorthodox, antiestablish-
ment dissidents, but relatively ordinary in their views on other matters. It
has been suggested that a number of the positions in the creed would have
been rejected by the Waldensians after they made their break with Rome,
in particular what is said about the relationship of Old Testament to New,[29]
infant baptism, and the validity of sacraments performed by unworthy
ministers. [30]

These 'credal statements' might exceed the brevity Bernard deems to be
characteristic of the *symbolum fidei*. Paul is appropriately called 'little Paul',
he comments, for they made him an abbreviated word in handing on the
symbol of the faith: *Bene 'Paululum', quia verbum abbreviatum fecerunt ei,
symbolum fidei tradentes*.[31] But our latter-day apologetic 'creeds' are none-
theless arguably credal statements for all that. They are marked by the selection of topics on which their authors have been challenged and a certain
defensive 'angling' of what is said. It is true, of course, that the Niceno-
Constantinopolitan Creed has similar characteristics, but that is the Church's
official version and not the defence of an individual. The key mark of a heretic or a schismatic is that he is set *apart* from the Church by his position.

The Unbeliever

'You show yourselves altogether unbelieving and faithless,' *omnino incredulos
vos exhibetis et infideles*,[32] Bernard reproves his listeners in a sermon. But he
does not confuse weak belief with true unbelief.

What is the duty of the faithful Christian towards someone who appears
to him not to be among the flock of Christ, whose soul seems in danger? Peter
the Venerable thought it was essential to be proactive, vigorous. His *Contra
Petrobrusianos Hereticos*, against the contemporary 'Henricians', was written in an early draft about 1138 but not sent out, because Peter was dissatis-
fied with it. In the prefatory letter which accompanied it when it was at last
published, he exhorts the provincial bishops to be energetic in keeping an
eye out for heresy and to fortify the faith with strong columns.[33] His *Adversus Iudeorum Inveteratam Duritiem* is an '*omnium gatherum*' of the standard

texts of the Jewish-Christian dialogue, containing nothing strikingly new, but having a clear purpose of fortifying with materials for argument those whose practical task it was to seek conversions and to defend the Christian faith.[34] Peter the Venerable is passionately protective of that faith. 'With what face, with what conscience,' he asks, could he come to the altar of Christ if he had been meek and gentle with the butchers of the faith?[35]

About some categories of unbelievers, there could be no doubt, for they were unbaptised, had never been Christians in name at all. Those who were not Christians were destined for hellfire, and the Christian apologist must take a view on his duty to seek to help them. Bernard recognised such a duty. He held that God intended his salvation to be offered to all.[36] Bernard knew of two categories of unbeliever of this sort: Jews and Moslems.

There could, at this date, be no notion of mutual toleration or of mutual respect, or of 'interfaith dialogue' designed as such. Yet there was dialogue. The Jews were local and familiar. They could be met in the streets of the cities of Europe. Indeed, there is evidence that there were meetings and discussions for mutual interest. Dialogue was therefore possible. Anselm conducts a dialogue with his friend and former pupil Boso in the *Cur Deus Homo* in which Boso seems to play the part of a Jew arguing against the necessity of the Incarnation. Gilbert Crispin, abbot of Westminster and another former pupil of Anselm of Canterbury at Bec, wrote a dialogue between a Christian and a Jew which is almost certainly indebted to real conversation.[37] Peter Abelard was the author of a dialogue involving a Christian, a Jew, and a 'Philosopher'. Hermannus Judaeus, a convert to Christianity, wrote, with the zeal of a convert, an account of how he had been won over by argument in conversation over an extended period. Andrew of St. Victor made a rather different use of the opportunity to meet Jews, as did Peter Abelard, in consulting them over the interpretation of the Old Testament text.

On the other hand, there was a 'bad press' to be dealt with, and talking to Jews was not uncontroversial. There was the baggage of negative assumptions to be got out of the way. The historical record of persecution of Jews on the grounds that they had been responsible for the death of Christ had not ended in Bernard's day—there were to be episodes with the Second Crusade. Bernard says the Jews should not be blamed for that death.[38] There was also a temptation to exploit their wealth in getting up funding for the Crusade, which rode on the back of the argument that their wealth could be regarded as forfeit because of their great offence. There were many who were ready to take advantage of that.

Bernard wrote to the archbishops of France and Bavaria 'on the matter of Christ, in which is our salvation': *de negotio Christi, in quo est utique salus nostra*.[39] It is praiseworthy that these prelates should be filled with zeal for God (*zelus Dei*), but there should be due moderation. 'The Jews are not to be persecuted,' he says. The psalm instructs us, 'Do not kill my enemies' (Psalm 58.12). It is better to try to *convert* the Jews than to attack them.[40]

Islam, Bernard 'encountered' at one remove, through his preaching of the Crusade. There was no long tradition of a half-kin relationship here, as there was between Christians and Jews. The Moslems could be seen as temporary usurpers of the Holy Places, fit objects for crusading zeal. It was not Bernard but Peter the Venerable, abbot of Cluny from 1122, who was sufficiently interested to enquire into the contents of the Koran and to arrange in 1143 for it to be translated into Latin so that Christian theologians would read it.

Schism and Heresy

Schism is a heresy. Augustine held it to be the most serious of heresies, for it divides the body of Christ. Bernard was less acutely aware of the importance of that. He was not dealing with the equivalent of Donatists on the doorstep. But that does not mean that he did not take the idea of schism seriously. He saw a *schisma* as an oppressive threat to the Church.[41]

The only example known to Bernard of a formal schism in the full technical sense of a division of the Church was the division between the Eastern (Greek) and the Western (Latin) Churches which dated from 1054. Bernard makes an observation on the Greeks. He says that they are 'with us and not with us'. By this he means that they are united in faith with Rome (though he thinks not perfectly), but not in harmony with it (because of the schism). This 'with us but not with us' line is close to what Augustine had to say about the Donatist schism in the North Africa of his own day, and no doubt Bernard took the sense of it from him. For Augustine understood that unity in the faith may persist even where there is a breakdown of a common order. That is why schismatics, if baptised with water and in the name of the Trinity, are deemed already baptised when they return to the *catholica*, the 'catholic Church'.

Schisma in Bernard also refers to papal schism.[42] This was another type of 'schism', common in this period of the Middle Ages, created by rivalry

between pope and antipope and a relative commonplace in Eugenius's lifetime. Letter 132 to the clergy of Milan argues vehemently that the schism
must be ended in order to return to catholic unity. Bernard writes to the
people of Milan to say that he is grateful to have been invited to negotiate
the peace.[43] He himself spent years trying to win secure tenure of the papacy for Innocent II, perhaps the most serious schism of his lifetime.

Even those of us who are *in* the Church are inclined each to seek his own
advantage, Bernard points out. There is too much personal ambition. That
is one reason why Eugenius is so beset with lawsuits by vexatious persons
wanting to get public attention for their problems. But Bernard can remain
confident that though the garments of Christ are divided, the tunic of Christ
remains whole, without seam, because it has been woven all in one piece from
the top.[44]

Bernard's keen interest was in lost sheep. His principal concern was
characteristically with the danger that internal strife in the fold itself would
damage the faith and set at risk the salvation of individuals.

Among the 'heretics' likely to mislead the sheep in this way whom
Bernard identifies are the Cathar dualists of the south of France and northern Spain and Italy. Awareness of Catharism came to Bernard late in life.
He partly sums up Cathar beliefs in the Song of Songs sermons (6–7) in which
he explores the evidences that God *works* through the flesh and through
material things and has good purposes for them. That must mean that the
Cathars are wrong in deeming them to be a creation of an evil God.

It is an offence of the Cathars, Bernard suggests, to abstain from the good
foods God has given us to eat. The Cathar motivation for fasting is culpable;
it is inspired by a repugnance for all that derives from the flesh, and therefore it shows ingratitude to the Creator. Fasting is not necessarily wrong.
But right fasting is that which is undertaken in reparation for sin. Bernard
reminds Pope Eugenius that these heretics have not so far responded to attempts to win them back to the fold by preaching to them.[45]

Bernard was also in contention with a variety of heretical sects of an 'anti-
establishment' persuasion whose members tended to the view that souls
could be saved without the assistance of the sacraments, and therefore of the
Church's hierarchy. This was the mainstream line of reforming thought
which stretches from the Waldensians or Poor Men of Lyons at the end of
the twelfth century to the Lollards in the late fourteenth and fifteenth centuries and to the reformers of the sixteenth. In Bernard's day, these lines were
not yet clear, and there were various attempts to get a working focus of the

reforming endeavour directed at the perceived corruptions in the Church. Bernard himself could on occasion speak with the 'reformers' here.[46]

About 1143, Everwin of Steinfeld wrote to tell Bernard of a recent unpleasantness at Cologne involving heretics, which had left him upset and troubled.[47] The heretics claim to be the sole true Church, following in the footsteps of Christ, imitating the true apostolic life. They live in poverty. They are vegetarians. They consecrate their food and drink at meals, as Christ consecrated the bread and wine at the Last Supper. They baptise not only with water, but also with fire and with the Holy Ghost, claiming that all believers who have been baptised and are among the elect have power to baptise others. They oppose the established practices of the Church in administering the sacrament, condemning baptism and marriage as they are usually understood.

Another group of heretics is found in the Rhineland, too, who disagree with the first. Their position is altogether more radically opposed to orthodoxy. They deny that priests have the power of consecrating bread and wine because, they say, the pope is no longer Peter's true successor; he is corrupted by his engagement in worldly affairs, and all his priests with him. They condemn infant baptism, saying that Christ alone baptises the believer, when he is of age. They think that the Church has lost the power of consecration. All the other sacraments they hold invalid.

The first group had been brought to trial. Two of its members, one calling himself their bishop, had defended their heresy before the archbishop of Cologne and certain magnates. They claimed that they were true followers of Christ; they declared themselves willing to belong to the orthodox Church if their arguments could be worsted in debate with the Church's apologists, but if not, they said that they were prepared to die for their faith. The mob took them and burned them, and they went to their death, says Everwin, not only with patience, but with joy. He is disturbed by these events, because he cannot understand why these men, obviously in error, showed a spirit and a piety which is not to be found even in good Christians, as a rule.[48] He describes the teaching of the heretics in outline and also mentions another sect in the area, whose teaching is different.[49]

He begs Bernard to write him a defence of the faith. There can be nothing more important, he presses; Bernard cannot say he is too busy, and if he says that the 'tower of David' is already sufficiently fortified, Everwin answers that its fortifications are not obvious to simple and slow-witted men such as himself (*nos simpliciores et tardiores*). There is a need for a plain man's guide to heresy, which will enable such honest Christians to make themselves prepared, and ready to resist the arguments the heretics may put to them.[50]

At the time Everwin's letter arrived, Bernard had been preaching on the meaning of the 'little foxes' of the Song of Songs (Canticles 2.15) in the sixty-fourth of his series of sermons on the Song of Songs. He had already explained that the *vulpes parvulae* could be interpreted either as temptations[51] or as heretics.[52] Now he continued, extending his reflections, considering how heretics should be dealt with by faithful Christians.

Heretics, he explains, should be captured not by force of arms, but by arguments to refute their errors (*non armis, sed argumentis, quibus refellantur errores eorum*).[53] Every effort should be made to reconcile them to the Church, for God's will is that all men should be saved.[54]

One of Bernard's most developed sequences of exposition on heretics occurs in Sermons 64ff. of the Song of Songs series. The little foxes which spoil the vines have to be caught and brought out into the open so that they can be recognised for what they are. For this fox is a pest with a unique characteristic. Once it is known for what it is, it is powerless to do further harm.[55]

The trick is not to drive the foxes away but to catch them, to entrammel them in arguments which refute their errors. Then they may themselves be brought back to the fold as true faithful. That is why the text says not 'catch the foxes' but 'catch us the foxes'.[56] Christ wants the foxes caught for himself and his Bride, the Church. That means that if someone acts as an apologist for the true faith in debate with a heretic, his purpose should be to persuade the heretic he is wrong and teach him the right way to think. As James says (5.20), if someone causes a sinner to be converted, that will cover a multitude of his own sins. Only if he will not be converted when two or three attempts have been made is this fox to be driven away.[57]

Bernard was obliged in the interests of consistency to offer this final option, for it was exactly what he did himself in his dealings with Abelard. And such an outcome is not entirely negative, for as Bernard points out, it strengthens the faith to clarify it, to explain for others why the heretic is wrong so that his heretical viewpoint may at least not gain a foothold in other minds and hearts.[58]

Bernard felt strongly about the inexcusable ignorance of those who are too lazy to learn divine truth.[59] The man who, trained and learned (*exercitatus et doctus*), takes issue with a heretic should have the intention of converting him clearly before his mind. He has done his work well when he overcomes the heretic's resistance and convinces him, confutes his heresy, distinguishes clearly between the truth and what merely appears to be true (*verisimilia a vero clare aperteque distinxit*), and makes it obvious how wicked his teaching is.[60]

In Sermon 65, Bernard apologizes to his listeners for preaching yet a third sermon on the foxes and then explores the deceitfulness of heretics, their subtlety, their vanity. He shows the good Christian how to see through them. They are seducers of the spirit,[61] flatterers who can present evil as though it were good. They are full of tricks.[62] They are seducers, dangerously attractive, tempting women to leave their husbands and husbands to leave their wives to join sects and communities of weavers with their women.[63]

In the same sermon, we meet the modern heretics as displaying a new *secrecy*, something the heretics of old did not tend to, says Bernard, for they preached openly in the marketplace. The new heretics are not interested in renown for themselves but only in the destruction of others.[64] Bernard is here teaching something which is the reverse of the *disciplina arcani* of the early Christian period. If teaching is of God, he argues, it ought to be freely and openly shared. Christ told his disciples to go out and preach. It is only that which is not of God which needs to be hidden.[65]

Sermon 66 begins with another apology: *Ecce ego ad vulpes istas*: 'Here again I am talking about those foxes!' Now Bernard examines the beliefs of the heretics Everwin has described to him—their teaching on marriage, on the baptism of infants, on purgatory, on prayers for the dead, on the invocation of saints.[66]

His method of meeting Everwin's request to simplify his teaching for simple men is to sharpen and compress his arguments until they are little more than indignant statements of the absurdity of such heretical claims; he wants to produce a strong, clear impression in his listeners' minds of the kind of thing the heretics are saying, so that they may recognize heresy when they meet it. He excuses himself that he has allowed his talks about the foxes to go on so long, with the end in view of painting a picture in bold colours which his listeners will remember.

Bernard as Polemicist

Bernard was a chief member of a 'reforming' party which showed steady hostility to Stephen de Garlande and to Abelard.[67] That suggests a proactive habit in seeking out wrongs to be righted and trying to do something about them. But Bernard's chief anxiety was over threats to the trust and confidence of ordinary Christians in the teaching of the Church about their faith. He often got into polemics because correspondents asked him to, underlining the danger until he could resist them no longer.

And on the face of it, Bernard was truly reluctant to be drawn into controversy. He held out against it at the time when attempts were made to draw him into the campaigning for the Second Crusade.

The polemic about the Second Crusade involved preaching. The set-piece performances at Sens and Rheims which we shall be looking at in a moment were also 'live'. But for the most part Bernard's polemical activities were conducted by letter. Bernard was not the only person who could write letters of attack. It appears from a letter to Chancellor Haimeric that someone had been making trouble in Rome about Bernard. He wonders whether he should be glad or sorry about being treated as an enemy. He knows that if you tell the truth people will dislike you. Bernard had certainly been 'blowing whistles', and as far as we know, doing it quite openly.

In an evasive letter to Gerard, abbot of Pouthières, Bernard begins by saying that he does not recollect ever having written anything to the count of Nevers which was hostile to Gerard. If he did write any letter, he concedes, it was done not to accuse but to help the abbot. Bernard argues defensively that Gerard can have no reason to accuse Bernard of injuring him if he, Bernard, has merely tried to encourage the count and strengthen him in his pious intention. 'In fact,' he ends, admitting that he did write, 'I think I did right to impress upon the count what his responsibility consists in here.'[68]

So he has drawn attention to the discredited 'steward' who had been squandering the Church's goods at Châlons; he has forced Fulbert to withdraw at Cambrai; he has restored the Lord's sanctuary to him at Laon, for it had become a 'brothel'.[69] He claims that he has done all this with a proper unconcern for what people will think of him. He is not disturbed to be blamed where the blame is undeserved, just as he wants no praise if that is not deserved.[70]

Whatever the route by which Bernard was drawn into his various polemical activities and however he came to understand his duty, there must remain a question whether what he was doing involved a witch-hunt. In fairness, it is Bernard's honest presumption that interfering letters are for the good of those they concern, and he wrote them as actively to defend as to attack. Bernard wrote to Innocent II on behalf of the archbishop of

Canterbury and the bishop of London. He tells him that Theobald is a good man who has become involved in a dispute through no fault of his own and who cannot defend himself.[71] Bernard could, on this evidence, be self-justificatory. And he certainly put energy into his campaigns, once launched. Bernard's polemical correspondence is considerable, both in its quantity and in its scope, especially the raft of letters he sent pursuing Abelard's condemnation after Sens, which we shall be looking at in a moment.[72] Its polemical character was sometimes heightened by the zeal of secretaries instructed to write a given letter, who wrote it at a higher temperature than bernard himself might have done.[73]

Practical Dispute Resolution:
Peter Abelard and Gilbert of Poitiers

The encounter between Bernard and Peter Abelard stood for something rather bigger than the jousting of a prominent and notoriously controversial academic and a highly visible churchman-in-politics. It marked a key stage in the uneasy story of the relationship between theological scholarship and the teaching office of the Church. These tensions were to heighten in the later Middle Ages. They have not diminished in the late twentieth century, where a prominent theologian may still find his books condemned by Rome and attempts made to silence him. Bernard does not present the issue as one of Church versus academe. In his mind, the conflict was between truth and falsehood, respect for orthodoxy of faith and a cavalier willingness to take risks with the truth out of intellectual curiosity.

The themes of the debate were, for the most part, those at which we have been looking in the chapter on 'positive theology'. In every age, theological controversies centre on the topics of the moment, fashionable issues which have become contentious, often because of a clash of personalities or the intransigence of a leader of thought who has refused to retract an argument when the ecclesiastical authorities have challenged his teaching. Yet one becomes such a leader of thought chiefly by resisting such censure.

The two scholars we are now concerned with, Peter Abelard and Gilbert of Poitiers, were not intransigent, in the sense that neither *set out* to challenge orthodoxy. As scholars, both had been exploring questions which were leading them to answers of some subtlety and complexity in areas of the use of theological language. They were trying to get a more exact understandng of the meaning of orthodox teaching, chiefly on the Trinity, and to find words in which to set out their conclusions. But revising formulations which lie at the heart of the faith looked dangerous to the ecclesiastical authorities. It was also a danger that these were working teachers, lecturing to the next generation of theologians and churchmen, and likely to influence their thinking.

When they were called to account, both scholars protested their innocence. They said they were not heretics. They said they had not been teaching the unorthodoxies they had been alleged to be teaching. Gilbert in particular offered to put it right if he could be shown to be in the wrong. But it was more important to the Church that the appearance of dissent should be visibly put down than that the exact teaching of these two should be clarified. Both were destroyed by the battle, personally and professionally. Theologically, nothing was settled, for the conceptual difficulties with which they were wrestling are inherent problems of Trinitarian theology, and the advancing skills of the period in logic and language were genuinely showing up new aspects of those problems.

The trial at Sens in 1142 was not the first time Peter Abelard had been in trouble. In 1121 he had been tried at the Council of Soissons. It has been suggested that the Church's authorities consciously saw that there were important questions to be settled about the powers of a synod or council to determine theological controversies. The ecclesiology of centuries would appear to have established that principle beyond doubt, but the papacy was now keen to establish a hegemony. To that end, it made sense to seek to treat such a hearing as a trial, with a 'judge' in the form of a papal legate. At Soissons, Abelard himself preferred to be tried by the collective judgement of the synod and resisted the authority of the legate. He was shocked to discover that the legate, Cono, was not proposing to read his book on the Trinity before judging him on its contents. 'As soon as I came to the city,' Abelard says, 'I handed over my little book to the legate for him to read and consider. But he immediately instructed that it be given to the archbishop and my enemies, so that they might judge me.'[74] He was shocked to perceive that the legate was comparatively unlettered, certainly not sufficiently literate to judge his work (*minus quam necesse esset litteratus*), and that he depended upon the archbishop's advice.[75]

His 'enemies' diverted attention from the question whether what he had been teaching was indeed heresy. They concentrated instead upon the question whether he had committed an offence simply by reading the text in public and allowing copies of it to be made, when the pope had not explicitly approved it.[76] (There was, of course, no routine expectation that the pope should approve every book published, but this book of Abelard's was a refutation of Roscelin of Compiègne, and Anselm of Canterbury had got approval for his own refutation of the same controversial teacher from the pontiff, thus setting a precedent.)[77]

There was also a move, at the instigation of Cono, to get Abelard removed to the abbey of St. Denis for a conference about his book. Abelard was in favour of that idea, because he still innocently believed that there was nothing afoot but an open-minded enquiry to discover whether his book did or did not contain heresy. He had not yet understood that he was being pilloried for blasphemy, accused of 'thought-crime',[78] that the question was not whether he was in fact guilty of these things, but whether the faithful would be edified by seeing them condemned, without reference to the actual content of his teaching and writing. Arguably, he lost his good name without its ever being discovered whether he deserved to do so. Bernard, when he entered the lists against Abelard two decades later, also seemed to take the view that a man's teaching was of less importance than his attitude, that a proud and contentious person ought to be condemned as a heretic in any case.[79]

Soissons, therefore, taught Abelard that the pope's man could not be relied upon to protect his interests. After Sens, Abelard seems to have changed his mind about the authority to make such determinations, and he appealed to Rome for a judgement to override that of the council. But again, even though he had friends at the Curia (such as Guy of Castello, the future Pope Celestine II, and Hyacinth Boboni, who was later to become Pope Celestine III), he found that independent fair judgement was not to be had; there appeared to be nowhere to go where his enemies could not reach with their influence.[80]

William of St. Thierry was probably present at this trial at Soissons. He was now, at the beginning of the 1140s, at Signy, no longer a Benedictine but a Cistercian. He initiated the attack which led to Abelard's fresh trial, in which, this time, Bernard was actively involved. William had been, he says, very shocked by Abelard's *Theologia*. He could not concentrate on the commentary he was working on, upon the Song of Songs. His inner calm was shattered by this outward strain.[81] So he wrote a treatise, a *Disputation* against Peter Abelard.[82] The accusation was that Abelard was teaching 'new doctrines' on subjects central to the faith, such as the Trinity, Christ, the Holy

Spirit, grace, the sacraments.[83] William wrote out passages from Abelard's work with which he said the Fathers disagreed, and he supplied passages from the Fathers to prove it. He sent a copy to Geoffrey, bishop of Chartres, and another to Bernard.[84] Abelard was insulted to have his *Theologia* spoken of as a *stultilogia*.[85] And he did not like being vilified in leading ecclesiastical circles. Bernard seems to have learned first of opinions of Abelard which disquieted him from this *Disputatio adversus Petrum Abaelardum* of William of St. Thierry.[86]

There are several accounts of the events surrounding Peter Abelard's second 'trial' at Sens, twenty years after the first, not only the contemporary ones of Geoffrey of Auxerre, Bernard of Poitiers, and Otto of Freising, but also echoing reverberations decades later, such as the story told by Walter Map of a dinner with Thomas Becket and two Cistercian abbots in 1163.[87]

The letter from the bishops of France[88] says that Bernard preached against Abelard to the students of Paris.[89] That would make him in part an instigator of the battle.

There is a Scriptural duty upon Christians to seek to make peace with their enemies. On the face of it Bernard tried the method of talk and reconciliation first with Abelard, in the spirit of Matthew 18.15.[90] However, Geoffrey of Auxerre says that the reason why Bernard wanted at first to handle the Abelard affair quietly and privately is that that was his usual way. Bernard would have preferred to get Abelard to see the error of his ways more tactfully. Geoffrey calls this Bernard's usual way of doing such business (*solita bonitate et benignitate desiderans errorem corrigi, non hominem confundi, secreta illum adminitione convenit*). He did not want the man publicly humiliated.

The letter from the bishops of France says that there was first a meeting of Bernard and Abelard alone and then a meeting with two or three witnesses.[91] It seems that Bernard did call a private meeting of the bishops the evening before the council, where he won them round to his side. It has been suggested that he used the simple device of presenting them with the series of propositions under discussion and inviting them to condemn them one by one as heretical.[92] That would have had the result of making it impossible for them not to support him in public on the morrow, and of blurring the distinction between the question whether a given view was indeed heretical and the question whether it was a view Peter Abelard in fact held. Abelard was turned from attacker to defender at a stroke. He found himself faced with the task of publicly defending propositions already condemned by the bishops present. Bernard of Poitiers gives a different account of this episode of the evening before the trial. He pictures it as a drunken after-dinner mock trial, marked by loud jeering.[93]

The archbishop of Sens now wrote to Bernard at Abelard's instigation, to invite him to the *congressio* which was to be held, 'Where in the presence of himself and his fellow-bishops he could, if he was able, establish the wickedness of Abelard's teachings': *quo ille in praesentia eius et coepiscoporum suorum deberet, si posset, statuere prava dogmata sua.*[94] Bernard's first response was to say that Abelard's own writings were sufficient condemnation (*sufficere scripta eius ad accusandum eum*); and that in any case it was not his office but that of the bishops to make the decision: *nec mea referre, sed episcoporum, quorum esset ministerii de dogmatibus iudicare.*[95]

One may tease a lion and then draw back when it begins to lose its temper and bare its teeth. Did Bernard's reluctance proceed from a sense that it is inappropriate to hold public disputations on theology, or from a fear that he could be outclassed and lose? 'I refused because I was a child and he a practised warrior from boyhood, and also because I thought it unfitting that the secure truths of faith should be subjected to nit-picking logical analysis.'[96]

It does not seem as though the meeting with Bernard encouraged Abelard to change his opinions or his ways. Geoffrey says that Abelard was indeed won over, and that he repented and promised amendment. But once out of Bernard's presence, he changed his mind: *resiliit a proposito saniori.*[97]

The informal meeting for the purpose of reconciliation could of course be used as a cover for another kind of informal meeting, with a very different purpose. Bernard more than once used the device of the private meeting in advance to 'fix' an outcome. If he did it before the Council of Sens in 1140, he did it again before the 'trial' of Gilbert of Poitiers in 1148.

Abelard wanted his name cleared. He was eager to defend his teaching. It was at that point, says Geoffrey, that Abelard went to the archbishop of Sens, who was about to hold a council, and asked him to invite Bernard to it, so that they could have a public debate.[98] For Bernard then not to appear would have been to put victory into Abelard's hands; Abelard made sure that the invitation to the meeting was widely known.[99]

This call for a public encounter would have created a forum in which there would be something very like a *litis contestatio*. There would be a public questioning of fundamentals of the faith, with Bernard turned into the accuser, his own reputation at risk if Abelard won.[100] For these pragmatic and diplomatic reasons, perhaps, Bernard appears to have been genuinely reluctant to go. But the archbishop of Sens agreed to Abelard's request.

Bernard's reluctance to appear at Sens may have a number of explanations, not least that he was not sure that he could outperform Peter Abelard in the flesh, but certainly not that he thought it an inappropriate forum.

His eventual capitulation and consent to go may also have several explanations. He himself says only that he came to fear that his absence might be misunderstood, might indeed become a stumbling block to the faithful; that his enemy would swell up to a larger size if he was not there to curb him; and that the error might become still further established if there was no one to refute it.[101] His reasons thus have to do with protecting the faith and the faithful.

So he went to Sens. He says that he went unprepared (*imparatus . . . et immunitus*), except that he held in his mind the promise of Luke's Gospel 21.14, that he would be told what to say at the moment when it needed to be said (*Nolite praemeditari. . . .*).[102] The 'art' in this was to appear at a disadvantage so that if he 'lost' in the encounter it would seem a smaller loss.

Bernard's own perception of his campaigns against heretics was undoubtedly that he had given the heretics a fair hearing by coming to their writings or the reports of their writings and opinion with an open mind and finding them unorthodox. He says in a letter to Innocent II that when he examined it, he found Abelard's teaching to be what it was said to be. But the disclaimer does not in itself make Bernard's motives pure.[103]

Was there really public diffusion of the controversies of the day to an extent which seriously threatened the faith of simple people? Heresy is seen as a disease. Henry of Sens spoke of the infection and contagion of the people.[104] Abelard was accused of making sacred things seem commonplace. He gets people discussing his teachings in the marketplace.[105] In the letter of the bishops of France to Innocent II, it is explained that 'throughout France, in cities, villages and castles, the doctrine of the Trinity is being argued about not only by scholars and within the schools, but even *triviatim*, casually, by everyone'; even children and the uneducated are talking about it.[106] (It is a paradox that Bernard complains both that Abelard thus lays sacred things before those unfit to see them and that he corrupts the faith of simple people; these simple people appear to be both the faithful and the 'swine'.)[107] At Sens, it seems, a great crowd collected in the church on the day: *adfuit dies et ecclesia copiosa convenit*.[108] There are indications of a suprising degree of popular interest. That tallies with what we know of the public enthusiasm for set-piece battles in the sixteenth century. Johannes Eck, for example, was always 'good theatre'.[109]

On the day, the meeting at Sens was crowded. Many came—the king, Louis VII, Count Thibaut of Champagne, and William II, count of Nevers, according to Otto of Freising's list.[110] It is open to question whether this was indeed a council 'in session'. The list of *erroris capitula* was presented to Abelard. He was given the choice to deny that he held the errors, to correct them humbly, or to prove that they were not errors but truth, using reasoning or the testimony of the Fathers (*rationibus pariter et sanctorum testimoniis Patrum*). Peter Abelard, say the bishops of France, was presented with *capitula* with the intention that he should deny that he had written them or, if he admitted that they were his, either prove them correct or alter them: *Ut ea magister Petrus vel a se scripta negaret; vel, so sua fateretur, aut probaret, aut corrigeret; visus diffidere magister Petrus Abaelardus, et subterfugere, respondere noluit*; though he had a chance to defend himself, they say, he simply walked away.[111] It has been pointed out that when he did that, he was walking away from the place and the judge he himself had chosen.[112] But it turned out that they were not what he had chosen.

The account Bernard gives in his letter to Pope Innocent stresses that the *capitula* of purported extracts from Abelard's works were produced in full view of the council, *in praesentia omnium*.[113]

What were these propositions? The *Capitula Haeresum* which has come down to us include the use of the image of the brass seal to represent the Trinity (I) and the assertions that the Holy Spirit is not of the substance of the Father (II); that Christ did not take flesh (IV); that God ought not, and cannot, prevent evil (VII); that the human race does not inherit guilt from Adam but only the liability to punishment (VIII); that the power of binding and loosing works only on earth and not in heaven (XII); and that the Father alone is omnipotent (XIV).[114] If Abelard had said these things, that would indeed have opened him to serious charges of unorthodoxy. But he said he had not.

Abelard left while the propositions were being read, and his followers left, too. This was strategically his best move, for it was a statement that this was to be no fair trial of the issues. It prevented his being condemned, as he certainly would have been, after he had presented his account. A condemnation in his absence would be easier to counter later. It is unclear whether the council did in fact formally repeat the condemnations of the informal meeting.[115]

An attempt was made to turn Abelard's departure against him by the publicity machinery of the other side. We read how 'it seemed that Master Peter Abelard was unsure and deceitful and he did not wish to respond': *visus est diffidere magister Petrus Abaelardus et subterfugere, respondere noluit*.[116]

Peter the Venerable, one of the few who appears to have been able to remain friends with both Bernard and Abelard, advised Abelard, who called at Cluny, probably on his way to Rome to appeal to the pope, to meet Bernard and make his peace with him. It was done.[117] But the pope still condemned Abelard.[118]

After Sens, there was a pincer movement to pin Abelard into a corner once and for all. The bishops of France wrote to tell Innocent that Bernard of Clairvaux looked at the writings of Peter Abelard, first by himself, and then with the assistance of others. They describe what happened at Sens. They suggest that Peter Abelard wanted to make a notable occasion of it. He called his supporters together for a showdown. But 'the bishops convened at Sens to honour and revere the side of truth': *convenerant ad nos Senonis fratres et suffraganei nostri episcopi, ob honorem et reverentiam sanctarum*.[119]

That there was a publicity war of sorts afoot seems sure. Berengar of Poitiers was a keen satirist.[120] His *Apology* names Abelard and Bernard. He wrote a tract against Benedict of Marseilles's heretical teachings, now lost, and other writings which survive. The *Apology* seems just to post-date Sens. He strongly favours Abelard's side. He describes Abelard as *praeceptor meus*. It is Abelard, in his view, who is *catholicus*, not Bernard's side. Indeed, Bernard is attacked as someone who knows little of the liberal arts. Bernard is the heretic. He has taught the preexistence of the human soul.

Berengar sees himself as a prophet, warning, exhorting, criticising. That is perhaps the most plausible basis for identifying a satirist in this period. There are topoi familiar elsewhere in writings after 1100.[121]

The publicity war carried further substantive points. Those in Berengar of Poitier's defence of Abelard are that it is unfair to condemn Abelard for one or two opinions on which there is no settled orthodoxy, when the Fathers are not reproached for publishing views of uncertain orthodoxy in their day which the Church has subsequently not endorsed.[122]

After Sens, Bernard wrote to everyone he could think of to try to prevent Peter Abelard's winning his way into the protection of the papal court. A heretic can prove a viper in the bosom of the Church. Bernard warns those at the papal court not to entertain Abelard, because he is coming to the Curia not to heal his wounds as he pretends, but to cover up his offences with smooth words.[123] Bernard urges correspondent after correspondent not to allow Abelard to win protection from the Curia.[124] He warns Haimeric that, Abelard having sought refuge with the Curia, 'the Church's enemy is now resting in its bosom'.[125]

There are ethical questions about this kind of letter writing. In the twentieth century, it could be regarded as a witch-hunt, a nasty little attempt by a man in an influential position to destroy the career and reputation of an enemy. Bernard certainly had no conscious malicious intent. He saw what he was doing as God's work, protecting the faith and defending the faithful. That rings from every line. Bernard's most substantial letter (190) against Abelard was sent to Innocent II. There were letters to senior persons in the Curia, probably Letters 188 and 338 (not sent until after the Council of Sens).

Gilbert of Poitiers

What had Gilbert of Poitiers said which was likely to lead the faithful astray? In sober fact, probably only arguments of a subtlety more likely to confuse than to mislead. He had, for example, seemingly tried to suggest that there must be some unifying 'divine stuff' 'by which' God is whatever he is. *Divinitas* is the divine nature. He was accused of elevating *divinitas* to the status of a God, making a fourth in the trinity. In one of his sermons for All Saints' Day, Bernard speaks of the majesty, power, eternal goodness, and divinity of God.[126] He does not run himself into the Gilbertian dilemma of seeming thus to imply that these substantive attributes are themselves Gods or fourth and further persons of the Trinity.

John of Salisbury's is the most valuable of the three surviving accounts of the encounter between Bernard and Gilbert of Poitiers at Rheims. Otto of Freising writes of it, but he was away on Crusade at the time and so cannot give an eyewitness account. John was there, and he had respect for both parties.[127] He describes the summoning of Gilbert of Poitiers 'to answer the abbot of Clairvaux' on matters 'already brought up the year before at Paris'. Certain statements in the bishop's commentaries on Boethius had been causing offence. John says that there was also disquiet about the reproduction of those ideas in the writings of Gilbert's pupils. He does not identify these pupils, and it is unlikely that Gilbert, known for the obscurity and difficulty of his arguments,[128] was breeding adherents in the way Abelard arguably did,[129] but this fear that contagion would spread was always a strong moving force in working up indignation against putative heresy.

Gilbert's accusers were Suger, abbot of St. Denis, and the two canons of Poitiers, Calo (later bishop there) and Magister Ernaldus, who bore a nickname (*Non Ridentis*) presumably reflecting the lack of a sense of humour. It is not difficult to envisage the legendary and seemingly ubiquitous internal warfare of cathedral chapters having a shaping role in the launching of this attack.

John of Salisbury was certainly disinclined to believe Gilbert a heretic. He knew him to be a thinker and writer whose ideas were not always clear to others, but he was sure they were clear to Gilbert himself (*cuius ei licet plurimos lateat, ratio non constaret*).[130] He had a high respect for Gilbert's learning as a man who after sixty years' study knew more of the liberal arts than anyone else: *circiter annos lx expenderat in legendo et tritura litterarum, sic in disciplinis liberalibus eruditus, ut eum in universis nemo precederet.*[131]

John of Salisbury saw agreement as the proper end for theologians. There could be no other fit outcome, since in the life to come there can be no disagreement about the truth. To be in heaven is to be face to face with the same truth (*quia simul semper optatum inspiciunt veritatem*),[132] and it cannot be imagined that the citizens of heaven will find themselves all facing in different directions. He suggests that Bernard and Gilbert will be in agreement now in heaven, though rather with the implication that Gilbert will now agree with Bernard: *et ut arbitror nunc ab abbatis et aliorum sanctorum sententia non discordat.*[133] But that does not, of course, mean compromise. There must be agreement, but it must be in the truth.

Before the public hearing at Rheims, Bernard called all the most eminent of those who were to be present to meet him privately in his lodgings. John is clear that it was beforehand (*antequam*).[134] Otto of Freising and Geoffrey of Auxerre describe this meeting as taking place at a later stage. Even if that is so, the device is substantially the same: that of planning in advance in secret how to achieve the desired outcome at a public hearing. John is noticeably insistent that he is speaking the truth here. He says that among those present were the archbishop of Canterbury, Theobald; Geoffrey of Bordeaux; Henry of York; the abbots Suger of St. Denis and Baldwin of Châtillon-sur-Seine; the Thomas who was archbishop of Canterbury at the time John was writing; and the present Roger of York.[135]

Bernard's address to them began by pressing upon them their duty to remove all scandals (*scandala*) from the Church of God. He invited them, perhaps disingenuously, to tell him if he has been wrong in the case he had brought (*ut eum corriperent si in causa contra magistrum Gislebertum suscepta videretur errare*). If he had, he said humbly, it was because he had been swept along by charity and zeal for the faith.[136]

Bernard used with these senior churchmen an argument to which he had frequent recourse in writing the letters he sent round after the Sens episode with Abelard. He stressed to them their duty to defend the faith. The *prelati* of the Church, he argues, have a duty to lay down their lives for the sheep in the way mere members of religious orders do not: *tenentur animas ponere pro ovibus suis*.[137]

Having thus set the scene, he offered to read them the *articuli*, so that they could judge whether or not there was cause for concern. The method he followed was in deliberate imitation of the method of promulgating decrees or laws. He read out statements on which he said he disagreed with the bishop of Poitiers. As he read each *propositio*, Geoffrey of Auxerre wrote it down and then read it back. He then read out the question: *placet vobis?* The answer *placet* was returned. The meeting thus bound itself point by point to the position that Bernard was orthodox and Gilbert unorthodox.

The logical flaw in that inference was of course that the meeting had not been invited to condemn Gilbert's opinions, but merely to endorse opinions which Bernard asserted were contrary to Gilbert's. Some of those present may have perceived this; John of Salisbury records that not everyone was happy with the method: *displicebat gravioribus modus iste*. But he claims that they were afraid to displease Bernard by saying so.[138]

As the sequence went on, there was an expression of disquiet from Robert de Bosco, archdeacon of Châlons. Bernard had read as his fourth assertion that the properties of the Persons are the Persons themselves, the Father, paternity, the Son, filiality, the Spirit, proceeding, and so on. Robert de Bosco pointed out that Anselm of Laon and his brother Ralph, and Gilbert the Universal, and Alberic of Rheims, and Gilbert Crispin had all been unsure whether this idea went beyond anything in the Fathers. It was not absolutely clear that the Fathers themselves would have considered it heretical. He exhorted the meeting to be careful not to make a hasty decision (*ut in re tanta non precipitarent sententiam*).[139] That brought the sequence of *placets* to an end. But Bernard had achieved enough to compromise the council, in that he had got support on key points from senior persons in the hearing of their peers.

When this story reached the cardinals, they were angry with Bernard and those who had met with him. They agreed to support Gilbert of Poitiers instead of Bernard. This was partly out of indignation at the implied slight to themselves. They pointed out that exactly the same device had been used by Bernard when he attacked Peter Abelard. He had not deferred to the apostolic See, which had experience in dealing with this kind of problem: *que consuevit machinationes huiusmodi reprobare*.[140] They spied in what Bernard had done the intention of forming parties or factions, with the English and Gallic bishops becoming his followers.[141] John of Salisbury says that only Alberic, bishop of Ostia, among the cardinals, spoke up for Bernard. But Bernard was quick. He heard of this talk of schism. He went to the pope *familiariter* and put it to him that he should show zeal against the heretic.[142]

At Rheims, according to the account of John of Salisbury, Bernard faced in Gilbert of Poitiers an opponent who could not be foot faulted or rattled. Gilbert had ready arguments, and they were sound. He could not be tripped up on his logic. He was impressively firm. If there were statements he could not be led to admit, however hard he was pressed, he merely asserted that he had not read it but was willing to accept the faith and doctrine of the Holy See.[143] Those present said that they had never heard anyone like him.

The attack was not over, however. On a subsequent day the pope instructed Henry of Pisa, a subdeacon of the court, to read the list of the bishop's errors again. The bishop expostulated that he ought to be judged on his own works, not the writings of other people, for these were not his words. He cried that no one, and especially not a bishop, ought to be condemned without either being convicted or having confessed to the offence.[144] He was not a heretic, he said. He would never be a heretic, because he was always ready to accept the truth and to follow apostolic doctrine: *acquiescere veritati et apostolicam sequi doctrinam*. The definition of a heretic identified someone who displayed intellectual pride (*mentis elatio*) of a sort which led to contumacy and brought about disputes and divisions: *et in contentionis et scismatis presumptionem pariens*.[145] He was no such person.

He described key features of his own conduct which showed him not to be a heretic. He had always taught openly, never in secret. He was willing to submit to correction if he had taught error in any of his published works.[146]

John of Salisbury floats the idea that Gilbert might not have been wholly sincere in his protestations that he was willing to recant if anything he had written could be shown to be heretical. His adversaries found it hard to understand what he said, so some thought he might be taking refuge in verbal subtleties (*quod astu et obscuritate verborum occultabat perfidiam, et religionem iudicis circumvenerate arte*).[147] But it may well be that he was indeed being confronted by a lecturer's nightmare, the reading aloud of a summary by a pupil which misrepresents what was said in the lecture. 'I have several pupils', he exclaimed, 'who have heard me lecture but have not understood a word I have said' (*minus intellexerunt*). They have written down their own interpretation. It is not what Gilbert has taught. He, too, would anathematise what is said in the list of accusations.

At Rheims in 1148 a dramatic 'cutting up' of the list of accusations was performed in full sight of all present, by the subdeacon. The pope, perceiving that the numerous members of the laity present might well misunderstand this, explained to the crowd in the vernacular that this did not mean that *Gilbert* had been condemned, but that the *arguments in dispute* had been condemned.

The attempt by Bernard to discredit Gilbert of Poitiers did not come to an end with the Council of Rheims. Bernard went on campaigning, as he had done against Abelard after Sens. He often spoke openly against the bishop (*contra episcopum sepe locutus est palam*), says John of Salisbury. He also wrote against him (*in suggillationem eius*) in his letters, in the *De Consideratione*, and in the Sermons on the Song of Songs. John defends him on the grounds that he wrote in zeal for the faith and in charity.[148]

When Gilbert's error was condemned by apostolic judgement and the authority of the universal Church, Gilbert was asked whether he accepted the condemnation. He submitted to it (*consentiens*), publicly refuted what he had written before, and affirmed that he would submit his opinion to be corrected by the Church.[149] Thus does Geoffrey of Auxerre describe the Gilbert of Poitiers episode in his *Vita Prima* of Bernard. But his is a partisan account, because his chief purpose was to praise Bernard's actions. Geoffrey of Auxerre was passionately Bernard's man.

There is a question, of course, about the use of a council as itself a forum for trial or for making theological rulings. There are precedents for both. It must be entirely acceptable to use a council to resolve a question about faith or order. That has the warrant of the earliest Church (Acts 15). The Fourth Lateran Council of 1215 was to condemn Joachim of Fieore on the same understanding of its role and powers.

The Characterisation of the Heretic

These events and the debate surrounding them enable us to draw out a number of features of the ideas in play about the nature of heresy itself and the behaviour which distinguishes heretics. For there is inevitably in systematic campaigning against a 'bogeyman' a tendency to draw with a bold brush a picture of a stock character. A 'typology' of heretics is strong in twelfth-century polemical writing. As Alan of Lille also found a little later, when an author wants to identify an opponent as a heretic, it is convenient to be able to point to an established heresy and explain that that is what the opponent also believes. Abelard has the same opinions about Christ the mediator as did Nestorius, accuses William of St. Thierry.[150] Among other things, that made it possible to wheel the Fathers in to the defence. To call the Cathars 'Manichees' was to be able to draw upon an immense amount of assistance from St. Augustine. But even where such identity of 'opinion' with the classic heresies is not apparent, there may be means of identifying heretics from their behaviour and characteristics.

That can be achieved even when on the face of it their behaviour is praiseworthy. It may be important in making a case to be able to say that heretics are deceptive, indeed deliberately deceitful. Arnold of Brescia could give a plausible account of himself, but that does not allow us to infer that he was on the side of truth. Bernard says that Arnold's behaviour was designed merely to allow him to enjoy a private supper with Satan on the blood of souls.[151]

Less equivocal signs of being a heretic abound in the Bernardine accusations. One is a tendency to wander. Peripatetic teachers are likely to be unorthodox.

Heretics are also dangerous to associate with. They contaminate others. When Bernard wrote to Guy, legate in Bohemia, to say that he has heard that the cardinal is befriending Arnold of Brescia, he warns him not to let Arnold create the impression that he has the cardinal's protection, so that Guy appears to be countenancing what Arnold says. Bernard flatters Guy with two suppositions: that he does not know that Arnold is there; or that he does know and is hoping to convert him to more orthodox views. That is dangerous, says Bernard. If Guy is seen in conversation with Arnold, people will think Guy approves of him. Then he will have a certain standing, and Guy's reputation will go down with Arnold's.[152] Guy has to understand that to be on Arnold's side is to speak against the pope and indeed against God. Bernard is sure that when Guy understands this, he will act firmly and do his duty.[153]

Heretics can be very persuasive. Abelard is superficially clever.[154] Bernard insists that because Abelard expects the protection of the cardinals and clergy of the Curia, it is important that they show him he is wrong.[155]

Heretics stick together. Master Arnold of Brecia and Master Peter Abelard have made common cause against the Lord and against his anointed.[156] Heresy is infectious.[157] A heretic who writes is extremely dangerous, because his writings remain and can be passed to future generations.[158] Heretics are treacherous, for they are betrayers of Christ.

Heresy leaves dirty marks. Bernard encourages Guy, cardinal legate in Bohemia, to take stock of the evidence that Arnold of Brescia is a heretic in the dirty footprints his teaching has left wherever he goes.[159]

Heresy thus has long-term effects. One of the reasons why it matters if the faith of simple people is damaged is that such a taint lingers, *quo semel est imbuta recens servabit odorem testa diu*, quotes Bernard in a letter to Chancellor Haimeric.[160]

To be new is to be dubious in theology.[161] Bernard's accusations against Abelard and Arnold of Brescia frequently return to that theme.[162] At the same time, heresies are very old. The heretic opens up old traps so that people may fall into them again.[163]

John of Salisbury makes a comment which shows up the crudity of this stock argument in the context of the twelfth-century debate. He realises that what seems heresy now, when it is first said, may become familiar and acceptable with time, that there is development in theological thinking, although he could not have put it in the terminology of a John Henry Newman. Now several usages are positively hackneyed in the schools, he notices, which when Gilbert of Poitiers first used them were regarded as profane innovations: *publico nunc plura scolarium teruntur usu, que tunc ab ipso prolata videbantur esse prophane novitates*.[164]

MORAL THEOLOGY, LAW, AND JUSTICE

Faith and Works, Action and Contemplation

Bernard had read Anselm. He borrows Anselm's image at the beginning of the *Cur Deus Homo* of a picture which has not been painted upon a solid base, but upon the air,[1] although he uses it for a different purpose: to emphasize the difference between an empty, listless following of Christ, and a process of purposeful pursuit until the Christian is embraced by Christ himself with solemn joy and then 'fed' in a bliss of fullness of life.

The spiritually active soul 'runs after' Christ in two ways. One is by prayer and contemplation. William of St. Thierry, in a further echo of the hermetic tradition,[2] describes three conditions (*status*) of those who pray, and he encourages the Christian to become familiar with all three. They are the 'animal', the 'rational', and the 'spiritual'. William chiefly has in mind the kinds of things to be prayed for in each of these *status*. The 'animal' man, for example, prays for wordly promotion and wordly goods. Each, as he prays, sees God in the manner which fits the direction of his prayer.[3] Bernard has a great deal to say about *oratio* and *meditatio* and *contemplatio*, but chiefly about *oratio*. It is something of a commonplace in his letters for him to ask, rhetorically, whether a sinner's prayer can be of any avail (*si quid potest peccatoris oratio*).[4] That is, of course, a serious theological question, and linked with it in Bernard's usage is the assumption that a pure desire will make prayer more powerful. Prayer consists more in purity and desire of the heart than in say-ing a great deal.'[5] There is also a sense that the common prayer of the Church, the prayer of the community of the faithful, is especially heard by God.[6] But most important of all is the inspiration of the Holy Spirit. God himself should whisper in our prayers.[7]

Next after *oratio* in the frequency of Bernards comments in this area comes *meditatio*. Meditation differs from prayer in that it is a perpetual attitude or orientation towards God, the soul constantly turning over the thought of the end and purpose of things and the delights which await it at the right hand of God.[8] It is meditation which teaches us what to desire, and by prayer we ask for it.[9]

Contemplatio is a perhaps more focussed *meditatio*, an *admiratio maiestatis*, a wondering at Gods majesty.[10] But with *contemplatio* we come to the other method of 'running after' God, which involves more active means. *Contem-platio* is a confident *intuitus animi*, an intuition of the mind about something, *consideratio*, a focussed exploration, a working out.[11] On one interpretation, says Bernard, the 'flower' of the Song of Songs (2.5) may be taken to be faith; the fruit is good works. There is no fruit without a flower. There is no good work without faith, for it is impossible to please God without faith (Romans 14.23). Yet faith is not enough on its own. Without good works, faith is dead (James 2.20), and so a flower is barren unless it produces fruit. Thus the 'waiting soul' is consoled by good works rooted in true faith (I Timothy 1.5) during those times when the light of her direct contemplation of the Beloved is withdrawn and the Bridegroom is absent.[12]

In this way, action can be seen not only as complementary to contempla-tion, but also as necessary to the full living of the spiritual life in this world. Anselm opened his *Proslogion* with a call to his reader to 'escape for a while ' from the business of his life, to enter into the chamber of his soul and close the door, and quietly be with God. But he recognised that there must be an opening of the door later, and a return to the business.

Bernard explicitly draws the parallel between faith and works, contem-plation and action, in the terms which had become a convention of exegesis. The two are sisters, Mary and Martha.[13] Thus Bernard links the active with the contemplative in the religious life. The pairing is important to lay Chris-tians and secular clergy, too, on the analysis Bernard gives here. But it is of central importance to the life of monks, who are professed to the spiritual life, that they do not allow contemplation to be crowded out by the business of daily life.

Bernard has personal experience of the way in which the waiting soul may be torn away from contemplation by duties of an active kind to fellow Christians. It does not disturb him, he says, when he is taken away from the preparation of a sermon to deal with the need of one of his monks to discuss a problem with him. He sees the seed germinating in the monk and is glad of the interruption.[14]

In the Sermons on the Song of Songs, Bernard lists a series of 'kisses'. The kissing of the foot (*osculum pedis*) is repentance. By the kissing of the hand, Christ raises man to newness of life. The kiss of the mouth is mystical union with Christ.[15] Practical theology concerns the way a Christian life should be lived so as to obtain the best chance of heaven.

To look at things that way is to make an assumption, to hold that God *rewards* right living, which may mean that he takes into account right behaviour, good works. Bernard, like most monastic scholars of his day, would not take this to be straightforward. He recognises the need for grace, for fallen human beings cannot be good unaided. But he never follows this line of argument through to the point of saying that good works are things indifferent to God or man. The whole system of monastic life is founded on the opposite premise, that to deny oneself in this life improves one's chances of eternal reward—that to give alms, to fast, to do good works, benefits one's chance of heaven, pleases God, earns merit in his eyes. That belief appears to hold even for those, like Bernard, who take a strongly Augustinian pre-destinationist view. It was certainly not yet theologically controversial, for the heated opposition between the teaching that salvation was by faith alone and that it requires the making of an effort to live a good life was three centuries ahead. *Caritas* should be shown in action (*caritas in actu*); it is not merely a feeling (*caritas in affectu*),[16] Bernard stresses.

The example of Christ is the model for Christian ethics.[17] Charity should be disciplined and not hasty or impulsive,[18] just as Christ is mighty but meek.[19] Christ is forgiving.[20] Many lessons follow from that. The good man does not retaliate if injured; there is to be no sneering or mocking.[21] The blessed soul is the soul full of mercy and charity. It makes itself all things to all men. It regards itself as a broken vessel, and it seeks nothing for its unworthy self, striving only to serve others.[22] The blessed soul lives with others in such a way as to give them no ground for complaint. Its owner is kind and helpful to all.[23] The man or woman who sins against a neighbour, however trivially, sins against Christ. Even hints and whispers are bad.[24] True charity consists in this: that those whose needs are greatest receive first.[25]

It may be that what is needful is not merely being good in such ways, but going *beyond* what is strictly required and putting oneself at risk of pain. Suffering for Christ is meritorious. Innocent is being persecuted like all the 'innocent', Bernard reassures the pope in question.[26] All those who live in Christ suffer persecution, says Bernard.[27]

There is thus a tropological[28] theology of great subtlety and complexity in Bernard. He had a high model here in Gregory the Great's *Moralia in Job* and one very familiar to his monastic readers.

This takes us back to a question we looked at under 'positive theology' in considering the task of the Church. What is God 'doing' about completing the work of salvation achieved once and for all by the death of Chrst, and making the world as good as he intended it to be when he created it? The self-imposed constraint upon him is that it has always been his purpose that human beings should love him freely and not because they have to. It would not serve the divine purpose to compel people to be good, although he could certainly do so if he chose.

There are, then, two areas to look at in Bernard's moral theology. The first is the question what, if anything, is innately right and good, and the second the question what is required of the person, that is, the Christian who seeks to do right in the sight of God so as to please him.

Virtues and Vices

The star of Jacob illuminates the whole world and penetrates into hell, warming minds rather than bodies: *calefaciens magis mentes quam corpora*, says Bernard. It encourages the virtues and scorches the vices: *fovet virtutes, excoquit vitia*.[29] And virtues are important. God's people will have virtues in heaven, so Bernard is confident that the acquirement of the virtues takes us through the gates of heaven.

The *De Consideratione* contains a little treatise on the virtues in which classical principles are given a fresh direction and a new principle of coherence. It was not difficult to say in outline what were deemed to be virtues. Cicero conveniently put into Western medieval hands the four cardinal virtues of prudence, justice, fortitude, temperance.[30]

Bernard perceives that the four virtues of Cicero's book *On Duty* (the *De Officiis*) go together. To keep to the middle way of prudence is justice, temperance, and fortitude: *Ergo modum istum tenere iustitia est, temperantia est, fortitudo est*.[31] The person who seeks justice finds prudence, conquers fortitude, and possesses temperance: *Itaque iustitia quaerit, prudentia invenit, vindicat fortitudo, temperantia possidet*.[32]

Bernard insists on the interconnectedness of justice with the other Ciceronian virtues of temperance, prudence, and fortitude.[33] He defines justice in terms of not doing to others what one would not wish to have done to oneself, or not denying someone else what one would wish to have for oneself. This is the principle of Matthew 7.12. It is also a principle of equitableness, the very essence of loving one's neighbour as oneself, to make a habit of putting oneself in the other's place.[34]

The connection of justice with temperance is through the will. Unless the will is under control (by consideration), it will not refrain from excess and then it will not be able to give the other person his just deserts. Unless the will is thus 'tempered', it may go too far in justice, for it is possible to be excessively just by being excessively severe (Ecclesiastes 7.17). Conversely, justice is needed to temper temperance itself, for it is always a danger that acts of visible temperance will become divorced from the motivation which ought to animate them. Those who fast so that others may see them doing it are reproved by Jesus in the Gospel (Matthew 6.16). They did not fast justly because they were trying to please not God, but men.

And it takes fortitude to restrain the will so that it goes to neither extreme.

This reflection brings Bernard to a discourse designed to bring prudence into its proper place in this scheme. But it also contains an analysis of the interrelationship of the virtues, in which he postulates a sort of ethical trinity. He argues for a 'mean' which is both proper to each virtue and uniformly and fully shared by all three so far discussed. Perhaps this mean is a common core of virtue? That will not quite do, argues Bernard, because the virtues do not unite by sharing a single virtue; it is rather that each completely and fully possesses it. It is of the essence of each, for without it no virtue can be what it is. Bernard tries to show that prudence occupies a special place among the virtues as the virtue which is the discoverer of this mean, this common element of all virtue.

The four virtues also moderate one another. For justice itself, in order to be just, imposes a limit by temperance: *denique et ipsi iustitia, ut iusta sit, temperantia modum imponit*.[35]

Nevertheless, the virtues can become disjoined. The person who makes an outward observance of virtue (for example, who eats moderately) but is not 'just' in his thinking seeks to please man, not God: *erat in cibo temperantia, sed non iustitia in animo, quia non Deo placare, sed hominibus intendebat.*[36]

Rupert of Deutz points out that there can be a fear and disturbance of the spirit which does not come from God. The point he wants to make is that there are equivalents of the four cardinal virtues of temperance, fortitude, prudence, and justice and those conjoined 'feelings' (*animi passiones*) of which the mind is capable (*gaudium, spes, dolor*), which the pagan philosophers recognised.[37] Rupert of Deutz again links the *quattuor virtutes principales* with the pagan philosophers (*ethnici*) in the *De Gloria et Honore Filii Hominis super Matteum*,[38] this time to point out that they could not understand the virtues in their spiritual sense because they did not know them within the Christian tradition: *sed non secundum caelestem vel spiritualem, ipsarum dignitatem cognoscere meruerunt.* Again, in the *De Sancta Trinitate*, Rupert links these four virtues with *mundana philosophia.*[39]

To these four cardinal virtues were routinely added the theological virtues of faith, hope, and charity, with their New Testament warrant.

For each virtue there is an opposing vice. Against love stands lust, and so on. The notion of this opposition was conventionally developed into a graphic picture of warfare, a battle in the soul. Prudentius's *Psychomachia*[40] of the fourth century was imitated by Alan of Lille in his *Anticlaudianus* in the generation after Bernard. The idea was pervasive even when not developed in so dramatic a way: the virtues are armed for battle. They have the shields and armour of strong men (*virtutes armantur ad proelium, habent clypeos et armaturam fortium*),[41] says Bernard. The burgeoning virtues (*nascentes virtutes*) are even depicted by Bernard as standing victoriously over the corpses of the vices on the battlefield: *cadavera vitiorum.*[42]

'Virtue' in medieval usage means not only the opposite of vice but also a disposition of mind. It is derived from 'power'. Bernard lists the orders of the angels, which include the 'powers' (*virtutes*).[43] In one of Bernard's definitions, that sense is strong. He speaks of virtue as a *vigor animi* possessed by a person who can stand firm with reason, or for the sake of reason: *immobiliter stantis cum ratione vel pro ratione.* Or it can be seen as 'in itself' a tendency to direct everything according to reason: *vel sic: vigor animi, quod in se est, omnia ad rationem cogens vel dirigens.*[44] Power held on a steady course for good becomes in this other sense 'virtue': *eiusmodi non natura virtutes sed usus facit.*[45] Already, in Aristotle, and quite independently of the Christian tradition, *habitus* is more than a disposition to behave in a certain way; it is an ingrained or innate characteristic,[46] a *habitus animi*.[47] Bernard speaks of a *humilis habitus*.[48] 'I glory in tribulations, if I am found worthy to suffer them for the Church' (*si quas dignas habitus sum pro Ecclesia pati*), says Bernard.[49] Virtue thus goes to character as well as behaviour (where one might speak, for instance, of a *histrionicus habitus*).[50] There is a hint of that in the usage by which one speaks of a monk's 'habit', for a monk's habit is more than an outward garment. 'Our habit, which is usually taken to be a sign of humility, is carried in our times as a sign of pride,' laments Bernard in his *Apologia*.[51] Do not be misled by a man with a sad face, a lowly outward dress (*vilis habitus*).[52] Conversely, *turpitudo* can also be a habit of mind, a coloration of the whole with vileness.[53]

Will, Consent, and Intention

In Peter Abelard's view, discovering the intention with which something was done was of the first importance in determining whether or not it was rightly done. It was an important plank of Peter Abelard's ethical platform that he believed that the consent to evil is what makes something wrong. 'He says nothing is a sin unless there is consent to evil' (*Dicit nullum esse peccatum, nisi in solo consensus mali*), says William of St. Thierry accusingly.[54]

Now Abelard was saying nothing here with which Augustine could not have agreed. It is a fundamental Augustinian principle that it is the will of rational creatures in which lies the origin of evil. Bernard does not take issue with the arguments of Abelard's *Scito Te Ipsum*, although he knew of it. His strictures are of a more practical and pastoral sort. But nevertheless, he goes some way with Abelard along the road of intention-ethics. It is for you to commit vices or, if you order things aright, to practise virtues, he explains: *tuum est aut, abutendo et confundendo, facere vitia, aut, bene ordinate que utendo, virtutes*.[55] He, too, thinks that purity of heart consists in a right intention.[56] Intention, Bernard explains, is made up of the will to do an act and the reason for doing the act.[57] 'Search your heart and discover your intention; test its truth': *tende cor tuum, discute intentionem, consule veritatem*.[58]

There was a substantial medieval investment in a notion of sins as capable of being listed, objectively definable acts which if committed would put a person in the position of being a sinner. That did not eliminate the need to look at the circumstances in which a sinful act was done and to take into account the consent and motivation of the individual. But it did place a premium on the act itself.

That view is highly visible in the penitential codes. The penitential articles issued after the Battle of Hastings of 1066, for example, make various distinctions. If someone kills in battle, knowing that he has done so, and knowing how many men he has killed, he shall do penance for a year for each life. He shall do forty days' penance for each of those he knows he injured but does not know for sure that he has killed. If he is not certain how many he has killed or injured, at the bishop's discretion he shall fast one day a week for life. If someone has injured no-one but would have done so if he could, he shall do three days' penance.[59]

Bernard could be an out-and-out pragmatist. Sometimes it is necessary to give in against one's better judgement. Samuel unwillingly anointed Saul to satisfy the people, because they insisted on having a king.[60] There is something approaching a situation-ethics in this. An ethical difficulty arose for Guy, abbot of Trois-Fontaines, who had been greatly upset by a mistake which had resulted in there being no wine in the chalice when he came to consecrate it at Mass. 'You should, I think, consider your own intention rather than the dignity of the sacred matter,' Bernard advises, 'because the motive not the matter, the intention and not the results of the action, constitute its moral character'. Bernard has talked the matter over with his own prior, and they can see no greater fault on Guy's part than ignorance; the servers are guilty of carelessness; but there has certainly been no malice involved. Bernard offers Guy a second principle to set beside the first: 'You surely know that as there is no good but what springs from the will, so there can be no great evil in a matter which is clearly involuntary.'[61]

It seems that Bernard believes that circumstances should make a difference. It would be wrong to seek to persuade or to bribe someone to do something which is contrary to justice, Bernard points out to Pope Honorius, to whom he is writing about the Church of Dijon. But there is no point in pressing a just cause with someone who is already a lover of justice.[62] Just as it is wicked to tempt someone with persuasion or a bribe to act unjustly, so it is, in the same way, unlikely to impress a lover of justice to strive for justice from similar motives.[63] He will do the right thing anyway.

Motivation was important to Bernard, too. He writes to congratulate Hugh, count of Champagne, who has become a Knight of the Temple. 'If you have become a knight instead of a count, and a poor man instead of a rich, for God's cause (*causa Dei*), I congratulate you, as is right.'[64] The right motivation is always love of God. Bernard wrote to Hugh Farsit about Humbert. 'I took up his cause with your count,' he says, 'for love of God, trusting in your charity.'[65]

But the problem with motivation is that only God truly knows what it is. Letter 126 to the bishops of Aquitaine was written against Gerard of Angoulême. Perhaps, says Bernard, Gerard will say that Bernard is judging him on grounds of mere suspicion and has no right to blame him for the secrets of his heart. For Bernard cannot know those and he cannot have any proof of what he says. In this area, Bernard might have learned a good deal about the subtleties of the question of motivation from Abelard's 'Ethics', the *Scito teipsum*.

We must turn now from the personal and inward to the social and outward, to questions of justice considered not as a virtue but according to law.

Law and Justice

God is ultimately the legislator, the judge of conformity with the laws of right behaviour, and the authority which rewards and punishes. In a sermon for the Epiphany, Bernard says, 'Here is the regulator of conduct, the judge of merit, the giver of eternal rewards': *hic rector est morum, in iudicio discretor meritorum, in regno distributor praemiorum*.[66] Ecclesiological elements are conjoined. Bernard makes a list of the six wings of the seraphim described in Isaiah 6.[67]

There is a 'law of the Gospel'. The person who does not take away a stumbling block when he can makes of himself a transgressor of the law of the Gospel: *transgressorem te facies iuris Evangelii*.[68] The man who refuses to obey God's law is the enemy of that law. 'See the enemy going before Satan (*praeambulans Satanae*), the Son of perdition, adversary of right and law (*adversator iuris et legum*)',[69] cries Bernard.

A person is seeking to make his own law when he puts his own wishes before the eternal law; indeed he is trying to imitate the Creator by making his own will into law.[70] This accusation of making one's own law is a repeating theme of Bernard's. 'He is a law unto himself; I can do nothing with him', he complains in a letter: *sui iuris est: iam non est in mea potestate*. 'He leads his life in the town and that is where he finds his companions': *sed in civitate vita eius et conversatio*.[71] By contrast, when the law of God enters into the individual soul at its conversion, it makes its owner will to obey it.[72]

Nothing could more effectively underline the importance of the eternal dimension of all this than the recognition of the penitential system that the soul after death, and without its body, will have no means of physical expression, and so, even though it will most bitterly repent, it will have no means of doing penance.[73]

Mercy and Justice

In Sermon 55.1 of the Song of Songs series, Bernard compares the gazelle and the fawn with mercy and justice.[74] The gazelle is not only fast; it is keen-eyed. It is prudent. It sees where it is going. This is Christ the judge. The waiting Church fears him as the gazelle, for nothing can remain unseen when he comes.

The fawn is equally quick, rushing into the embrace of the Beloved. This is Christ the merciful. When Christ was born an infant, he appeared as a fawn.

This balancing of justice and mercy is of the essence of Bernard's approach to the question of law, for it is inseparable from his idea that law is 'lawful' insofar as it expresses the divine nature. Eternal law is God himself, changeless, always right as well as always just. The natural laws of the universe, which govern creation, are of God's making and reflect the divine purpose for creation. They are orderly, because they inform order. Human laws ought to model themselves on that standard and seek, in the implementation of justice, to fulfill the deep laws of God.

But sure as he is of the divine mercy, Bernard is highly conscious of God as *judge*, and of the divine parameters of justice. It could hardly be otherwise, when he read so much involving that terminology in the Old Testament. Bernard was angry with Pope Innocent, who, once he began to win a stronger position, broke promises made when he was in need of support.[75] Who shall judge between us, Bernard cries to Innocent. If I had a judge before whom I could bring you, he said, I would soon demonstrate to you what you deserve. There is a tribunal of Christ, but God forbid that I should summon you before that. A soul for which Christ died must be lost to please Cluny, laments Bernard, in the case of a young monk who wants to be a Cistercian.[76] But there will be further judgement. God is a judge who will not be deceived.[77] Bernard knows the Ciceronian definition that justice is giving to each his due. *Iustitia vero quae est, nisi quae cuique reddit quod suum es*t.[78]

Law Codes and Knowledge of the Rules

There is limited information to be had in Bernard's writings about his direct knowledge of legal texts. It is instructive to look across to Lanfranc and Anselm in England to get a sense of what was happening in this period by way of self-education of senior clerics who had to deal with the practicalities.

The continental European scene of the Carolingian to eleventh-century periods had been marked by various attempts to compile lists of canons. The problem was that there was no corpus. It had to be created, out of canons of councils and decrees of popes, in circumstances where no one could say which councils' decrees were universally binding and which had merely *local* authority. (Anselm understood the rules of territoriality of episcopal jurisdiction. On William, bishop-elect of Winchester, Anselm writes to King Henry. The king had sent the bishop out of England. If he has thus sent him away, Anselm cannot consecrate him.)[79]

Burchard of Worms made an early attempt to list and to systematise. But the divisions were pragmatically rather than theoretically-conceived. He was interested, for example, in the powers and duties of bishops, because those kept being called into question by events. About 1050 a collection in seventy-four Titles was put together, in which can be perceived early stirrings of a centralizing tendency in the greater emphasis on the role of the papacy in the government of the Church. By the era of Gregory VII (1073–85), that had become paramount.[80] Lanfranc's Letter 39 is to Pope Gregory VII. In it he recognises his canonical subjection to the universal primate. 'My mind ought to submit to your precepts in all things, and in every way, according to the precepts of the canons': *mens mea preceptis vestris in omnibus et per omnia secundum canonum praecepta subiaceat*.[81]

Papal plenitude of power could, paradoxically, strengthen the position of other 'primates', senior bishops of provinces such as archbishops and patriarchs. Lanfranc points in a letter to various canons stressing the authority of the primates. 'There are many other things about the supremacy and power of archbishops in these texts and also in the authentic writings of other orthodox Fathers': *sunt alia plurima de excellentia et potestate primatum atque archiepiscoporum tam in prefatis scripturis tam in aliis orthodoxorum patrum auctenticis libris*.[82] Eadmer's narrative of 'recent events' has Anselm insisting that he cannot be metropolitan of the whole of Britain, since York's archbishop is metropolitan in his province; but he can be primate.[83]

Gratian's *Decretum*, which became the definitive canon law collection, was completed immediately before Eugenius's pontificate began. Behind it lay a series of collections, stretching back to the Carolingian period. Ahead lay the era of the professional law schools at Bologna and of the kind of papal headhunting in those schools in which Innocent III was to engage in the period up to the Fourth Lateran Council of 1215. Already in Eugenius's day, as Bernard comments in Book 1 of the *De Consideratione*, the ambitious were anxious to obtain the kind of useful 'professional exposure' to be got from being seen as an advocate in a case where the pope was judge.

Lex, ius, consuetudo, are all familiar usage in Anselm. Anselm writes to Urban II in 1098. He fears that it will appear that he has gone against the law of God, canonical and apostolical authority, and even voluntary custom.[84]

Iure is often used by Anselm simply for 'rightly'.[85] But it has its legal connotations, too.[86] Sometimes these are puzzling. 'And certain other things pertaining to the law of priests'. *Et quaedam alia ad ius sacerdotum pertinentia*,[87] clearly contains a technical term.[88] perhaps drawn from the Council of Carthage of 404. *Lex* for Anselm is preeminently *lex dei*.[89] In a letter to Henry, king of England (with a very similar text written to Matilda, queen of England), Anselm puts squarely his insistence that his first duty is to the law of God. He can have made no promise which could override that, whether in his baptism or in his ordination.[90] No agreement which is against the law of Christ ought to be followed: *nullum pactum servari debet contra legem Christianitatis*.[91] Monks have to distinguish between the law of God and their Order's Rule.[92]

For Anselm, custom establishes an 'ought'. 'He ought to do this by custom' (*se hoc facere debere per consuetudinem*);[93] 'He owes by custom': *debet per consuetudinem*.[94] The obligation derives in part from the antiquity of such custom: *vos contra ecclesiasticam consuetudinem in tam grave secundum antiquam consuetudo*;[95] There is *consuetudinem antecessorum*.[96] There is *ex antecessorum consuetudine professi sunt*.[97]

Abelard wrote to Bernard on the subject of discrepancies between the Gospels. Bernard objected to a liturgical innovation at Heloise's convent of the Paraclete. 'Who is ignorant,' says Abelard (correctly), 'that there are numerous different customs in the celebration of the divine office in the Church' (*diversas et innumeras Ecclesiae consuetudines*). Even the clergy differ in their practice among themselves. That means that Roman rules do not run everywhere.[98] *Consuetudo* in the legal sense is not an issue of interest to Bernard. But he does recognise that *consuetudo* may be a 'bad' habit (*prava*

consuetudo,[99] *pessima consuetudo*) as well as a rule falling short of formal legislation, designed for a good purpose.[100]

If we turn to the concept of a 'case' (legally speaking), we find a conjoining of 'case' and 'cause' natural to the Latin vocabulary. Anselm consciously
lived his life in the *causa dei*, 'God's cause'. That included making decisions
on such questions as whether to accept election to Canterbury. He wrote to
the monks of Bec, on his election to Canterbury, that in a *causa dei* such as
this he did not dare to fail to take advice.[101] He continued in the natural
presumption that everything he subsequently did as archbishop was in God's
cause and that all the bishops under him ought to take the same attitude. It
was also in the *causa dei* that he wrote to the bishops of Ireland asking them
to send him, as their primate, cases of a legal sort which they were unable to
deal with themselves. If they do not, there is a danger that stumbling blocks
will be created and the 'cause of God' which Anselm ought to be fostering
will in fact suffer.[102]

Causa was a term familiar to Anselm both in a wider and in the technically stricter narrow sense of a legal 'case' or dispute 'between' parties. He
wrote to Pope Paschal about the dispute between Chartres cathedral and the
local countess: *de causa quae est inter Carnotensem ecclesiam et comitissam
Carnotensem*.[103]

But most important of all for his own understanding of the legal framework, he came to see his own dispute with the king as a *causa*. He wrote to
Ernulf, prior of Canterbury, to thank him for his help with this *causa*.[104] To
Pope Paschal, the bishop of Tusculum, and Cardinal John, Anselm wrote
of the 'cause which is between the king of England and me': *causa [quae est]
inter regem Anglorum et me*.[105] In the second of these letters, he added a
gloss: *immo inter illum et libertatem ecclesiae dei*, 'more: between the king
of England and the liberty of the Church of God.' It might be a legal case in
which he was involved, but it was a bigger issue than that joined between
the parties. It was, if we may take the *ecclesia* as then firmly constituting a
sector of the public domain, a 'public law' issue.

Anselm's obligations to the king depend, as he understands it, upon the
maintenance of right order, the *rectus ordo* which is so strong a feature of
the argument of the *Cur Deus Homo*. The king will have none of the pe-
cuniary dues to which he is entitled from the archbishopric until he re-
stores what he has taken from it and canonically reinvests his archbishop
in person.[106]

Robert of Limminges has become a monk. Anselm grants his wife, during her lifetime, the lands he held of the archbishop. The important point is that she held them of the archbishop, not of Anselm. She will continue to hold them if Anselm dies, because the grant he has given is binding upon his 'canonical' successor.[107] Here we see Anselm's sense of 'right order' extending to a perception of the distinction between office and person.

There were clarifications of the theology of ministry at the Council of Westminster of 1102. Archdeacons are 'deacons' (the emphasis is that they are not priests). No archdeacon, priest, deacon, or canon may take a wife, or if he takes her, remain with her. Since a subdeacon is not a canon, he may take a wife, but he is bound to live with her chastely once he has taken a vow of chastity. No one is to be ordained subdeacon or above without taking a vow of chastity.[108] A priest in an illicit relationship with a woman may not celebrate the Eucharist, and no one should hear his mass if he does so.[109] All these are rulings which go to orderliness and ultimately to 'right order'.

Anselm, as we might expect, is alert to the ground rules of the theology of ministry and the concomitant branch of 'order'. In a letter to the king of Ireland, he describes how bishops are being consecrated without a see to go to and how they are being ordained as though they were priests, by a single bishop and not by three. Those thus instituted are, Anselm instructs, to be deposed from their office, together with those who have ordained them: *cum suis ordinatoribus ab episcopatus officio deponi praecipient*. He does not recognise—and probably did not know of—the *chorepiscopus*. He insists that it is for good reason that three bishops are required in the ordination of a bishop. It is a guarantee of their *fides*, *vita*, and *sollicitudo*. He also takes it to be fundamental that a bishop must have a *parochia* and a *populum: cui superintendat habeat*.[110] Anselm protests in a letter to Ralph, bishop of Durham, about 1008 that the bishop-elect of St. Andrews cannot be consecrated before the consecration of the archbishop-elect of York: *hoc nec debet nec potest canonice fieri ab eodem electo archipiscopo, nec ab alio per illum, priusquam ipse fiat archiepiscopus canonica consecratione*.[111]

There were frequent jurisdictional disagreements *within* the Church. Lanfranc's Letter 47 is to Herfast, bishop of Hereford. Gregory VII instructed Lanfranc to intervene when Herfast attemped to assert his jurisdiction over an exempt abbey. Lanfranc tells Herfast to leave the abbey alone so that he, Lanfranc, can deal with the matter as it is his duty to do and arrive at a judgement in due form by canonical authority: *quoadus res in nostram audientiam veniat finemque congruum canonica auctoritate nostrique iudicii definitione recipiat.*[112]

But the great issue of the day, for Anselm as for Bernard in the next generation, was the relation of Church to state jurisdiction. Anselm went to King William Rufus in 1094 to ask for a council to be called. 'There has not been a general council of bishops in England since you were king,' he points out in the words of Eadmer's *History of Recent Events*, 'nor for many years before that.' Meanwhile things have gone from bad to worse. If things are not taken in hand, 'the whole land will soon be a Sodom'. He suggests that his pontifical authority and the royal authority should act as one to call a council: *sed conemur una, quaeso, tu regia potestate et ego pontificali auctoritate, quatinus tale quid inde statuatur.*[113] The thrust of Anselm's diplomatic letter is to seek to bring both powers on board. It blurs the question who has jurisdiction.

But the tendency in the administration of justice is the other way, to separate the jurisdictions. The distinguishing feature of medieval Church trials is the person before whom they are heard (*coram episcopo, coram archidiacono*).[114] That provides a foundation for a group of rights to be attached to the bishop, and it is noticeable that creeping usurpation of those rights, by lay as well as monastic authorities, was being vigorously checked as it came to be recognised what its implications were.[115] A strong motive for such usurpation was the fine (or share in the fine) it could capture for the usurper.[116]

It seems from pre-Conquest evidence that shire and hundred courts heard both ecclesiastical and secular cases. Bishops were also barons. They could preside over secular courts. Lay and ecclesiastical witnesses might appear side by side.[117] But a bishop already seems to have had a right or duty to deal with certain types of offence both as to judgement and as to penalty. Synods could be courts.[118] But a chapter of priests could be a synod. A synod could be held in the chapter house of the cathedral.[119] There is little to suggest that synods were used routinely as courts[120] (as that at Reims was to be, in the case of Gilbert of Poitiers in 1148).[121]

William I issued an ordinance to regulate the jurisdiction of bishops in England. He removed ecclesiastical causes from the shire, where the hundred court involved judgement by laymen. Such pleas were now to be reserved to the bishop and the archdeacon.[122] William I's main concern was to ensure that laymen were tried in lay courts and did not seek to slip in under the arm of the Church for that purpose.[123] There is evidence of separate ecclesiastical courts after this date.[124] But even by the end of Henry I's reign, it is not always clear what law was being administered in ecclesiastical courts, and the crisp identification of courts as courts is not easy. The *Leges Henrici Primi*, which derive partly from a compilation of Anglo-Saxon laws,[125] still do not distinguish between a tribunal to try lay and a tribunal to try ecclesiastical cases.

The jurisdiction of the Church in the immediate post-Conquest period was primarily over moral offences, the relation of sin and crime being in every generation a vexed question.[126] But at the same time, it was literally tested 'on the ground' in disputes about property rights and the holding of lands. Most of the cases known to us involve property, for these were the ones recorded in the charter evidence.[127]

That, then, was the scene. Bernard was not unaware of such practicalities. He also took some initiative in encouraging the popes to use their appellate jurisdiction to uphold reform at Langres and York. But he was trying to focus Eugenius's attention on something bigger. What was occupying Eugenius's time more than anything else were his duties as a judge. In a period when law was blossoming as a vocational discipline and breeding advocates keen to be seen in the highest court of appeal, these duties increasingly went with the papal office (indeed loomed large upon the time of a pope).

So Eugenius was sitting up late into the night to hear litigation and getting up the next morning to begin again on the same task. By not putting a stop to this, Bernard tells Eugenius, he is paradoxically not doing his duty, but allowing himself to be led astray from it.[128] The test he should be applying is the character of the litigation he is hearing. Paul the Apostle said that he had made himself a slave to all (I Corinthians 9.19). But he did not mean it to be an apostolic duty to become the servant of those who were seeking financial gain, the simoniacal, the sacrilegious, fornicators, the incestuous— all the kinds of unjust person at present trying to use the pope's judicial powers for their own ends.[129]

Bernard tries to make Eugenius think about the nature of true justice. It is, he says, something which builds up rather than knocking down, as so much adversarial wrangling in the courts is apt to do.

God's law is perfect, converting souls (Psalm 18.8). Justinian's is a very different thing.[130] Moreover, God's law enjoins such activities as praying and teaching, and for these most important episcopal responsibilities Eugenius needs time. Above all he needs to make a well-proportioned distribution of his time to the purposes God's law sets.

Moreover, he is behaving in a manner which is a breach of the right order of things. Eugenius is a successor of the Apostles, and he is behaving in a low and contemptible way in frittering away his time on these unworthy occupations.[131] Paul wrote to Timothy to remind him that no one who is fighting on God's side ought to involve himself in the business of the world (II Timothy 2.4). And in fact if Eugenius does so, he is, ironically enough, diminishing his standing as a judge. A judge who behaves in such a way as to dishonour his office, Bernard points out, is hardly likely to be taken seriously. His very judicial authority will be lessened.[132] On the other hand, if he sets his standards high and judges only those things which properly belong to eternity, he will see that there is simply no place for him to adjudicate on the petty selfish concerns which at present take up all his time and energy. Bernard goes so far as to say that Eugenius actually does not have authority over property at all, but only over sin.

The search for balance, which is the defining task of consideration, is particularly important in the administration of justice Bernard says, bringing Eugenius back to the practical questions he is addressing to him. The present time is even more difficult for a pope than the days of Gregory I, when spiritual danger threatens. Now the dangers are actually with us. There is fraud, deceit, and violence everywhere. Accusations are often false, and it is hard for the helpless to find a defender. The powerful oppress the poor. It is the duty of Christians to protect the weak, to administer justice in such a way as to remedy injustice (Psalms 102.6 and 145.7).[133] Here Bernard echoes a theme of contemporary legal thinking, as it picked up from the Platonic tradition the principle that justice is above all a device for ensuring that the strong do not always win.

Procedure

There is some discussion in Bernard of the shortcomings of the legal process as he knows them. This provides an interesting sidelight, one-sided though his immediate purposes inevitably make it, upon a story of which we hear otherwise mainly in terms of the procedural manuals of the twelfth century and the outcomes of notorious trials.

Procedure was defined only in a rudimentary way at this date.[134] But there is an emphasis in Chapter 5 of the English *Leges Henrici Primi* upon the need for due process in all types of cases, ecclesiastical and secular (*legaliter et ordine pertractandis*).[135] The compiler of the *Leges Henrici Primi* knew about the *nemo iudex* rule of natural justice. The accusers, the defenders, the witnesses, the judges, must be different persons (*alii; alii*).[136] No judgement is to be given by a judge who has not been approved by the accused.[137] *Iudices sane non debent esse nisi quos impetitue elegerit.*[138] No one is to be judged in his absence. *Nec in re dubia vel absente accusato dicta sit sententia.*[139] It shocked Bernard that a judgement should be given when only one party had been heard and the other was absent.[140]

The accused must have a reasonable period in which to prepare his case, and an opportunity to make his defence: *et respondendi vel defendendi licentiam legitimam habuerit.*[141] There should be no trial until the judge has been agreed on. *Nec prius audiatur vel iudicetur quam ipsi eligantur.*[142] A trial has to be conducted according to rules, and it has to be properly initiated. There has to be a formal accusation and due process: *Nec oportet quemquam iudicari vel dampnari priusquam legitimos accusatores habeat . . . locumque defendendi accipiat ad abluanda crimin*a.[143] Christ knew that Judas was a thief, but because Judas was not formally accused, he was not found guilty; he was not cast out.[144]

The accused may request adjournments.[145]

There must be a right of appeal.[146] Where there are lawsuits, there are bound to be attempts to appeal against the judgements arrived at. This is a problem for Eugenius, who is himself the last point of appeal in the whole world. Bernard is concerned about this. He wants to see appeal as a mechanism for protecting the oppressed from the oppressor. It would be entirely fitting that the very invocation of Eugenius's name should have the effect of freeing the oppressed and stopping the cunning persecutor in his tracks. But sometimes appeals are trivial or are made with the intention of doing down the innocent, and Eugenius must be alert to this danger.[147] There was a tradition in Roman law that he who brings a case unjustly should himself be punished for the offence of which he accused someone else (*lex talionis*). Bernard thinks it perfectly just that a man who wants to injure his neighbour should find that he has harmed himself.[148] Appeals, he insists, are allowed to the injured, but not to those who want to injure others. So it is to be inferred that anyone making an appeal who is not demonstrably injured is doing it for the wrong reasons. More: appeal can be used as a device to inhibit local bishops from doing justice, for fear of the case being dragged to Rome.[149] On the other hand, if Eugenius were to diminish the authority of the appeal structure, he might prevent justice being done in that way. As always, Bernard argues for a balanced and moderate and sensible use of the device.[150] It is true that Eugenius has powers of dispensation. But those were given him so that he might build up the body of Christ, not so that he might destroy it.[151]

If accusers lay more than one charge against a cleric, they shall not be allowed to proceed with the remainder if they cannot succeed with the first.[152]

A bishop is not to be condemned except by seventy-two witnesses.[153] For a cardinal priest, forty-four witnesses are needed; for a cardinal deacon, twenty-six; for a subdeacon, seven. No one may judge a pope.[154]

Once a secular trial has started, it has to finish, but an ecclesiastical case may be halted for good cause.[155]

These are all principles which recur and are developed in the manuals on process stretching forward into the thirteenth century. We have no evidence upon which to credit either Lanfranc or Anselm with their development in England, but these principles of fair procedure must have had their blessing.

Upon the foundation of this assumption that there are divine ground rules, Bernard rests an evident understanding of some of the ground rules of the systems of justice operating in the courts of the day, including the rules of natural justice. There was a legal question whether one young monk was ever in fact a child oblate. He had been promised to Cluny, but he was not living there. He had never arrived. He entered the Cistercian order from the world, not from Cluny.[156] There has, in Bernard's view, been no proper 'judicial review' of this problem. When the pope pronounced judgement, there was no one present to argue the other side; the person judged was absent; the defendant was absolved without making satisfaction; the purpose of the suit was to allow the robber to keep the spoils.

There are other rules to do with keeping a balance of mutual recrimination between protagonists. In his letter to Robert of Châtillon, his nephew, Bernard wrestles with Robert. Robert, says Bernard, has injured him. But he, Bernard, is going against all the rules of justice in casting himself at Robert's feet, although he is the injured party. He does not ask why Robert has left him. He only grieves that he does not return.[157]

Bernard criticises the adversarial wrangling of advocates, in which both sides are prepared to lie to make their cases. They use their eloquence to bring about an unjust outcome, their wisdom to achieve an evil end. They adduce evidence which goes against the facts and is no more than a web of calumny, destroying the reputations of innocent people. Truth has simplicity. These advocates entangle it in complexity. Nothing, Bernard stresses, so readily reveals the truth as a simple, straightforward presentation of the facts.

So Bernard recommends Eugenius, first, to be selective about the cases he hears, and, second, to decide them carefully but with brevity.[158] Here he goes against the advice to judges which is to be found in contemporary manuals and collections, to be thorough and patient, so that no material evidence is left unexplored. But he is dealing with a judge whom he deems unlikely to be able to tell the difference between thoroughness and time wasting. He tells him to choose the cases he hears on the basis of deservingness. That of a widow or a poor man is the kind of case he should judge himself. He can appoint other judges for cases which deserve a hearing but do not deserve his personal attention. And about others he can make the decision that they do not deserve to be heard at all.[159]

Bernard is alert to the problem of the danger of bias in judgement. He does not think that Eugenius can be bought with money. But he fears that he may be partial in the sense of favouring sinners instead of judging cases on their merits. Credulity is a common fault in judges, Bernard finds.[160]

POLITICAL THEOLOGY

Church and State

According the Bernard, the highest orders of the angels show us the way we might fly up to God in spirit if we were not weighed down by bodily pressures. They also show us something about God which we might otherwise not see, for they reflect him upon whom they eternally gaze. In the ardent love of the seraphim, for example, we can see a reflection of the way in which God loves with divine generosity, hating nothing he has made.[1]

Bernard knows the Ps.-Dionysian orders of angels,[2] and he introduces them into the discussion in Book 5 of the *De Consideratione*.[3] They are described as having distinct roles in the heavenly hierarchy and in their relation to humanity.[4] Bernard approves of the idea of a divinely-appointed diversity in things. Just as the soul sees with its eyes and hears with its ears and smells with its nose and so on, so God brings about different ends through a variety of spirits.[5]

Here among the angels are models of the just judge. The thrones reflect the divine justice in which God sits, causing no fear among the innocent, the execution of his justice never frustrated, so that those who are subject to it can rely upon the serenity of their judge, his absolute love, and the knowledge that there will be no mistakes and no prejudice against them.[6]

Bernard uses the angelic order of the virtues as a test-bed for a definition of what virtue really is. It is a power.[7] In the virtues we see displayed the eternal divine force through which all things have their being, which gives life, invisibly moving all things and sustaining the whole of creation. Moral virtue is an aspect of this power in the universe.[8]

But Bernard finds himself with a problem, in that it seems he is called upon in living his own life to discharge the duties which belong to those who ought to be concentrating on contemplation, as well as those which fall to people who ought to be doing active, practical things for good in the world. We have seen him wrestling with that problem throughout this book.

Nowhere does he confront this dilemma more squarely than in the *De Consideratione*, where he looks at it in the search for an answer to the question how the active life can be led with a proper Christian set of priorities. Beneath the battle for control of the 'two swords' of secular and spiritual authority lies a deeper conflict. The spirituality of the monastic life required time for prayers. But Bernard's busy-ness, as he was only too well aware, cut into the spiritual life which was always his conscious vocation, and he could see that such distraction was a danger to others, too. In the first book of the lengthy letter he wrote to Pope Eugenius III, he explores it trenchantly. He puts himself in Eugenius's place, or, as he says, he hopes it is the place in which Eugenius, like Bernard, is already conscious of finding himself in difficulties. Eugenius had been a monk of Clairvaux, and later abbot of St. Vincent and St. Anastasius. To Bernard, he was still a novice in the spiritual life. 'I share your grief about the demands of your office,' Bernard begins. Then he adds that he hopes it is indeed grief, for so it should be. Eugenius has until recently been able to enjoy the pleasures of the solitary life. He should actively miss them. It is common experience that pain is dulled by repetition. Yet pain is useful and can be just, that is, necessary and appropriate. It is more likely to lead to salvation than is dullness of heart. It is important that Eugenius does not simply get used to his present busy life.

Christians, Bernard believes, would, if they were in their right minds, 'always, everywhere, and completely prefer to everything else' that which is of unique and supreme value. He explains to Pope Eugenius III how to pursue this infinitely desirable thing by 'consideration' (*consideratio*).

This is a word he almost certainly borrowed, for the pastoral purposes of what follows, from Gregory the Great, who uses it at the beginning of his Pastoral Rule (*Regula Pastoralis*). For Bernard's *De Consideratione* is his own treatise on 'pastoral care', written not by a pope for himself and his fellow bishops but by an abbot for a pope who had once been one of his monks.

'Consideration' is an alert balancing of the demands of action and contemplation, explains Bernard. It acts on the mind which exercises it, purifying it and helping it to focus its efforts. The considering mind is a mind in control. It feels but is not carried away by feeling. It directs actions appropriately. It restrains excesses. It fosters good behaviour. It expands in knowledge both human and divine.[9]

The habit of taking time for consideration gives a dignity and orderliness to life. Indeed, its effect is in every way orderly. Where there is confusion, it brings it to order; where there are omissions, it fills them; where things have become disorganised or scattered, it collects them together again; it finds out what is hidden; it discovers the truth; it discloses lies and deceit. It takes stock of what has been done and makes plans to complete what needs to be done. It foresees adversity and is full of fortitude in the face of adversity when it comes.[10]

The Two Swords

Bernard's book *On Consideration* began as a letter to Pope Eugenius III, but it became a statement of a position on the relationship of the head of the Church not only to the state but indeed to the whole world, at a crucial stage in the development of papal claims to plenitude of power.

The first and supreme duty of rational creatures is to love God. To that end it is natural to 'look up'. This presumption of the essential rightness of hierarchy in a created world carries on downward. It is hierarchically appropriate for men and women to love their neighbours as themselves, because they are one another's equals in the hierarchy of creation. Those who share the same nature should have the same advantages. For that reason, you should be prepared to share your goods with your neighbour.[11]

At the same time, this is a hierarchical love. To love one's neighbour with perfect justice, one must do so in God.[12] *Dignitas* is not merely something which confers a privilege, a right to be looked up to; it is a power of domination, says Bernard. For all creatures fear man.[13] But the guiding motivation and binding principle ought to be love, not fear. Humanity's duty to love God derives from his having loved his people first.[14]

God deserves to be loved best, indeed without limit.[15] That means loving him without a hope of reward, although in fact he is not loved without reward,[16] and there is an immeasurable benefit to the human lover in the loving. A great debt is owed by the creature which is not only 'created' but also 'saved' from the consequences of its own sin. (That sin turned mankind into a tribe of beasts, and so God has, in effect, saved both men and beasts.)[17]

So the almost unbalancing 'generosity' of God in giving a reward to those who love him is further thrown into the realm of unmerited divine giving by the gift of salvation. It is rational to love God. Everything points to it. That means that man as a rational being will naturally and properly tend that way.[18] God is the reason for loving God.[19] Despite all that is so freely offered, this high obligation is not fulfilled unless God is loved for his own sake, and not for the benefit to his human worshipper which comes from loving God.[20] Self-love must ultimately become a love for the sake of God and not for the sake of self, if it is to fulfill its true function.[21]

It is a breach of *rectus ordo* (right order) not to love God best. The wicked, as it were, walk round in circles. They naturally want what will satisfy their desires, but they foolishly reject what will do so.[22] The righteous man walks in a straight line.[23] What we may call Bernard's 'political theology' is, like Augustine's, geared to the eschaton. It is never *merely* this-worldly.

Despite this high-mindedness, Bernard's political theology had an immensely pragmatic, this-worldly dimension. A number of Cistercians who became bishops, archbishops, and papal legates entered the hierarchy of the Church and got control of powerful positions in Bernard's day and after. By the end of Bernard's life, there had been 19 Cistercian cardinals and 152 bishops and archbishops (of whom 20 became Cistercians after resigning their sees, taking to Cîteaux as a place of retirement). These are not on the whole individuals who were also prominent in the development of a Cistercian spirituality. Nor were they, in the main, writers. They crossed a Rubicon. They were or became political leaders.[24]

Bernard not infrequently had a hand in this development, especially after 1130 when the schism began and his own influence in politics increased. Clairvaux monks were prominent in the list. After Bernard's death in 1153 and for the rest of the twelfth century there was a noticeable drop in these numbers.

So, Bernard was active in the political arena of his day. He was an extremely practical politician. But his tactical moves were always comprehensively underpinned by his understanding of the ground rules. And the ground rules were theological.

In Bernard's political thinking, the theme of the two swords was a leading idea. He mentions it three times, in his treatise for the Templars (III.5) and in a letter to Eugenius III in which he explains that as Peter's successor, he has two swords—the spiritual one, drawn by his own hand, and a temporal one, drawn at his command.[25] The third occasion, the discussion in the *De Consideratione*, we shall come to in a moment. Baldwin of Ford also wrote in his sermons that there are two powers which rule this world (*due potestates quibus hunc mundus regitur*), royal power and pontifical authority (*regia potestas et pontificalis auctoritas*), and that these are the two swords of the Gospel.[26]

The 'two swords' motif had a patristic background.[27] But in the twelfth century it had a topicality created by the raising of awareness of the complexity of relationship between authority in the Church and authority in the state.

Bernard reflects in the *De Consideratione* on the 'two swords' analogy of the relationship between Church and state, first used by Gelasius I. Luke's Gospel describes the incident where two swords were produced at Jesus' arrest, and Jesus said: *Satis est*, 'It is enough.' This text was taken as a justification for the theory that it is the divine intention that there should be two kinds of power in the world, the spiritual and the secular. The debate then turned on their ownership. Does God entrust both to the papacy, so that the pope gives one to the emperor at his coronation, or does God give each his own sword directly?

Within the hierarchy of Church and state set out in the *De Consideratione*, Bernard takes the pope to be supreme over all secular powers. In a letter to Conrad, king of the Romans, he reminds a secular ruler sharply of this principle. He speaks of his duty to show reverence to the supreme and Apostolic See and to the representative of St. Peter, just as he would wish it to be shown to him by those beneath him in the empire.[28]

Bernard was born into a world extremely conscious of a fundamental conflict of authority between spiritual and temporal, Church and state. During his youth, it erupted in ugly scenes between pope and emperor, in which both behaved in ways unworthy of their offices (even if only because they were undignified). At Canossa in 1077, the emperor Henry IV was brought to kiss the pope's stirrup so as to get the ban of excommunication lifted, a gesture with far-reaching feudal implications. Conversely, in 1111, Paschal II conceded the right of investiture to the emperor, so that he could get out of the imprisonment in which the emperor was holding him. But he himself was guilty of excommunicating the emperor without going through the appropriate process, which was designed to ensure that excommunication was deserved. He simply used it as a weapon.

We touched in looking at Bernard's life on the fact that the 'investiture' conflict was to a large extent about control of property.[29] When someone was appointed to a bishopric, he held in that capacity lands and rights equivalent in extent and status to those of a secular baron. In many respects, he behaved like a worldly lord, not least in his involvement in affairs of state and in the entourages of kings or emperors. He would normally come from one of the ruling families of the area. So the placing of someone in a see was a political appointment. Moreover, the ruler who controlled the appointment to a see could use his powers to give himself a periodic source of extra revenue. It became quite usual to leave a bishopric vacant for a year, so that the king could enjoy the income. The overlap or conflict of interests causing the tension between secular and spiritual was thus in part unavoidable.

But there were distinct elements in the making of a bishop, not all of which could properly be in the control of a secular power. A king or emperor might choose a candidate, but strictly that candidate had to be accepted by the people or he could not properly be their bishop. More importantly, no secular ruler had authority to celebrate sacraments. Ordination was at this date uncontroversially regarded as a sacrament. The making of a bishop was seen as the completion and perfecting of the ordination which had made him a priest.[30] So when kings and emperors presumed to go so far as to invest a new bishop with the ring which symbolised his union with the Church and with the staff of his pastoral office, they were intruding upon an area which belonged entirely to the Church's part in the commissioning of a new bishop. Out of the desire to keep control of the property (the 'temporalities') of the see came a tendency to invade the 'spiritualities', and that was intolerable both ecclesiologically and practically to the Church.

This very practical and pressing example of the conflict of interest of the worldly and spiritual reached some sort of resolution with the Concordat of Worms in 1122, when an attempt was made to distinguish the elements in the process of bishop making which properly belong to each and to keep secular rulers on the right side of the line. The temporalities were to be looked after by secular authority, and the spiritualities by the Church.

This was only the most vivid contemporary example of a conflict which had many other ramifications. In 1134 Bernard wrote to Louis the Fat to censure him for his attempt to prevent the bishops of France attending a council which Pope Innocent had called at Pisa, and which was to be held in May of 1135. Louis had argued that it would be too hot. But the real issue was whether he had authority to prevent the bishops' attendance. The kingdoms of this world and their prerogatives can remain intact, argues Bernard, only as long as they do not contravene divine ordinances and dispositions.[31]

Moreover, the king is jealous for no reason; he has nothing to fear from the bishops' attendance. His royal interests and his royal honour are not threatened.[32] If there is something the Apostolic See has done which has upset him, then it is sensible to allow his bishops to attend, Bernard argues, so that they can intercede at the council and seek to have changed or revoked any decrees which have offended the king.[33]

There are two connected fundamentals of Bernard's political theory as it unfolds here. The first is that Bernard was Augustinian in his assumption that the account of things he had to give embraced eternity and time alike. Augustine's *City of God* has as its citizens all God's people, dead, living, and yet to be born, and the unfallen angels as their natural companions. The other city includes all those excluded from that city because for one reason or another they are not God's people. Bernard's *De Consideratione* is his *City of God*. In it he addresses the same embarrassing problem that on the face of it, with the disaster of the Second Crusade, a Christian power has failed in the world. Augustine's contemporaries, educated pagan Italians in exile in North Africa, were challenging him for an answer to the question why, if the Christians were right about God, his omnipotence, his goodness, this Christian God had allowed a Christian Roman Empire to fall into the hands of barbarians. Bernard's contemporaries needed an answer to the question why the Second Christian Crusade had failed to win back the Holy Land for Christendom. For both, the context can only be God's providential plan, and the answer must be that within that plan there are considerations so great that no apparent disaster figures largely beside them.

As we have seen, Bernard's second great underlying assumption has to do with *rectus ordo*. This was both a notion familiar to Bernard in his reading of Gregory the Great and an Anselmian idea. And in Anselm it is very strong. Harmony and fittingness (*convenientia*) are powerful ideas in the twelfth century. We should try to ensure that our voices are in harmony with God's own word and voice, suggests Bernard.[34]

If one has power legitimately but uses it wrongly, that is a breach of right order. Authority has limits.[35] There is a balance of power and duty. On the other hand, there are no limits to the duty of obedience.[36]

Abuse of power can be identified only when it is clear what would be a *proper* use of power. Bernard gave much thought to the question what the authorities in Church and state ought and ought not to do, but on some points the principles appeared to him to be noncontroversial.

Bernard was fierce with those who, as it seemed to him, abused their powers or used them improperly. 'Your own will is law,' he accuses Henry, archbishop of Sens. 'You are thinking of power and not of the fear of God. . . . How could you have unfrocked a man who had not even been summonsed, let alone convicted in court?' he asks. He enquires whether Henry thinks no one will notice what he has done. 'Do you think the whole world is as devoid of a sense of justice as you?' he asks.[37]

One way of abusing power is to use a mailed fist when there are alternatives which make it unnecessary to use force. Bernard writes to Duke Conrad of Zeringen, discouraging him from extreme action. He had been contemplating warfare against Amadeus I, count of Geneva. Bernard tells him that Amadeus has offered to submit to judicial arbitration and to make satisfaction to Conrad for all he has against him.[38]

If a use of power goes beyond or against the purposes for which God has granted it, it may be emptied of potency. If Conrad goes ahead regardless, invading Amadeus's territory, destroying churches, burning down buildings, shedding blood, that will make God himself angry. If God is angry, Conrad will lose the war anyway, however great his military strength.[39]

Moreover, God will be the judge if Conrad slaughters his people in this way in an unjust cause.[40] The underlying understanding here is again that the world in which politics operates is both eschatological and of the here and now. On the one hand lies a practical proposal for dispute resolution, placed squarely on the table; on the other is a threatened sanction at the supernatural level. In Letter 124 to Hildebert, archbishop of Tours, Bernard seeks Hildebert's support for Pope Innocent. But Hildebert had a quarrel with the king and did not want to support a pope who had the king's allegiance. Bernard's argument is that since those who are of God's party have freely chosen Innocent, anyone who stands against him must be Antichrist or his follower.[41] Again, pressure is being put on in a this-worldly context, with other-worldly sanctions looming. The divine source of all legitimate power must never be forgotten, and it is taken for granted that God has not simply handed it over but continues to hold the ends of the strings.

It is also an abuse of power involving a breach of right order to exercise a spiritual authority in a secular context or vice-versa, or to confuse the two. Stephen of Garlande's family were friendly with King Louis the Fat. Stephen was holding both high office in the secular sphere and high office in the Church. He was a seneschal (steward) and also a deacon and archdeacon of Notre Dame and dean of Orléans. Bernard wrote to Suger, abbot of St. Denis, to express his disquiet. He stresses that it goes against the Gospel to serve both God and mammon, to be so heaped with ecclesiastical preferments as to seem almost one of the bishops, while simultaneously being so much involved in military affairs as to take a personal precedence over the army's very commanders. Moreover, Stephen seems to take more pride in his secular than in his ecclesiastical positions.[42] In a letter to Suger of St. Denis about Stephen of Garlande, Bernard adds the rider that Stephen is confusing distinct states of life in trying to be both a minister of God and a minister of the king. He abuses both positions by choosing the honours but not the labour of the army in one, and the revenues but not the service of religion in the other. He disgraces both positions in this way.[43] Here is a man trying to live in two worlds in this life, and the reasons why that is wrong are spelt out against the dimension of eternity.

Polity in the Church

Bernard's Theology of Ministry (part I)

Primacy, Oversight, and Authority   In Letter 330 to Pope Innocent, written after Sens, Bernard speaks the language of stewardship. The Bride of Christ weeps. The Bridegroom delays. In the meantime, the Bride is entrusted to the 'friend of the Bridegroom', the pope. The same argument from friendship to the Bridegroom is used with Stephen, cardinal bishop of Palestrina.[44]

Bernard also speaks the language of 'proper humility' in connection with his ideas of stewardship. The Holy See has never thought it a loss of face to change a ruling drawn from it on false pretences, claims Bernard, writing to Pope Innocent II on behalf of the archbishop of Trèves.[45] In this way of looking at the role of the pope, his power is played down, and dramatically

played down if we contrast it with Bernard's gigantic claims for papal plenitude of power in the secular arena.

Bernard was, in practice, both a strong adherent of the view that the pope
holds a monarchical primacy, and an advocate of the Augustinian 'with us
and among us' school of leadership in the Church. Who am I to write to a
bishop? Who am I to be disobedient to a bishop? Thus does Bernard approach the discussion of a bishop's office in a letter. The letter has a sting in
the tail. He points out that if he does not write 'above himself' by addressing
a bishop, he will be disobeying the orders of one superior to him, for a bishop
has asked him to write.[46] This little courtesy reveals the confidence Bernard
has in these positionings and, more importantly, his confidence that his ecclesiastical 'lord' may come to him as a source of senior advice.

There is a great deal in Gregory the Great about the *rectores* of the
Church, but again and again, a high doctrine of the power of prelates is
coupled with an emphasis on mercy alongside justice—as it is in Gregory's
doctrine of God. Bernard pairs the 'fathers' of monasteries, their abbots, with
the lords of castles—rectors of souls with princes of provinces—with an
uneasy sense that the parallel should not be so close as it often appears.[47]
Nevertheless, Gregory the Great's ideas of a *rectorship* of the episcopate go
with his assumption that oversight is authoritative, a service of the Church
which is also a ruling of the Church. Gregory's world was different from
that of Bernard, but the perception of the dilemma this creates is the same.
In Book III of the *De Consideratione*, Bernard explores at length the central
paradox of his doctrine of papal authority: that Eugenius is to preside and
yet not to rule.

In Bernard's thought there is a secure starting place on the subject of 'rule'.
God is uncontroversially *rector* and *gubernator* of the world, coupling rule
with governance.[48] Christ did not make the Roman prelate his superior, but
he did put him very high, attributing to him the powers of Christ, for he is
Christ's vicar on earth.[49] Bernard drew from Gregory the Great a clear sense
of the roles of oversight of the ordained ministry. When invited to reply to
Abelard at the Council of Sens, one of the grounds on which he at first refused was that it was not an abbot's but a bishop's task to make rulings on
matters of faith: *nec mea referre, sed episcoporum, quorum esset ministerii de
dogmatibus iudicare*.[50] Bernard does not use the term *rector* a great deal. In
the *Life of St. Malachy*, Malachy is described as *ipse rector, ipse regula fratrum*,[51]
but the play there is upon the setting of a rule of conduct by example, rather
than upon governance.

Bernard wrote a letter on the duties of bishops (Letter 42, *De Moribus et Officio Episcoporum*) in which he presents bishops with a high doctrine of their authority. He reminds them: 'You have received the keys of the Kingdom' from God himself (*Deo auctore, vobis traditas*), according to the rite of that strong woman of the Book of Proverbs,[52] who is taken to represent the Church.[53] Everyone agrees that not all those called to the ministry are chosen by God among his elect: *eligi et ad regnum*.[54] On the other hand, the bishop's is a ministry, not a dominion (*ministerium . . . non dominium*).[55] It is for service, not for rule alone.

The bishop may have a high authority in the Church, and the pope a higher, but they are required to exercise wisdom. Without prudence and goodwill there is no perfect counsel: *absque prudentia et benevolentia non est perfecta consilia*.[56] And without counsel, the office of a bishop and his pastoral charge cannot be fitly (*digne*) discharged.[57]

The bishop has a responsibility which requires prudence and thoughtfulness in its discharging, because the balance which is of its essence is not easy to keep. The episcopal task and the pastoral cure cannot be worthily carried out without thought (*sine consilio*).[58]

The bishop should seek in all things not to dishonour his ministry. He should be zealous for that honour. *Probetis zelum, ministerium honoretis*.[59] It is his ministry's honour he should look to, not his own,[60] and that means that he should not seek fine vestments, impressive horses, large palaces, but the adornments of good conduct, spiritual studies, good works, chastity, and charity.[61] A bishop or a pope ought to be simple. Bernard advocates simplicity of life and dress for the bishop who asks his advice in the matter.[62] The bishop is to be a faithful *pontifex*, or 'bridge-maker', through whose hands the good things of this world pass, and the divine good things come to his people, and the vows of his people are brought to God, while he keeps back nothing for himself.[63]

But that is merely an outward and visible sign of the inward and spiritual reality that the bishop ought in all things to be activated by charity. They should be as sweet (*dulces*) as they are powerful (*potentes*), so that they may protect their people courageously.[64] Purity of heart consists in love of God and love of one's neighbour, Bernard reminds prelates.[65]

Love for himself appears not to be a proper consideration for a bishop in Bernard's eyes. Whatever passes through his hands, whether the divine beneficence towards man in the sacraments or the vows of men to God, the prelate should keep nothing for himself.[66] Bernard does not think that this is incompatible with loving himself as he loves his neighbour.[67]

Primacy and Collegiality   The appeal to a higher authority—in one instance an apostolic licence—may be an admission of being on uncertain ground.[68] No one not uneasy in his mind would have needed to seek such authorisation.[69] But the inference takes us to the question of primacy and collegiality. Bernard had a sense of himself as an 'abbot among his peers.'[70] That was a reflection of an organisational choice of the Cistercian order and not of a profounder ecclesiology. If he had been a bishop, his hierarchical relationship to other bishops would not have been something he felt free to regard as a matter of choice. Bishops are necessarily 'brothers'; whether they like it or not, they share collegially in the governance of the Church. Eugenius is not lord of other bishops, but one of them.[71] That is in line with Augustine's strictures about how he is a bishop with and among his people.

But Bernard was clear—no doubt for reasons not unconnected with the recent memory in Europe of the moves made by Gregory VII and the Investiture Contest—that the pope is special among bishops: that there is a *singularis primatus* of the pope,[72] that it is *unicus*,[73] and that it therefore carries a *primatus praerogativa*,[74] or *singularis praerogativa*, which is a divine gift.[75] Primacy in the Church is thus ultimately a token of the divine recognition of the dignity of man: *considero quanta praerogativa Deus dignavit hominem*. God has placed a human authority over all lands and all other animals.[76] The prerogative is one which, *mutatis mutandis*, extends in some sense to the faithful at large. Bernard speaks of the 'divine prerogative' by grace in the hearts of the elect.[77]

But he asks a searching question about the Trinitarian basis of such a claim. Authority on earth must reflect the nature of God, or it cannot be divine. Where is the primacy of the Father where there is the equality of coeternity in the Trinity?[78] The passion to rule corrupts.[79] Eugenius must remember that the authority he bears is a *responsibility*. God creates a balance of power in the Church which preserves its order. The people made you prince of the Church, Bernard tells Eugenius, and they did it not for your benefit but for their own.[80] Eugenius has not been given his elevated position so that he can give orders. The proper use of authority is to get things done, not to lord it over others. Jesus was quite explicit about this, Bernard points out, when he said that his disciples were not to be like the kings of the nations (Luke 22.26).[81] To behave like a lord in the apostolic office would be a usurpation.[82] The spiritual labour to which his duties put Eugenius ought to be as hard as sweaty manual labour.[83]

Now clearly, this is in startling contrast not only to the papal 'style' of the age, but also, on the face of it, to much of what Bernard was to go on to say about papal supremacy later in this treatise. Bernard is keen to stress the supremacy of Peter (and therefore of his successors) over all others. He points out that even James, the Lord's brother, gave place to him.[84] So it is important to keep in mind in the background of his account the force of the governing principle that 'rule' for popes must be above all service. To come back to our point of departure: they are stewards. They have to render account.[85] All the prerogatives of the pope and his personal dignity are held in trust on behalf of his sheep.[86]

Person and Office   There is a key discussion of the relationship of person to office in the *De Consideratione*. This is extremely important in an ecclesiology which places great stress on the personal character of the episcopal office, that is, which insists that oversight in the Church properly belongs to individuals commissioned to carry pastoral responsibility for their sheep as shepherds, and that at ordination something happens to alter permanently the relationship in which that person stands to the community of the Church. You are still what you were, Bernard instructs Eugenius. You were born a man and elected a pope. That did not so transform you that you ceased to be a man. Your humanity is still there, but something has been added to it.[87] If Eugenius is asked who he is, he will have to reply that he is a bishop, rather than that he is Eugenius. But it is surely of his essence that he is a man, rather than that he is a bishop?[88] Moreover, he ought to pay attention to what sort of person he is by birth and regard what has been added to him as 'garments' he can take off. This does not have the implications it might seem to for Bernard's theology of episcopacy. He is not saying that ordination does not effect an indelible change, merely that the trappings of honour and the both literal and metaphorical fine raiment which go with it are not of its essence, and not of the true being of the person who holds the office, either. Bernard elaborates by tying the idea to the theme of humility. Eugenius may be pope, but he is still common dirt in the eyes of God, and he should never forget that.[89]

But there must be obedience, too. The body-politic image is convenient here. Bernard is able to use it to underline the disorderly results of any officer in the Church getting out of place in his behaviour. This is what he believes is happening as prelates become reluctant to submit themselves to papal authority or to that of those above them in the hierarchy of the Church. They cause the churches to cry out that they are being mutilated and dismembered. Abbots are free from the jurisdiction of bishops, bishops of the jurisdiction of archbishops, archbishops of that of primates. It is Eugenius's responsibility to preserve the proper degrees of honour within the hierarchy. Then honour will be rendered to whom it is due (Romans 13.7).[90]

But how is Eugenius to tell whether he is getting the balance right between accountability to the whole people of God and the preservation of hierarchical order? Bernard sets out for him three 'considerations', to take in sequence. He should ask whether what is in hand is lawful, whether it is fitting (in the strong medieval sense of harmonious with 'right order'),[91] whether it is likely to be profitable or beneficial. The position of Christian philosophy, Bernard argues, is that the latter can never be the case unless the first two conditions are also fulfilled. But the converse is not true. Lawfulness is not necessarily a token of fittingness or of *utilitas*. If Eugenius makes his will the law, there is no guarantee that he will not act on a whim, and then the second and third criteria would not apply. In fact, he would be debasing himself to the level of a beast if he thus chose to act without reason.[92]

Eugenius's role of *episkopos* (overseer) requires him to be vigilant over the whole Church, ensuring that the people obey their clergy, and the clergy obey God.[93] We have seen already that Bernard assumes a hierarchical ecclesiology which separates the clergy from the laity in what is required of them within the household of God.

Eugenius's role of overseer also requires him to watch over the observation of the rules of internal order in religious houses (those houses directly answerable to the pope and not to the local bishop) to see that there is no straying from the faith, and it is also his duty to bring it about that there is a flowering of good priests in the Lord's vineyard, bearing fruit in the obedience of faithful people.[94]

This is a counsel of vigilance, for it is not enough to make laws; there has to be some effort to ensure that they are obeyed.

Bernard envisages an accountability which extends to a kind of suspension even of bishops if they do not exercise their office as they should. They in their turn are 'responsible' for the faults of those subordinate to them. Consequently, if they do not do something about those faults, they should abstain from the exercise of their episcopal office until they have imposed the penalty prescribed by the Apostolic See, says Bernard.[95]

In Book IV Bernard turns to the pontifical household, those who are 'around' Eugenius: the *curia* and the city of Rome, as well as his own entourage. They are, because more intimate with him, in need of a different kind of handling from the Church at large. And if they behave badly, that reflects directly upon him.[96]

Bernard defines a custom as that which has been done not only once but again and again. But it can, in the same way, die out. He has in mind the once honourable custom of shepherds devoting themselves to their sheep for no reward but that of seeing them thus prepared for their God. In the Church of his own day, he observes, a different custom has arisen. Now everyone is interested not in sanctity but in honour and even profit.[97]

Mater, Magistra, *and* Magisterium   'Your breasts are better than wine'.[98] Tradition says that the Bride is speaking to the Groom here, and it is his breasts which are spoken of. On this understanding, Gregory the Great says that the breasts of the bridegroom are holy preachers. *Ubera sint praedicatores sancti*.[99] Bernard, on the other hand, applies the text to the Bride. He makes the breasts still preachers but now the Church's preachers. Among those preachers, Bernard would rank himself. Preaching was exegesis for Bernard as for his patristic predecessors. Indeed, if one were to seek the exegetical record in Bernard's work, that is where one would begin.

The Roman Church is mother of other churches, says Bernard. She is not mistress. (*Domina*, not *magistra*, is the Latin here, for the Fourth Lateran Council recognises the Church as mistress in the second sense, that is, as teacher of the faithful.)[100] The prelate himself ought to be a teacher and also a learner to whom Christ himself is the master of all the paths of life: *His sunt magistri mostri, qui a Magistro omnium vias vitae penius didicerunt, et docent nos*.[101]

Does the pope have any distinctive function as a teacher? It is too early to expect to find the term *magisterium*. In Bernard's view, the pope's present and continuing task is the same as that which the prophets were the first to attempt. They left work for the apostles to do after them, and the apostles have, in their turn, left labour to be completed by succeeding generations.

So this is an inherited duty, in a tradition of high honour and concomitant high obligation.[102]

The way for Eugenius to carry out this task, Bernard explains, is not by going out physically himself, but by intellectual and spiritual contemplation of the world, looking carefully to see whether trees are fruitful or barren. When he has a clear picture, he should act, rooting out what is not bearing fruit of the Lord.[103]

There is, in Bernard's view, above all a responsibility to call men to God, a missionary task. The Jews Bernard sets aside as unreachable, at least for the moment, until all the gentiles have 'come in.' But for the rest he thinks it is a matter of simple justice that unbelievers should be offered Christ if they do not possess him, and believers brought back to Christ if they have begun to go astray from him.[104]

Bernard's Theology of Ministry (part II)

The Making of a Minister   Christ as priest and shepherd was uncontroversially the model for ministry. Whether a priest has a sacrificial duty was not the matter of dispute in this period which it was to become in the sixteenth century, nor was 'pastor' a term preferred to *sacerdos*, 'priest'.

How, in Bernard's view, is a minister 'made' after this model? The ground rules are clear. It is a matter of vocation. God calls. To Bruno, archbishop-elect of Cologne, Bernard writes to offer advice as to whether he ought to accept the bishopric offered to him or not. If the call is from God, says Bernard, no one can have authority to tell him to disobey. If the call is not from God, no one can have authority to tell him to accept. Only the Spirit knows whether the call is from God. Bruno has a bad past record. But he has skills which Bernard believes it is his duty to use. He is being called from the depths to the heights.[105]

The people also 'call' a minister. Bernard writes to the clergy of Sens about the appointment of a new bishop they have to make. You have to find a new pastor, he says. You must take the advice of the suffragans. You have to await the consent of the religious in the diocese. He wants them to arrange 'this matter which is everyone's business' with everyone's help. He wants them to proclaim a fast and call everyone to consult together.[106]

In practice, the relationship between the selection of persons, the ordination, the placing in a given local office with the cure of souls, caused end-

less medieval difficulty. That was what the Investiture Contest was principally about.

Unworthy Ministers   Bernard disapproves of the practice of promoting
inexperienced juveniles just because they have powerful families (*ob
sanguinis dignitatem*). At first they are more pleased to have escaped the
schoolmaster's rod than to be in their new positions. Then they begin
to 'get the hang' of their tasks, but they are governed more by *ambitio*
and *avaritia* than by any true sense of their duties.[107] This was one contemporary manifestation of a perennial problem in the life of the
Church, that of the minister who does not behave as a minister should.

The 'unworthiness' of a minister can be 'carried' in an ecclesiology which
deems the effective power in the Church to be grace. God can work in frail
vessels. 'Peter sinned a great sin, perhaps the greatest, and he was immediately forgiven, and in such a way that he lost nothing of his primacy. Paul
who had so attacked the Church was called to the faith by the very voice of
the Son, so that he might be made a fit vessel (*vas dignum*) to bring his name
to the gentiles.'[108]

But unworthiness in ministers is not to be taken lightly. Bishops have a
duty to be alert to unworthiness. The insolence of the clergy which Bernard
deplores is, he fears, encouraged by the negligence of bishops.[109]

It is a commonplace of twelfth-century satire (as of less sophisticated
forms of complaint) that there is a positive crisis of clerical unworthiness.
Complaints mainly take the form of worries over displays of wealth and
pomp. But, conversely, the contention is also found that there is a lack of
respect for clergy and especially for the higher clergy. Bishops everywhere
are shamed and despised. That means that when they seek to make a ruling, no one takes any notice. That in turn brings papal authority into dis-
repute. Bernard says this in a letter to Innocent II designed to cause him to
take action, but the general principle was one he had much at heart.[110] It is
the thrust of the *De Consideratione*, particularly in its later books, that the
maintenance of a high papal authority is essential to the preservation of an
order in the Church which reflects the eternal and cosmic order.

Unworthy ministers will not necessarily accept reproach in the right
spirit, whether it comes from pope or from bishop. In Letter 152 to Innocent II, Bernard writes on behalf of the bishop of Troyes, who had got himself into trouble through trying to reform the clergy. There have been re-
prisals. False witnesses have stood up to accuse him.[111] This was a familiar

problem and a reason why more witnesses were always required for trials of senior clergy than for others.

There are subtler forms of unacceptable clerical conduct. 'I am a weakling to be scandalised,' confesses Bernard in a letter to Ulger, bishop of Angers. Ulger has a quarrel with the abbess of Fontevrault, over a piece of property. The issue, says Bernard, is not whether you are in the right or in the wrong, but whether you could have handled this more quietly. The greater the name, the greater the scandal.[112] It would be to Ulger's credit not to value his own high standing. But this apparent act of humility is not to his credit if he carries it so far as to offend God. Creating scandal is an offence to God, and if Ulger does not try to diminish the scandal, he is not fulfilling his ministerial duties.[113]

Bernard draws a parallel in this letter with the teaching of Christ about turning the other cheek. Christ would seem to be saying that it is a fault in Christians to go to law against one another. Should they not allow themselves to be defrauded? He has held a mirror up to you, says Bernard. This is the light of the Sun of justice. This small property is not worth the cost in damage to the Church. Be more jealous for your good name, he urges.[114]

War

The Christian, says Bernard, has to be a soldier, for there is a war to be fought against evil. 'When war is declared by the virtue of the mind against the vices or demons, we do not call that remarkable, even if it is praiseworthy': *Sed et quando animi virtute vitiis sive daemoniis bellum indicitur, ne hoc quidem mirabile, etsi laudabile dixerim.*[115] But that does not give a licence to kill, or even a dispensation. There can be no doubt that Christ's spiritual soldiers, fighting evil, are doing his will. But if the war becomes reality and the fighting involves real bloodshed, a number of questions may arise about the virtue of the activity.

A frequent dilemma of medieval Christianity is the opposition between the commandment 'Thou shalt not kill' and the requirements of a warlike society, a society set up in such a way that the Church could become unavoidably involved in wars through the requirement to supply so many knights for the knight-service due in 'rent' for land.

What are the circumstances which create a dispensation for the Christian to kill? It cannot be argued that a Christian is never allowed to lift a sword

in anger, for the Gospel tells soldiers to be content with their pay and therefore countenances their profession (Luke 3.14) (this notwithstanding the
acceptance that killing in battle is a sin for which penance is appropriate).[116]

Defending the Faith

Another route by which the Christian may escape from the dilemma that
he may not kill but must sometimes fight is to see legitimate warfare in terms
of defending the faith. The angels stand by as watchers and protectors; the
Lord himself is there as helper and supporter, he who teaches your hands to
fight and your fingers to wage war: *Adsunt angeli spectatores et protectores:
adest ipse Dominus adiutor et susceptor, qui doceat 'manus tuae ad proelium et
digitos tuos ad bellum*.[117] Let us go to the aid of our brothers, lest if they
fight without us they may perhaps be victorious without us: *Procedamus in
adiutorium fratrum, ne si forte sine nobis pugnent, sine nobis vindicant*.[118]

The enemy of the Cross of Christ is also the persecutor of the Church,
and so Bernard argues that it is appropriate to speak in terms of an active
defence.[119] The friends of the Bridegroom must protect the Bride against
her enemy the heretic, particularly an enemy pretending to be a Christian
and therefore a friend.[120] If the attacker is not a Christian heretic but an
unbeliever from another faith, Bernard sees the Christian soldier's task as
protective, the prevention of the disruption of the peace of God. Let both
swords of the faithful fall on the necks of the enemy, he exhorts, so as to
destroy every high thing which exalts itself against the knowledge of God.[121]
Indeed, once the enemy has been cast out, and only then, God will return to
his house.[122]

Augustine was willing to go further than the defensive posture and think
in terms of war being justified if it was to recapture land taken unjustly or
otherwise to redress an injustice. In Bernard's day there was a further concept of 'holy war' which had a new, if not unprecedented vividness because
of the Second Crusade. Bernard sought to build on the encouraging foundation of the success of the First Crusade, at first not willingly, but eventually with sincere confidence that it was right to do so. In 1146, he preached
successfully to encourage and arouse enthusiasm for the Second Crusade,
at Eugenius's instigation. So when it failed in its objectives, he had to make
sense of what had happened, not only for himself, but also for those he had
led into the enterprise.

The failure of the Second Crusade was a major embarrassment. Bernard can only say that God's purposes are mysterious. He found his people faithless and rebellious (Numbers 20.10). He knew that, although they had set out on the Crusade, in their hearts they were constantly turning back. If we do not believe that the destruction of the Israelites was contrary to God's purposes, we should not think that of the failure of this Crusade either.[123]

Spiritual with Physical Warfare: The Templars

In Bernard's Europe, there was a special category of adherents of the religious life who lived by a Rule and were yet working soldiers, the Order of the Knights Templar in the Holy Land.

In the treatise he wrote for these Knights of the Temple, Bernard speaks of a dual metaphorical and literal knighthood. He claims that this is without precedent, unknown in past ages, because it involves its practitioners in both a spiritual and a physical warfare. The world is full of soldiers and monks, but there are few who are both. They are girded with both the swords of Luke 22.38. Such a soldier does not fear death—in fact he must desire it, and therefore when he fights in a physical battle he has unmatched courage. On his soul is the armour of faith, on his body the armour of metal. To die in battle as such a soldier is to die a glorious death.[124] To die an ordinary soldier may be the reverse of glorious. Ordinary warfare is conducted with pomp and display, caparisoned horses, painted shields, so that it cannot even be fought efficiently. A soldier needs strength, freedom of movement, and mental vigilance. The secular soldiery has its limbs entangled in fancy garments, so that it cannot move freely, and an uncertain conscience, because its members have dared to undertake their dangerous business on trivial grounds. Secular wars start as a result of moments of anger, out of a desire for an empty glory, or from the hankering after earthly goods. To die for such a cause is not the way to heaven.[125]

Because he fights for Christ, the soldier of Christ can regard himself not only as doing his duty for his Lord but even as a minister of Christ (Romans 13.4), Christ's instrument for God, Christ's avenger, defender of the faith and the faithful.[126]

In Bernard's view—as in Augustine's—Christ is glorified by the death of an unbeliever, and such a killing, far from requiring repentance and incurring penance, deserves divine reward. That does not mean, Bernard emphasises, that it is right to kill pagans if there is any other way of preventing them from harassing the faithful. But the persecution they engage in may not only damage; it may intimidate, so that the faithful may allow themselves to be led astray. [127]

The Templars' dwelling place is itself Jerusalem.[128] The Temple was once a fine building adorned with gold and precious stones. It is now adorned by the religious zeal and good behaviour of the Templars, who dwell in their own Temple.[129] The ancient witnesses, he says, were foretelling this new knighthood.[130]

Bernard is balanced on a line between the literal and the metaphorical, here. He is writing for a community of religious with a specific job to do in the Holy Land. But he is also writing for the wider community of Christians, for whom Jerusalem is much more than one small earthly city. When he cries 'Rejoice Jerusalem!' and brings together Old Testament texts[131] in a call to 'Jerusalem' to be glad and give praise because the Lord has comforted his people and ransomed Jerusalem, he has in mind the spiritual Jerusalem.

The Ethics of Soldiering

The ground rules of obedience under which the religious live have their counterpart in the discipline of soldiers and their duty of obedience to their superiors. That is perfectly exemplified, says Bernard, in the style of life of the new Order of the Templars. The Templars obey orders like proper soldiers. But they also live celibate lives as a community under religious obedience, without personal property, preserving the unity of the Spirit in the bond of peace.[132] They are industrious, occupying spare moments in repairing their armour or tidying up. They do not indulge in the usual soldierly leisure activities, dicing and hunting. The 'bond of peace' they share seems collegial. But Bernard stresses that the Templars do not make distinction of persons and defer not to those of more noble blood, but only to those whose merits earn respect.[133]

The bond of peace is also a bond of gentleness, and the Templars behave towards one another with mildness and forbearance; but in battle, the Templars must be fierce. Indeed they must be fiercer than other soldiers; they must fall upon the enemy as though they were merely a flock of sheep. Their motto is the motto of the Maccabees; they believe that a multitude may be vanquished by a few when the Lord is on their side, for it does not make any difference to God whether he has to enable them to overcome a large army or a small one. His power suffices.[134]

The Templars are thus a military paradox. They are gentler than lambs but fiercer than lions.[135]

Spiritual Warfare

One solution to the dilemma this creates for the Templars within their microcosm (and also for the macrocosm in which other Christians live) is to think in terms of a spiritual warfare only, in which there is no actual killing. The metaphor of the soldier of Christ is ancient. It is biblical (II Timothy 2.3).

The idea of an inner warfare, a battle between the body and its desires and appetites, and the soul which is aspiring to God, is present from earliest Christianity. Augustine never shook off the conviction that this was a part of the fallen human condition, although to be consistent he should perhaps have shed it with his Manicheism. The flesh is the enemy of continence, complains Bernard, on the same understanding.[136]

Our inward war is more than 'civil'; it is 'domestic', says Bernard: *bellum non civile, sed domesticum, spiritus adversus carnem et caro adversus spiritum concupiscens.*[137] An inward war is a dangerous quarrel: *bellum intestinum est et discordia periculosa.*[138]

Was Bernard's political theology consistent with the remainder of his 'theologies'? For it was here that he was most severely tested, here where pragmatism and the exigencies of practical politics most radically challenged his idealism.

CONCLUSION

What are we to make of Bernard of Clairvaux? Many of those who have written about him, in his own age and our own, have been disposed to adulation. He was a powerful and compelling figure. He has been loved and hated, but especially loved. To those who come to him looking to be moved, he is still persuasive, winning, capable of heightening the emotionality of a spiritual response and giving it that affect which he sought and in which he saw few dangers to the soul. He was not concerned that there might be dangers to the intellect, for unlike Anselm of Canterbury he did not come at the task of theological problem-solving with a mind which took pleasure first and foremost in the rationality, the calm sense of the solutions proposed. Anselm's delight in the discovery which he wrote down in the *Proslogion* was perhaps more cerebral than spiritual, although it certainly had a devotional content. Bernard minded most that his words should strike chords and make people enthusiastic for God. In that he was closer to the monastic tradition than to the coming academic practice of the later twelfth century.

All this makes him a good theologian and an important theologian, but only if we can share his priorities and regard it as more important not to rock the boat than to push the boat a little farther out to sea. That is one of the most important decisions a theologian has to take in any age, and if Bernard can challenge the reader to make it, one way or the other, he is still worth reading for something more than the beauty and cogency of his siren call to the faithful.

NOTES

De Diligendo Dei	*De Diligendo Deo*, LTR 3.
Diversis	*Sermones de Diversis*, LTR 6i.
Dominica 1 Nov.	*Sermones in Dominica 1 Nov.*, LTR 5.
Epiphania	*Sermones in Epiphania Domini*, LTR 4.
Festivitate	*Sermo in Festivitate Omnium Sanctorum*, LTR 4.
Grace	*De Gratia et Libero Arbitrio*, LTR 3.
Henrici Primi	*Leges Henrici Primi*, ed. L. J. Downer (Oxford, 1972).
Historia Pontificalis	John of Salisbury, *Historia Pontificalis*, ed. M. Chibnall (Oxford, 1986).
Humility and Pride	*De Gradibus Humilitatis et Superbiae*, LTR 3.
Klibansky	R. Klibansky, 'Peter Abailard and Bernard of Clairvaux', *Mediaeval and Renaissance Studies* 5 (1961), pp. 1–27.
Letter(s)	*Epistolae*, LTR 7–8.
Libellus	*Libellus de Diversis Ordinibus*, ed. G. Constable and B. Smith (Oxford, 1972).
LTR	*Sancti Bernardi Opera*, 8 vols., ed. J. Leclercq, C. H. Talbot, and H. Rochais (Rome, 1957–).
Malachy	*Vitae Sancti Malachiae.* LTR 3.295.
Marenbon	J. Marenbon, *The Philosophy of Peter Abelard* (Oxford, 1997).
Morris	Colin Morris, 'William I and the Church Courts', *English Historical Review* 324 (1967)
On Conversion	*Ad Clericos de Conversione*, LTR 4
Petri et Pauli	*Sermo in Solemnitate Apostolorum Petri et Pauli*, LTR 4.
PL	J. P. Migne, *Patrologia Latina*.
Pranger	M. B. Pranger, *Bernard of Clairvaux and the Shape of Monastic Thought: Broken Dreams* (Leiden, 1994).
Precept and Dispensation	*De Praecepto et Dispensatione*, LTR 3.
Psalmum	*Sermones in Psalmum Qui Habitat*, LTR 4.
Quadrigesima	*Sermones in Quadrigesima*, LTR 4.
RB	*The Rule of St. Benedict*, ed. G. Holzmer (Dublin, 1994).
SC	*Sources chrétiennes* (Paris: Editions du Cerf).
Sent.	*Sententiae Series*, LTR 6i–6ii.
SS	*Sermones in Cantica Canticorum*, LTR 3.
Templars	*In Laudibus Militis Templi*, LTR 3.
VP	*Sancti Bernardi Vita Prima*, *PL* 185.

INTRODUCTION

1. Bruno Michel, 'La considération et l'unitas spiritus', in Brague, pp. 109–27, at p. 110.

2. Letter 193. Bernard's letters can be retrieved from two sources: LTR 7–8, which are generally referenced in this book, and *Lettres*, tr. M. Duchet-Suchaux and H. Rochais, *SC* 425 (Paris, 1997).

3. Pranger, p. 31.

4. *SS* 20.1, a theme explored by Pranger, p. 22.

5. Pranger, p. 10.

CHAPTER I

1. Bredero, p. 91.

2. Bredero, pp. 91ff.

3. Eadmer, *Life of Anselm*, ed. R. W. Southern (London, 1962).

4. *PL* 185.573–88. Cf. Bredero, p. 95.

5. Bredero, pp. 103, 104.

6. Letter 310.

7. Bredero, p. 104.

8. On all this, see the introduction to William of St. Thierry, *Expositio super Epistolam ad Romanos*, *CCCM* 86, pp. xiii–xxiv.

9. *PL* 185.226.

10. J. Leclercq asks in *A Second Look at Bernard of Clairvaux* (Kalamazoo, 1990) whether the known facts of Bernard's life are at odds with the hagiographical account. Bredero's recent study, *Bernard of Clairvaux: Between Cult and History* (Edinburgh, 1996), makes a substantial addition to this debate.

11. *Libellus,* p. 3.

12. *Libellus,* p. 118.

13. *Libellus,* p. 3.

14. *Libellus,* pp. 19, 45.

15. J. B. Auberger, 'La législation cistercienne primitive', *SC* 380 (Paaris, 1992), pp. 181–208, at p. 188, and J. Marilier, *Chartes et documents de Cîteaux* (Rome, 1961), p. 43.

16. *SS* 52.7.

17. Cf. William of St. Thierry, *PL* I.2.17, *PL* 185.236.

18. See André Louf, 'Bernard abbé', *SC* 380 (Paris, 1992), pp. 349–79.

19. Malcolm Barber, *The New Knighthood* (Cambridge, 1994), p. 49.

20. See I. S. Robinson, *Authority and Resistance in the Investiture Contest* (Manchester, 1978).

21. He uses the phrase *plenitudo potestatis* in Letter 131.2.

22. See John of Salisbury, *Memoirs of Life at the Papal Court*, ed. M. Chibnall (Oxford, 1986).

23. See *CCCM* 90–92 for the works and some context for the life of this pioneering abbess.

24. Letter 195.

25. *Historia Pontificalis,* p. xviii.

26. Bredero, *Bernard of Clairvaux,* p. 4.

27. See notes on these figures in Bredero, *Bernard of Clairvaux*, and see P. Rassow, 'Di Kanzlei s. Bernhards von Clairvaux', *Studien und Mitteilungen zur Geschichte des Benediktiner-Ordens* 34 (1913), pp. 67–69; A. H. Bredero, *Études sur la vita prima de saint Bernard* (1960), pp. 15–23; and G. R. Evans, 'The *De Consideratione* of Bernard of Clairvaux, a Preliminary Letter', *Cîteaux* 35 (1984).

28. Bernard de Clairvaux, *Lettres*, vol. 1, pp. 24–26.

29. Martin Camargo, *Ars dictaminis*, *Ars Dictandi*, *Typologie des sources du moyen âge occidental* (series), no. 60 (Turnhout, 1991); Giles Constable, *Letters and Letter-Collections*, *Typologie des sources du moyen âge occidental* (series), no. 17 (Turnhout, 1976).

30. Bernard de Clairvaux, *Lettres*, vol. 1, p. 214.

31. Bernard de Clairvaux, *Lettres*, vol. 1, p. 26.

32. Bernard de Clairvaux, *Lettres*, vol. 1, p. 33.

33. Letter 387.

CHAPTER 2

1. *Quadrigesima* 2.1.

2. *Quadrigesima* 2.4.

3. Letter 81.

4. Letter 285.1.

5. Letter 280.2.

6. Galatians 2.6.

7. *Templars* VII, and cf. *Sent.* 3.127.

8. Letter 243.1. Cf. Letter 280.1 and *homunculus* in *SS* 45.2.

9. G. R. Evans, 'A Change of Mind in Some Scholars of the Eleventh and Twelfth Centuries', *Studies in Church History* 15 (1978), pp. 27–38.

10. J. Quillet, 'Aspects de la doctrine Bernardine de l'obéissance', in Brague, pp. 165–77, at p. 170.

11. See Evans, 'A Change of Mind', pp. 27–38.

12. See my *Augustine on Evil* (Cambridge, 1983) on this background.

13. *On Conversion* II.3.

14. Guibert of Nogent, *De Vita Sua*, ed. G. Bourgin (Paris, 1906).

15. Pranger, p. 6.

16. See, too, chapter 5.

17. *Sermones in Vigilia Nativitatis Domini* 5.1, LTR 4.

18. *In Resurrectione Sermo* 4.1, LTR 5.110–11.

19. *On Conversion* I.1.

20. Cf. Augustine, *Quaestiones Evangeliorum* 2, q.44, ed. A. Mutzenbecher, *CCSL* 44B; Augustine, *Ennarrationes in Psalmos* 132.5, *CCSL* 40.

21. Nicholas of Clairvaux. Letter 35, *PL* 196.1645, cf. Acts 17.25.

22. *On Conversion* II.3.

23. George Lawless, *Augustine of Hippo and His Monastic Rule* (Oxford, 1987).

24. Letter 1.

25. Letter 1.

26. Watkin Williams, *Monastic Studies* (Manchester, 1938), p. 1. On the Cluniac and Cistercian debate in the later twelfth-century dialogue between a Cluniac and a Cistercian, see also Williams, *Monastic Studies*, p. 61.

27. H. E. J. Cowdrey, *Popes, Monks, and Crusaders* (London, 1984).

28. *VP* I.14.

29. J. Leclercq, *La femme et les femmes dans l'oeuvre de S. Bernard* (Paris, 1982), pp. 31ff.

30. Letter 114.

31. Leclercq, *La femme et les femmes,* p. 29.

32. Leclercq calculates 40 occasions in 500 letters. Leclercq, *La femme et les femmes,* p. 13.

33. Letter 7.16.

34. *Dominica 1 Nov.* 4.1.

35. Letter 7.16.

36. Letter 7.15.

37. Letter 7.15.

38. Letter 42.

39. Letter 382.3.

40. *RB* 1.

41. Letter 64.1. Cf. Pranger, p. 33.

42. *Precept and Dispensation* II.5.

43. Letter 54.3.

44. Letter 52.

45. Letter 7.16.

46. Letter 195.

47. *SS* 26.1.

48. *Quadrigesima* 6.1.

49. *Psalmum* 11.9.

50. *Sermones in Assumptione Beatae Mariae Virginus* 2.1, LTR 5.232.1.

51. *Apologia* 8.

52. Letter 319.

53. *Csi* V.2.

54. *Sent.* 3.127.

55. *SS* 50.1.

56. Deriving from Apuleius. *Asclepius, De Philosophia Libri*, ed. C. Moreschini (Stuttgart, 1991).

57. *Cantica Canticorum* I.1, p. 19.

58. *Grace* 49.

59. *Csi* V.i.1–2.

60. Cf. *Sermo in Nativitate Beatae Mariae Virginus* 8, LTR 5.280.16.

61. *De Moribus et Officio Episcoporum*, Letter 42.8, LTR 7.107.12.

62. *De Moribus et Officio Episcoporum*, Letter 42.8, LTR 7.107.17.

63. *Homilia super 'Missus Est'* 1.5, LTR 4.17.24.

64. *Grace* 49.

65. *Sent.* 1.38.

66. *SS* 7.7.

67. *Grace* 49.

68. *Sent.* 3.8.

69. *Diversis* 69.2.

70. *Ut numquam mente excidat peregrinos vos esse, longe factos a patria, pulsos ab hereditate. Sermones in Epiphania Domini* 1.1, LTR 4.291.

71. *Sermones in Octava Paschae* 2.5, LTR 5.120.21.

72. *SS* 13.1.

73. Letter 42.

74. *Sermo in Festivitate S. Michael* 1.5, LTR 5.297.

75. On purgatory, see J. le Goff, *The Birth of Purgatory*, ed. A. Goldhammer (London, 1984).

76. On the *regiones*, see F. Châtillon, 'Regio dissimilitudinis', in *Mélanges E. Pochédard* (Lyon, 1945), pp. 85–102, and R. Javelet, *Image et ressemblance au douzième siécle,* 2 vols. (Paris, 1967).

77. *Sent.* 3.91.

78. *Apologia*, 28.

79. *Apologia* 14.

80. *Sed et in mandatis hominum rara aequalitas invenitur, cum pro variis necessitatibus vel utilitatibus agendorum, iniungentium affectio variatur. Precept and Dispensation* XV.

81. *Prodest, si devote suscipitur et tenetur; non tamen, si non suscipitur, obest. Precept and Dispensation* I.2.

82. *Precept and Dispensation* I.1.

83. *Precept and Dispensation* I.2.
84. *Precept and Dispensation* I.2.
85. *Precept and Dispensation* II.6.
86. *Precept and Dispensation* VII.13.
87. Letter 7.5.
88. *Precept and Dispensation* IX.21.
89. Quillet, 'Aspects de la doctrine', p. 165.
90. *Precept and Dispensation* X.23.
91. Letter 42.16.
92. *Quadrigesima* 1.6.
93. Letter 7.16.
94. Letter 94.
95. *Sent.* 3.120.
96. Letters 233.2 and 236.2.
97. But see P. Delhaye, *Le problème de la conscience morale chez S. Bernard étudié dans ses oeuvres et dans ses sources,* Analecta Medievalia Namurcensia, no. 9 (Namur, 1957).
98. Letter 1.9.
99. Letter 233.2.
100. Letter 280.
101. Peter the Venerable, *De Miraculis* 2.15, ed. D. Bouthillier, *CCCM* 83.
102. Letter 42.6.
103. *In tua lateat conscientia, Csi* II.23.
104. Letter 253.3.
105. *On Conversion* V.7.
106. *Sent.* 3.114.
107. *Humility and Pride* XLVII.
108. *Templars* II; *De Diligendo Dei* 34.
109. Letter 42.21.
110. Letter 7.2.
111. *Precept and Dispensation* IX.19.
112. *Precept and Dispensation* VII.13.
113. Letter 7.4.
114. Letter 7.3.
115. *Precept and Dispensation* IV.9.
116. Letter 7.3–4.
117. Letter 1.4.
118. Letter 7.4.
119. On this problem, see further under 'moral theology'.
120. *Precept and Dispensation* V.11.

121. *Precept and Dispensation* V.11.

122. *Si modus est oboeditionis tenor professionis, nec se valet extendere potestas imperantis, nisi quatenus attigerit votum profitentis. Precept and Dispensation* V.11.

123. *RB* 68.

124. *Legem nescit, terminis non arctatur. Precept and Dispensation* VI.12.

125. *Precept and Dispensation* V.11.

126. *Diversis* 41.2.

127. *Sermo in Vigilia Nativitate Domini* 6.4.

128. *Precept and Dispensation* XLIII.

129. Quillet, 'Aspects de la doctrine', p. 168.

130. *Precept and Dispensation* X.

131. *Precept and Dispensation* VII.16.

132. *Precept and Dispensation* VIII.18.

133. Letters 4, 5, and 7, in *Anselmi Opera Omnia*, 6 vols., ed. F. S. Schmitt (Rome-Edinburgh, 1938–68), vol. 3.

134. Letters 7, 28, and 287, in *Anselmi Opera Omnia* 3–4.

135. Ailred of Rievaulx, *De Spiritali Amicitia,* prologue.1, ed. A. Hoste and C. H. Talbot, *CCCM* 1, p. 287.

136. Ailred of Rievaulx, *De Spiritali Amicitia*, prologue.2, 6, and book I.1, *CCCM* 1, pp. 287ff.

137. Ailred of Rievaulx, *De Spiritali Amicitia*, book I.2–4, *CCCM* 1, p. 289.

138. Ailred of Rievaulx, *De Spiritali Amicitia*, book I.5, *CCCM* 1, p. 290.

139. Cicero, *De Amicitia* 20, ed. W. A. Falconer (London, 1971).

140. Letter 142.2.

141. *Quadrigesima* 4.2.

142. *Humility and Pride*, preface.

143. *Humility and Pride* I.2.

144. *RB* 7.10–66.

145. *Humility and Pride* IX.27.

146. See my *Getting it Wrong: The Mediaeval Epistemology of Error* (Brill, 1998).

147. *Humility and Pride* X.28–29.

148. *Humility and Pride* XI.39.

149. *Humility and Pride* XII.40.

150. *Humility and Pride* XIII.41.

151. *Humility and Pride* XIV.42.

152. *Humility and Pride* XV.43.

153. *Humility and Pride* XVI.44.

154. *Humility and Pride* XVII.45.

155. *Humility and Pride* XVII.47.

156. *Humility and Pride* XX.50–XXI.51.

157. See chapter 5 on Bernard's doctrine of the will.

158. *Precept and Dispensation* XI.26, on I Kings 15.23.

159. *Humility and Pride* XIX.49.

160. Letter 1.4.

161. Letter 1.4.

CHAPTER 3

1. Augustine's *De Genesi ad Litteram* was an important influence here. *PL* 34.245–483.

2. *Anselmi Opera Omnia* 1.

3. J. Verger, 'Le cloître et les écoles', *SC* 380 (Paris, 1992), pp. 459–73, at p. 460.

4. See chapter 6.

5. Letter 77.1.

6. *Videat forsitan nimius in suggillatione scientiae, et quasi repehendere doctos, ac prohibere studia literati. SS* 36.i.2.

7. Cf. William of St. Thierry, *Golden Epistle*, tr. Walter Shewring (London, 1980), II.iv.203, and Augustine, *De Immortalitate Animae* 6.10, *PL* 32.1021–33.

8. LTR 7.184.17–20.

9. See chapter 6.

10. *Historia Pontificalis,* p. 26.

11. N. M. Häring's introduction to his edition of Gilbert of Poitiers, *Commentaries on Boethius* (Toronto, 1969).

12. *Historia Pontificalis,* p. 27.

13. *Historia Pontificalis,* p. 26.

14. *Historia Pontificalis,* p. 26.

15. William of St. Thierry, *Disputatio adversus Petrum Abaelardum* 1, *PL* 180.249.

16. John of Salisbury, *Letters*, vol. 1, ed. W. J. Millor (Oxford, 1986), Letter 124.

17. Letter 336, to a certain abbot.

18. Letter 332.

19. *Sermo in Labore Messis* 3.4, LTR 5.224–25.

20. *Sent.* 2.1.

21. *Apologia* 5. Cf. LTR 3.97.

22. *On Conversion* I.2.

23. Letter 58.2.

24. *On Conversion* I.1.

25. *On Conversion* VI.11.

26. *SS* 74.3.

27. *Et prorsus sanguinis pro Christo effusio magnae cuiusdam fidei indubitat probatio, non Deo tamen, sed hominibus.* Letter 77.8.

28. *Iterum experiri vires, arma probare delectat.* Letter 129.3.

29. *Nonne nempe in tuo arbitrio est probare me vel improbare. SS* 13.6.

30. *Non enim 'iudicare' hic posuit, sed 'diiudicare', quod utique discernere et probare est. Diversis* 34.3.

31. Letter 162.

32. *Extinctae fidei nulla iam debeatur probatio, sed reprobatio.* Letter 42.15.

33. *Csi* V.iii.6.

34. *Csi* V.iii.6.

35. *Rationalis tunc est, cum in omnibus quae oportet de Christo sentiri, fidei ratio ita firma tenetur, ut ab ecclesiastici sensus puritate nulla veri similitudine, nulla haeretica seu diabolica circumventione. SS* 20.9.

36. Letter 190.i.1.

37. Letter 338.

38. E.g., *Proslogion*, in *Anselmi Opera Omnia* 1.98.1–15.

39. *Nam etsi constet in christiana utique philosophia non decere nisi quod licet, non expedire nisi quod decet et licet, non continuo tamen omne quod licet, decere aut expedire consequens erit. Csi* III.15.

40. *Diversis* 16.4, and cf. the organising principle of *De Consideratione*.

41. *Sermo de Voluntate Divina* 5, LTR 6i.39. *Haec enim vera est philosophia, et utraque cognitio proprsus necessaria ad salutem: ex priore siquidem timor concipitur et humilitas, ex posteriore spes et caritas generatur. Diversis* 5.5.

42. See my *Old Arts and New Theology* (Oxford, 1983).

43. Letter 190.

44. Letter 190.8.

45. See my *Philosophy and Theology in the Middle Ages* (London, 1993).

46. See my *Augustine on Evil* (Oxford, 1983).

47. *In Natali Sancti Clementis* 1, LTR 5.413.

48. *Diversis* 7.1.

49. *Petri et Pauli* 3.

50. *Csi* 1.12.

51. *De Diligendo Dei*, prologue.

52. *Sermo de Septem Donis Spiritus Sanctus* 5, LTR oo.

53. *Non sit molestum his qui sunt in lege periti, si parum doctis morem gerimus, ut exigit ratio caritatis. Sermones in Epiphania Domini* 3.1, LTR 4.

54. Letter 24.1.

55. *Csi* V.14.

56. *Philosophi gentium, plus iusto fisi et fixi in cordibus suis ob inanem fiduciam, in inanem dedere ruinam. Diversis* 5.4.

57. *Dominica 1 Nov.* 4.2, and Romans 1.21 and 1.28.

58. Ecclesiastes 1.2; *Sermo in Nativitate Sancti Johannis Baptistae* 7, LTR 5.180.

59. *Festivitate* 5.4.

60. Letter 523.

61. *Sent.* 3.57.

62. *Sent.* 3.108.

63. *Sed et illa eius stultitia, per quam ei placuit salvum facere mundum, ut mundi confutaret sapientiam, confunderet sapientes.* Templars XXVII.

64. *Grace* 20.

65. *Sermo in Ascensione Domini* 4.4, LTR 5.143.

66. *Petri et Pauli* 3.

67. *Csi* II.iii.6.

68. *Csi* II.vii.14.

69. *Diversis* 12.2.

70. *Csi* II.iii.6.

71. *Csi* II.iii.6; J. Reiter, 'Bernard de Clairvaux, philosophe malgré lui entre coeur et raison', in Brague, pp. 11–25, at p. 13.

72. Michel, 'La consideratione', p. 581.

73. Brague, *Saint Bernard et la philosophie*.

74. See chapter 5.

75. *SS* 5.2.8.

76. *Festivitate* 4.5; *PL* 64.159ff.; *Sermones in Assumptione Beatae Mariae Virginis* 2.5, LTR 5.

77. *De Diligendo Deo* 28.

78. F. Nef, 'Caritas dat caritatem', in Brague, pp. 87–108.

79. *De Genesi ad Litteram PL* 34.219 and 34.245.

80. Chalcidius, *On Timaeus*, ed. Waszink (Leiden, 1962), pp. 264 and 271.

81. *Erunt autem et tot speculativae philosophiae species, quot sunt res in quibus iustae speculatio considerationis habetur.* Boethius, *In Isagogen Porphyrii*, ed. C. Meiser (Leipzig, 1877), I.3, p. 8.

82. Augustine, *Enarrationes in Psalmos* 64.3, *CCSL* 39.

83. Augustine, *Enarrationes in Psalmos* 101, Sermo II.4., *CCSL* 40.

84. *In Heremiam Prophetam*, Book VI, *CCSL* 74, p. 381.

85. *Quod est ecclesia, in qua dominus spiritaliter inesse reverenda semper contemplatione monstratur.* Cassiodorus, *Expositio in Psalmos*, Psalm 2.166, *CCSL* 97, and Psalm 98.61, *CCSL* 98.

86. Cassiodorus, *Expositio in Psalmos*, Psalm 75.60, *CCSL* 98.

87. See my *Augustine on Evil*.

88. *Quando ab hac purgabitur confusione oculus cordis. Diversis* 28.7.

89. *Mundatur oculus cordis, cui se in sui puritate videndam veritatis promittit.* Humility and Pride VI.19.

90. *Quales oculi, qui contemplantur cogitationes . . . solent sentiri a cogitante, non audiri ab auscultante, non a contemplante videri.* Letter 42.22.

91. *Csi* I.iii.5.

92. *Csi* V.i.2.

93. Michel, 'La considération', at p. 112.

94. *Csi* V.ii.4.

95. *Csi* V.4.

96. *Csi* V.4.

97. *Csi* V.4.

98. *Csi* V.iii.5.

99. *Diversis* 115.

100. *SS* 49.4.

101. *Csi* V.3.

102. *Non dico agnitione, sed amicitia et familiaritate donata est, ut eius crebra colloquia et oscula mereretur, et nunc familiari ausu loquitur.* SS 38.3.

103. *SS* 52.2.

104. *SS* 52.3.

105. *SS* 52.4–5.

106. *SS* 82.8.

107. *Humility and Pride* VI.19.

108. *SS* 52.5.

109. *SS* 52.6–7.

110. *SS* 23.6; Pranger, p. 51.

111. Chapter 6.

CHAPTER 4

1. *Feria IV Hebdomadae Sanctae*, Sermo 8, LTR 5.61; cf. *On Conversion* I.2.

2. Letter 195.3.

3. Letter 252.4.

4. *In Natali Sancti Benedicti* 1, LTR 5.1.

5. *Cantica Canticorum* II.5, p. 21.

6. *Cantica Canticorum* I.3, p. 21.

7. G. Lobrichon, 'La Bible des maîtres du xii siècle', *SC* 380, pp. 209–36.

8. J. Dunbabin, 'The Maccabees as Exemplars in the Tenth and Eleventh Centuries, the Bible and the Medieval World', in K. Walsh and D. Wood, eds., *Essays in Honour of Beryl Smalley* (Oxford, 1985).

9. See Beryl Smalley, *The Study of the Bible in the Middle Ages* (3rd ed., Oxford, 1983).

10. On the library, see *La bibliothèque de l'abbaye de Clairvaux du xiie et xviiie*

siècles, vol. 1, *Catalogues et répertoires*, ed. A. Vernet and J.-F. Genest (Paris, 1979). See, too, A. Wilmart, 'L'ancienne bibliothèque de Clairvaux', *Mémoires de la Société académique d'agriculture des sciences, des arts et belles lettre du département de l'Aube*, 81 (1917), pp. 127–90.

11. J. Leclercq, 'Les manuscrits de l'abbaye de Liessies', *Scriptorium* 6 (1952), pp. 51–62, and J.-P. Bouhout, 'La bibliothèque de Clairvaux', *SC* 380 (Paris, 1992), pp. 141–55.

12. *Quo quidem non minus nos experientia propria quam divina pagina docet. On Conversion*, 30.

13. *In Octava Epiphaniae* 2.

14. *In Octava Epiphaniae* 3.

15. See further chapter 4.

16. See chapter 6.

17. *Sermo super Psalmum 'Qui Habitat'* 1.3, LTR 4.388.

18. *SS* 80.8.

19. *Dominica 1 Nov.* 4.3; cf. *Diversis* 110.

20. *SS* 19.4.

21. See my *Logic and Language of the Bible*, 2 vols. (Cambridge, 1984–85), vol. 1.

22. *Circumcisione* 3.11.

23. Letter 108.2. Cf. *Sermones in Dominica I post Octavum Epiphaniae* 1.3, LTR 4.314.

24. *'Et vox facta est': lucis et vocis testimonia facta sunt credibilia nimis, nec dubitare est de veritate, quae sese ingerit per utrasque, oculorum scilicet auriumque fenestras. Sermo in Conversione Sancti Pauli* 2, LTR 4.327.

25. *Sane ex deliberatione communi ascendit Veritas ad constitutam diem, sed ascendit usque ad nubes. Sermones in Adnuntistione Dominica* 1:10, LTR 5.23.

26. *In Annuntiatione Sermo* 1.10, LTR 5.23.

27. *SS* 15.8.

28. *Sent.* 3.109.

29. *Audiens proinde verbum Dei, multo magis attende loquentem intus Deum quam hominem foris, nam illa vox viva et efficax ipsa est vox Domini convertens animas. De conversione (textus brevis)* 2.

30. *Templars* VI.

31. *Quod signasse expressius videtur alia interpretatio. SS* 41.4.

32. *SS* 14.8, and Augustine, *Confessions* III.v.

33. One of the values of having the spiritual senses at the exegete's disposal is that they make it possible to get round the difficulty that the literal sense is sometimes repugnant (Augustine certainly found it so as a young man).

34. II Corinthians 3.6.

35. *Utrum saeculari sapientia et philosophicis traditionibus, seu etiam divinarum superficie Scripturarum, quam nimirum occidentem litteram vocat Apostolus. Sermo in Dominica Quattuor post Pentecosten* 3.3, LTR 5.203.

36. *SS* 7.5.

37. *SS* 53.5.

38. *Diversis* 97.2.

39. Letter 89.1.

40. See H. de Lubac, *Exégèse médiévale*, 2 vols. (Paris, 1959); Smalley, *The Study of the Bible*; Evans, *The Logic and Language of the Bible*.

41. *In Octava Paschae Sermo* 1.5, LTR 5.114.

42. *Diversis* 5.2, cf. *De Diligendo Deo* 11, LTR 3.128.6.

43. *Psalmum* 3.3.

44. *Sermones in Nativitate Domini* 4.2, LTR 4.265.

45. *Sermo in Dominica Quarta post Pentecosten* 2, LTR 5.202.

46. *Non timebis a timore nocturno, Psalmum* 6.1.

47. *Circumcisione* 2.3.

48. *Circumcisione* 1.3.

49. *Circumcisione* 3.11.

50. *Circumcisione* 1.4.

51. *Circumcisione* 1.4.

52. *Habes ergo unum in his omnibus appellationibus Jesum, nec omnino aut vocari posset, aut esse Salvator, si forte horum quippiam defuisset. Circumcisione* 1.5.

53. Cf. *laeva . . . iure vocatur non incongrue dexteram nominat. Festivitate* 4.2.

54. *Sermones in Nativitate Domini* 5.2, LTR 4.000.

55. *Diversis* 104.

56. Letter 7.2.

57. *Grace* 4.

58. *Grace* 6.

59. *Sermo de Septem Donis Spiritus Sancti* 5, LTR 6i.138.

60. *Diversis* 83.

61. *Ego tamen opinor non incongrue pennas istas agnitionem et devotionem intelligi posse, quibus in eum, qui supra ipsos est, Seraphim rapiuntur. Dominica 1 Nov.* 4.2.

62. *Nempe quod sequitur 'iudicia tua abyssus multa'* [Psalm 35.7], *non incongrue forte videbitur pedum posse appellatione signari. Dominica 1 Nov.* 5.9.

63. *Psalmum* 6.7.

64. *Quadrigesima* 4.2.

65. *Psalmum* 9.2.

66. *SS* 59.7.

67. *Psalmum* 9.2.

68. *Circumcisione* 2.1.

69. *Circumcisione* 2.2. *SS* 59.9.

70. *In Conversione Sancti Pauli* 6, LTR 4.331; I Timothy 1.15; I Timothy 4.9.

71. *Verbum enim consummans, et abbrevians in aequitate: quia verbum breviatum faciet Dominus super terram.*

72. *Adventu* 2, on Genesis 3.22.

73. *Adventu* 5.2.

74. *Psalmum* 9.8.

75. *In Annuntiatione Sermo* 3.7, LTR 5.39.

76. For example *Adventu* 6.2.

77. *Circumcisione* 2.3.

78. *Et nos enim, fratres, circumcidi necesse est, et sic nomen salutis accipere: circumcidi sane non littera, sed spiritu et veritate, circumcidi non uno membero, sed toto corpore simul. Circumcisione* 2.3, Luke 2.3.

79. Wisdom 11.1.

80. *In Circumcisione Domini Sermo* 1.1.

81. *Sermones* 2.2, *in Septuagesima* LTR 4.350.

82. *Humility and Pride* VIII.

83. *Cantica Canticorum* II.7, p. 23.

84. *Adventu* 1.11.

85. See chapter 3.

86. J. J. Murphy, *Mediaeval Rhetoric: A Select Bibliography* (Toronto, 1989).

87. *PL* 210, and see Alan of Lille, *The Art of Preaching*, tr. G. R. Evans (Kalamazoo, 1981).

88. *In Resurrectione Sermo* 4.1, LTR 5.110.

89. See C. Mohrmann, 'Observations sur la langue et le style de S. Bernard', LTR 2, pp. ix–xxiii, and V. Lossky, 'Études sur la terminologie de S. Bernard', *Archivum Latinitatis Medii Aevi* 17 (1943), pp. 79–96.

90. *Memorials of St. Anselm*, ed. R. W. Southern and F. S. Schmitt (London, 1969).

91. *De Consideratione*, preface.

92. *Precept and Dispensation* III.253.

93. *Sermones in Epiphania Domini* 1.2, LTR 4.

94. *Feria IV Hebdomadae Sanctae Sermo* 6, LTR 5.56.

95. Letter 11.1.

96. *Adventu* 3.1.

97. *Et in vita passivam habuit actionem, et in morte passionem activam sustinuit, dum salutem operaretur in medio terrae. Feria IV Hebdomadae Sanctae Sermo* 11, LTR 5.56.

98. *Sermones in Nativitate Domini* 5.1, LTR 4.000.

99. *In Resurrectione Sermo* 2.4.

100. *Quadrigesima* 3.2.

101. *PL* 180.250, chap. 2.

102. *Die ehelehre der schule des Anselm von Laon*, 2 vols. (Münster, 1919 and 1974), 1.3.

CHAPTER 5

1. On Peter of Blois's similar experience, see my *Reception of the Faith* (London, 1997), pp. 65–68.

2. See LTR 7.184 n.1 for the literature.

3. Letter 98.1–2.

4. Letter 98.1.

5. Letter 98.2.

6. Letter 98.5.

7. *PL* 180.249–82.

8. See chapter 6.

9. *Csi* V.vii.15.

10. *Csi* V.viii.19.

11. See pp. 000.

12. *Csi* V.17.

13. Rowan Williams, *Arius* (London, 1987).

14. *SS* 76.4.

15. This distinctness was successfully exploited by Anselm in the argument of his *De Processione Spiritus Sancti*, in *Anselmi Opera Omnia* 2.

16. Cf. William of St. Thierry, *Disputatio adversus Petrum Abaelardum*, 2, *PL* 180–250.

17. Aristotle, *Categories*, ed. N. P. Cook (London, 1962), and Boethius, *Commentary on the Categories*, *PL* 64.159.

18. *Csi* II.30, p. 492.12–15, the dimensions of length-breadth and height-depth are held as in the two arms of the fear and love of God. Cf. Michel, 'La considération', p. 110.

19. *Nativitatis Domini* 5.2.

20. Cf. William of St. Thierry, *Disputatio adversus Petrum Abaelardum* 2, *PL* 180.250.

21. *De Diligendo Deo* 35. Letter 11.3.

22. *Nam, dicente auctore*.

23. *SS* 80.8–9. Cf. Gilbert of Poitiers, *Commentaries on Boethius*, p. 76.

24. *SS* 80.8.

25. Letter 190, p. 19.

26. Letter 190, p. 19.

27. See my *Church and the Churches* (Cambridge, 1994).

28. *Die ehelehre der schule des Anselm von Laon*, 2 vols. (Münster, 1919 and 1974), 1.8, 9.

29. *PL* 188, and Anselm, *Dialogues*, vol. 1, ed. G. Salet (Paris, 1966).

30. *Aut si dividere quid conetur vel personas a substantia, vel proprietates a personis, nescio quomodo Trinitatis se profiteri cultorem possit. Csi* V.5.

31. *Csi* V.18.

32. Letter 190.i.2.

33. Letter 190, p. 18.

34. *Grace* 49.

35. *Sermones in Labore Messis* 2.1, LTR 5.220.

36. *Diversis* 45.1.

37. *Grace* 49.

38. *Diversis* 92.1.

39. *SS* 68.1.

40. *Grace* 9.28.

41. *Grace* 9.30–31.

42. *Adventu* 1.5.

43. *Grace* 10.32.

44. *Grace* 10.33.

45. *Die ehelehre der schule des Anselm von Laon*, 2 vols. (Münster, 1919 and 1974), 1.26. See, too, O. Lottin, *Psychologie et morale au xiie et xiii siècles* (Gembloux, 1959).

46. *Cur Deus Homo* 1.v, in *Anselmi Opera Omnia* 2.52.12–24.

47. *SS* 11.7.

48. Peter Abelard, *Commentary on Romans*, *CCCM* 11.

49. LTR 1.59.12–13.

50. *Adventu* 1.2.

51. *Adventu* 7.2. *Necessarius proinde salvatoris adventus, necessaria sic praeoccupatis hominibus praesentia Christi.*

52. *Nativitatis Domini* 1.2.

53. *Sent.* 2.4.

54. *PL* 180.269.

55. See R. W. Southern, *St. Anselm and his Biographer* (Cambridge, 1963), pp. 85–87, 93–97, 358–61.

56. *Cur Deus Homo* 1.vii, in *Anselmi Opera Omnia* 2.55–59.

57. Hugh of St. Victor, *De Sacramentis* I.viii, *PL* 176.307–9.

58. Letter 190.v.12–14.

59. Letter 190.vi.15.

60. Letter 182.

61. *Sent.* 3.115.

62. *Cur Deus Homo* 11.vi, in *Anselmi Opera Omnia* 2.101.

63. *Sent.* 3.23.

64. *Adventu* 1.7.

65. This question of necessity is raised by Anselm in the *Cur Deus Homo*.

66. *Adventu* 1.8.

67. Peter Abelard, *Commentary on Romans*, ed. M. Buytaert, *CCCM* 11, pp. 113.129–14.134.

68. *CCCM* 11, pp. 114.135–15.175.

69. *CCCM* 11, p. 115.179–91.

70. *CCCM* 11, p. 116.210–14.

71. *CCCM* 11, pp. 117–18.

72. Letter 190.v.11.

73. LTR 3.229.17–20.

74. LTR 3.230.8.

75. LTR 3.230.8–9.

76. LTR 3.230.12.

77. LTR 3.229.22–230.1.

78. *Grace* 5.14.

79. *Grace* 2.3–4.

80. *Grace* 2.4.

81. *Grace* 2.5.

82. *Grace* 3.6.

83. *Grace* 3.7.

84. *Grace* 3.7.

85. *Grace* 4.9.

86. *Grace* 4.9.

87. *Grace* 4.9.

88. *Grace* 4.10.

89. *Grace* 4.10.

90. *Grace* 4.11.

91. *Grace* 4.11.

92. *On Conversion* II.3.

93. *On Conversion* III.4.

94. *On Conversion* III.4.

95. *On Conversion* II.3.

96. *De Casu Diaboli*, in *Anselmi Opera Omnia* 1.266.

97. *Grace* 6.17.

98. *Grace* 7.22.

99. *Grace* 10.33.

100. *Grace* 11.37.

101. *Grace* 12.39.

102. *Grace* 12.39.

103. *Grace* 12.40.

104. *SS* 52.9–10.

105. *Grace* 13.44.

106. *On Conversion* X.20.

107. Letter 107.5.

108. *SS* 23.5.

109. *SS* 23.4; Pranger, pp. 66, 69.

110. *SS* 51.1.

111. *SS* 51.2.

112. *SS* 51.

113. *Homiliae super 'Missus Est'*, preface, LTR 4.13.

114. *Grace* 4.

115. *Grace* 5, Cf. *Ubi necessitas urget, excusabilis dispensatio est; ubi utilitas provocat, dispensatio laudabilis est. Csi* III.18.

116. Letter 113.1.

117. *Sermo de Septem Donis Spiritus Sancti* 1.

118. Letter 41.

119. *Magna siquidem nos necessitas de claustris ad publicum traxit, ubi et quod loquimur vidimus.* Letter 46.

120. *Grace* 14.49.

121. *Grace* 13.43.

122. *Grace* 13.42.

123. *Grace* 14.46.

124. *Grace* 14.49.

125. *Grace* 14.51.

126. Letter 107.5.

127. See earlier in this chapter.

128. *Grace* 14.49.

129. Psalmum 6.7.

130. *Grace* 4.10.

131. *Ecclesiasticus* 48.12; Malachy, preface.

132. Malachy, preface.

133. Malachy, preface.

134. Job 7.1.

135. Malachy, preface.

136. Malachy, preface.

137. *Psalmum* 9.2.

138. Malachy II.4–III.5.

139. Malachy III.6.

140. Letter 126.3.

141. *PL* 182.540.

142. Letter 189.4.

143. *In generali statu Ecclesiae. Psalmum* 6.7.
144. *Csi* V.18.
145. *SS* 80.8–9.
146. *Diversis* 11.1.
147. Letter 132.
148. *Csi* III.5.
149. Letter 190.
150. Letter 334.
151. On these, see chapter 7.
152. Letter 190.
153. *Festivitate* 2.6.
154. Letter 87.7.
155. *Cena Domini* 4.
156. *Grace* 36.
157. Letter 77.8.
158. *Sent.* 3.111.
159. *Diversis* 13.3.
160. *Sermones in Dedicatione Ecclesiae* 5.2.
161. *Cena Domini* 1.
162. Letter 190.
163. Letter 188.2; cf. Letter 397.1.
164. *Sermo* 3.4.
165. Malachy 7.
166. *Sent.* 3.97.
167. Letter 77.4.
168. *Cena Domini* 2.
169. *Diversis* 119.
170. *Cena Domini* 2.
171. *Cena Domini* 2.
172. *Cena Domini* 2.
173. *Cena Domini* 2.
174. *Cena Domini* 2.
175. Letter 77.i.1.
176. Letter 77.i.3; cf. Augustine, *Retractationes* I.25, *CSEL* 36.124–25, and *Quaestiones in Heptateuchum* III.84, *CCSL* 33.
177. Letter 7.i.1.
178. Letter 77.i.3.
179. Letter 77.iv.17.
180. Letter 77.i.3.
181. Letter 77.iii.10.
182. *Cena Domini* 1.

183. *Cena Domini* 2, 3.

184. *SS* 66.8.

185. *Cena Domini* 2.

186. Chromatius of Aquileia, *Sermo* 15, line 42, *Opera*, ed. R. Étaix and J. Lemarié, *CCSL* IXA (1974).

187. *Bede Homiliae Evangelii* II, Homilia 5, line 83, *CCSL* 120.

188. *Bede Homiliae Evangelii* II, Homilia 5, line 98, *CCSL* 120.

189. *Parabolae* 5, LTR 6ii.257. Cf. *Tria sunt operimenta altaris: de peccatis paenitentialis afflictio, quae est cilicium; de venia laudis et laetitiae magnitudo; quae est velut ae sonans; de gratia praeconialis iubilatio, quae rutilat velut aurum. Sent.* 2.143.

190. *Psalmum* 3.3.

191. Letter 78.11.

192. *Sermones in Octava Paschae* 2.10, LTR 5.100.

193. *PL* 178.1863–64; *SS* 26. Bernard's brother Gerard died in 1138.

194. See the end of Augustine's *De Civitate Dei, Dialogues* IV, *PL* 77.149.

195. *Grace* 4, 8.

196. *De Diligendo Deo* XI.31.

197. Letter 56.

198. *SS* 33.16; Letter 124; *SS* 72.5.

199. Letter 336.

200. Malachy, preface.

201. Malachy, preface.

CHAPTER 6

1. Matthew 18.

2. See my *Reception of the Faith*.

3. Letter 7.9.

4. *On Conversion* II.3.

5. 338, quoting Horace, *Epistula,* ed. H. Rushton Fairclough (London, 1978), I.ii.68.

6. *On Conversion* VII.16.

7. *On Conversion* VII.16–17.

8. *On Conversion* IX.18.

9. *On Conversion* IX.18.

10. See my *Alan of Lille* (Cambridge, 1983).

11. *PL* 185.31lC.

12. *VP* III.5.12–14.

13. *Anselmi Opera Omnia* 1.281.7–13.

14. *Anselmi Opera Omnia* 1.282.1–16.

15. LTR 8.17–9.10.

16. *PL* 185.310.

17. C. Burnett, ed., 'Confession Fidei "Universis": A Critical Edition of Abelard's Reply to Accusations of Heresy', *Mediaeval Studies* 48 (1986), pp. 111–39.

18. Only part of the work survives, Marenbon, p. 69. There is a complicating factor, in that Bernard's Letter 190 has the *capitula*. It is impossible to be sure whether these are identical with the ones produced in the council.

19. *Apologia contra Bernardum* 5–6, *CCCM* 11, p. 362.

20. Compare the recensions of the *De Incarnatione Verbi,* in *Anselmi Opera Omnia* 1–2.

21. *Apologia contra Bernardum* 5–6, *CCCM* 11, p. 362.

22. Peter Abelard, *Historia Calamitatum*, ed. J. Monfrin (4th ed., 1978), lines 714ff.

23. N. M. Häring, 'Capitula Haeresum Petri Abelardi', *Cîteaux* 31 (1980), pp. 35–50; J. Rivière, 'Les "capitula" d'Abélard condamnés au concile de Sens', *Recherches de théologie ancienne et médiévale* 3 (1933), pp. 5–22.

24. See later in this chapter.

25. Marenbon, pp. 69–70.

26. A Dondaine, 'Aux origines du Valdéisme: une profession de foi de Valdes', *Archivum Fratrum Praedicatorum* 16 (1946), pp. 191–235.

27. This text is found in a manuscript contemporary with Valdès, even before 1184. Biblioteca Nacional de Madrid, MS 1114. Dondaine, 'Aux origines du Valdéisme', pp. 195–96. The creed reappears in a letter of Innocent III of 1208, *PL* 215.1510–13.

28. *Inventor istius erroris apud [lugdunum] iuravit in manu cuiusdam cardinalis romane ecclesie, quod numquam de cetero sectam is tam teneret, nec haberet socius istius erroris*. Dondaine, 'Aux origines du Valdéisme', pp. 195–96; Troyes, MS 1068, f.130va.

29. *Novi et veteris testamenti, idest legis moisi et prophetarum et apostolorum, unum eundemque et deum auctorem credimus*. Dondaine, 'Aux origines du Valdéisme', pp. 197–99.

30. Dondaine, 'Aux origines du Valdéisme', p. 231.

31. *SS* 79.2.

32. *Diversis* 3.2.

33. *Contra Petrobrusianos Hereticos*, ed. J. Fearns, *CCCM* 10, p. 3.

34. *Adversus Iudeorum Inveteratam Duritiem*, ed. Y. Friedman, *CCCM* 58.

35. *De Miraculis* 2.15, *PL* 189.851–954.

36. *SS* 14.3–8.

37. *The Works of Gilbert Crispin*, ed. A. S. Abulafia and G. R. Evans (London, 1986).

38. Letter 158.2.
39. Letter 363.7.
40. Letter 363.6.
41. *Laborabat ea tempestate sub schismaticorum oppressione tota Burdegalensis Ecclesia*. *VP* II.6.
42. *VP* II.7.
43. Letter 133.
44. *Csi* III.i.5, and Letter 334, to Guy of Pisa.
45. *Csi* III.i.5.
46. See pp. 000.
47. Letter 472, *PL* 182.676–80, and see J. Leclercq, 'S. Bernard Docteur', *Collectanea Cisterciensia* 16 (1954), pp. 284–86.
48. *PL* 182.676–77 [1–21].
49. *PL* 182.677–78 [3–4].
50. *PL* 182.679C–D.
51. *SS* 64.i.1–ii.7.
52. *SS* 64.iii.8.
53. *SS* 64.iii.8.
54. I Timothy 2.4.
55. *SS* 64.iii.7.
56. *SS* 64.iii.8.
57. *SS* 64.iii.8.
58. *SS* 64.iii.9.
59. Letter 77.5.
60. *SS* 64.iii.
61. *SS* 65.i.
62. *SS* 65.iii.4.
63. *SS* 65.ii.5
64. *SS* 65.i.2.
65. *SS* 65.ii.3.
66. *SS* 66.i.1.
67. Marenbon, p. 28.
68. Letter 81.
69. Letter 54.1.
70. Letter 54.2.
71. Letter 211.
72. See later in this chapter.
73. Clanchy, pp. 316–17.
74. *Historia Calamitatum*, lines 827–35.
75. *Historia Calamitatum*, lines 855–57.
76. *Historia Calamitatum*, lines 848–51.

77. Anselm, *De Incarnatione Verbi*, in *Anselmi Opera Omnia* 2.1; cf. Clanchy, p. 301, and M. T. Clanchy, 'Abelard's Mockery of St. Anselm', *Journal of Ecclesiastical History* 41 (1990), pp. 15–16.

78. Clanchy's helpful phrase. See Clanchy, p. 304.

79. Clanchy, p. 310, citing Bernard's Letter 331.

80. On all this, see Clanchy, pp. 297ff. and 312.

81. *Neque enim integrum mihi fore arbitrabar tam delicato intus vacare otio, ipso foris fines fidei nostrae nudato ut dicitur gladio tam crudeliter depopulare.* See Klibansky, pp. 11–12.

82. *PL* 180.249–82.

83. *PL* 182.531.

84. Marenbon, p. 27.

85. See Klibansky, p. 15.

86. *PL* 180.249–82.

87. Walter Map, *De Nugis Curialium*, ed. M. R. James (1983), book 1, chap. 24, pp. 78–80.

88. J. Leclercq, ed., 'Autour de la correspondance de S. Bernard', in *Sapientiae doctrina. Mélanges de théologie et de littérature médiévales offerts à Dom Hildebrand Bascour, Recherches de théologie ancienne et medievale* (series), no. 1 (Louvain, 1980), pp. 185–98.

89. See, too, Klibansky, pp. 6–7.

90. See Marenbon, p. 29, and see L. Komer, 'Abaelard und Bernhard von Clairvaux in Sens', *Zeitschrift der Savigny-Stiftung für Rechtsgeschichte* 67 (1981), pp. 121–47, at p. 127. *Historia Pontificalis*, pp. 17–18.

91. J. Leclercq, 'Correspondance de S. Bernard', pp. 185–98.

92. Marenbon, p. 31.

93. Clanchy, pp. 308–10.

94. Letter 189.4.

95. Letter 189.4.

96. *Abnui tum quia puer sum et ille vir bellator ab adolescentia, tum quia iudicarem indignum rationem fidei humanis committi ratiunculis agitandam quam tam certa ac stabili constat esse subnixam.* Letter 189, and see Klibansky, p. 18.

97. *PL* 185.311C.

98. *PL* 185. 311A–B and *Letter to His Socii*, p. 7.

99. Letter 189, and Letter of French bishops, p. 189.

100. Marenbon, p. 30.

101. Letter 189.4.

102. Letter 189.4.

103. Letter 338.

104. Clanchy, p. 307.

105. Letter 332.

106. *PL* 182.540.

107. Letter 338, to Chancellor Haimeric.

108. *VP* III.5.

109. J. Verger, 'Le cloître et les écoles', *SC* 380 (Paris, 1992), pp. 459–73, at p. 460.

110. Otto of Freising, *Gesta Friderici*, ed. F. J. Schmale (1965), p. 228.2–4.

111. *PL* 182, 311, and 542.

112. Clanchy, p. 312; cf. LTR 8.429.

113. Letter 189.4; Rivière, 'Les "capitula,"' pp. 5–22.

114. *CCCM* 11, pp. 473–80.

115. Marenbon, p. 32.

116. Letter of French bishops. pp. 190.90–91.

117. Marenbon, p. 33.

118. Marenbon, p. 33.

119. *PL* 182.541.

120. R. Thompson, 'The Satirical Works of Berengar of Poitiers', *Medieval Studies* 42 (1980), pp. 89–138.

121. J. J. Murphy, *Medieval Eloquence: Studies in the Theory and Practice of Medieval Rhetoric* (Berkeley, 1978).

122. Thompson, 'Satirical Works of Berengar', p. 91.

123. Letter 333, to Cardinal Gregory, deacon of SS. Sergius and Bacchus.

124. Letter 335, to a certain cardinal priest.

125. Letter 338.

126. *Dominica 1 Nov.* 5.9.

127. *Historia Pontificalis,* p. xli.

128. N. M. Häring's introduction to his edition of Gilbert of Poitiers, *Commentaries on Boethius*.

129. D. E. Luscombe, *The School of Peter Abelard* (Cambridge, 1969).

130. *Historia Pontificalis,* p. 16.

131. *Historia Pontificalis,* p. 16.

132. *Historia Pontificalis,* p. 16.

133. *Historia Pontificalis,* p. 16.

134. *Historia Pontificalis,* p. 17.

135. *Historia Pontificalis,* p. 17.

136. *Historia Pontificalis,* p. 17–18.

137. *Historia Pontificalis,* p. 18.

138. *Sed verebantur abbatem et suos offendere, si non ei gererent morem. Historia Pontificalis,* p. 18.

139. *Historia Pontificalis,* p. 19.

140. *Historia Pontificalis,* p. 19.

141. *Historia Pontificalis,* p. 20.

142. *Historia Pontificalis,* p. 20.
143. *Historia Pontificalis,* p. 21.
144. *Historia Pontificalis,* p. 21.
145. *Historia Pontificalis,* p. 22.
146. *Historia Pontificalis,* p. 22.
147. *Historia Pontificalis,* p. 26.
148. *Historia Pontificalis,* p. 25.
149. *PL* 185.312.
150. *PL* 180.276, *Adversus Errores Petri Abaelardi.*
151. Letter 195.
152. Letter 196.1.
153. Letter 196.2.
154. Letter 193.
155. Letter 193.
156. Letter 330, to Pope Innocent.
157. Letter 331.
158. In Letter 330, to Pope Innocent.
159. Letter 196.2.
160. Letter 338, quoting Horace, *Epistola* I.ii.68.
161. Smalley, *The Study of the Bible.*
162. In Letter 330, to Pope Innocent.
163. Letter 331.
164. *Historia Pontificalis,* p. 17; cf. I Timothy 6.20.

CHAPTER 7

1. Letter 190.ix.25; and cf. *Anselmi Opera Omnia* 2.51.20–21.
2. See Apuleius, *De Philosophia Libri,* ed. C. Moreschini (Leipzig, 1991).
3. *Cantica Canticorum* III.11–12, p. 24.
4. For example, in Letters 6, 42.
5. *Sent.* 3.97.
6. Letter 365.2, *illa universalis oratio ecclesiae.*
7. *De Diligendo Deo,* 22, LTR 3.138.
8. *Sermo in Ascensione Domini* 4.7, LTR 5.143.
9. Sermo 110, LTR 5.433.
10. *Csi* V.32, LTR 3.493.
11. *Csi* II.5, LTR 3.414.
12. *SS* 51.2.
13. *SS* 51.2.
14. *SS* 51.3.

15. *SS* 3, and see William O. Paulsell, 'Ethical Theory in the Sermons on the Song of Songs', in E. Rozanne Elder and John R. Sommerfeldt, eds., *The Chimaera of His Age: Studies on Bernard of Clairvaux*, Studies in Mediaeval Cistercian History (Kalamazoo, 1980), pp. 12–22.

16. *SS* 50.3.

17. *SS* 21.2.

18. *SS* 49.5.

19. *SS* 15.6.

20. *SS* 22.8.

21. *SS* 29.5.

22. *SS* 12.1.

23. *SS* 60.9.

24. *SS* 29.4.

25. *SS* 50.3.

26. Letter 124.1.

27. Letter 83.2.

28. We have already touched on the 'tropological', or moral, among the figurative senses in exegesis. See, too, H. de Lubac, *Exégèse médiévale*, 4 vols. (Paris, 1959).

29. *Homily on 'Missus Est'* 2.17, LTR 4.34.

30. Cicero, *De Officiis*, ed. W. Miller (London, 1968), I.15–19.

31. *Csi* V.i.11.

32. *Csi* V.i.11.

33. See Cicero's discussion in *De Officiis* I.

34. *Csi* I.viii.10.

35. *Csi* V.i.10.

36. *Csi* V.i.10.

37. Rupert of Deutz, *De Sancta Trinitate et Operibus Eius* 42, in *Opera Spiritus Sancti* IX, *CCCM* 24, p. 2104.

38. Book 4, line 754, *CCCM* 24.

39. *In Leviticum* 15, *CCCM* 22, p. 856.

40. Prudentius, *Psychomachia*, ed. H. J. Thomas, 2 vols. (London, 1949), vol. 1.

41. Parables, *Analecta Sancti Odrinis Cisterciansis* 18 (1962), p. 55.

42. Letter 51.

43. *Csi* V.viii.

44. *SS* 85.4.

45. *Csi* V.ii.20.

46. There is a useful discussion of some of these principles in the introduction to *Peter Abelard's Ethics*, ed. David Luscombe (Oxford, 1971), p. xxxv.

47. *Grace* 3.

48. *SS* 16.9.

49. Letter 147.1.

50. *SS* 33.15.

51. *Apologia* 25.

52. Letter 248.2.

53. Cf. *SS* 41.1.

54. *PL* 180.276, *Adversus errores Petri Abaelardi.*

55. *Csi* V.ii.20.

56. *SS* 13.3.

57. *SS* 7.7.

58. Letter 1.9.

59. *Councils and Synods,* p. 583.

60. Letter 83.2, to Simon, abbot of St. Nicholas.

61. Letter 69.1.

62. Letter 14.

63. *Nam sicut tentare aliquid vel prece vel pretio adversus iustitiam ini-quum est, sic pro iustitia multum laborare apud iustitiae amatorem superfluum.* Letter 14.

64. Letter 31.

65. Letter 35.

66. *Sermones in Epiphania Domini* 2.2, LTR 4; cf. *Diversis* 50.1.

67. The six wings are *naturalis suggestio, legalis institutio, prophetalis assertio, evangelica sanctio, apostolica visio,* and *ecclesiastica consuetudo. Sent.* 2.137.

68. Letter 538.

69. Letter 520.

70. *Ut sicut ipse lex sui que iuris est, ita is quoque seipsum regeret.* Letter 11.5; cf. *De Diligendo Dei* 36.

71. Letter 307.1.

72. J. Kopper, 'Loi de la volonté et loi de Dieu', in Brague, pp. 153–64.

73. *On Conversion* IV.6. The evolving doctrine of purgatory of the twelfth century complicates this principle.

74. Cf. Song of Songs 2.9.

75. Letter 213.

76. Letter 1.6.

77. Letter 1.7.

78. *Quadrigesima* 4.2; *Csi* I.viii.11.

79. *Si illum expellitis de terra vestra, ut mihi non liceat eandem consecrationem canonice facere: videtur mihi quia dissaisitis me de officio meo, sine iudicio cur facere debeatis.* Letter 265, in *Anselmi Opera Omnia,* p. 180.

80. P. Fournier, *Les collections canoniques romaines de l'époque de Grégoire V*, vol. 2 (Paris, 1920).

81. *The Letters of Lanfranc*, ed. and tr. H. Clover and Margaret Gibson (Oxford, 1979), pp. 130–31.

82. *The Letters of Lanfranc*, pp. 152–53.

83. Eadmer, *Historia Novorum*, ed. M. Rule, Rolls Series (London, 1884), p. 42.

84. *Legem autem dei et canonicas et apostolicas auctoritates voluntariis consuetudinibus obrui videbam. De his omnibus, cum loquebar, nihil efficiebam, et non tam simplex rectitudo quam voluntariae consuetudines obtendebantur.* Letter 206, in *Anselmi Opera Omnia*, p. 100.

85. For example, Letter 39, in *Anselmi Opera Omnia*, p. 149, to Lanfranc; Letter 198, in *Anselmi Opera Omnia*, p. 88, to the bishops of Ireland.

86. *Archiepiscopi proprie iuris esse*t. Letter 170.51, in *Anselmi Opera Omnia* 4.

87. Anselm, Letter 336, in *Anselmi Opera Omnia* 5, p. 272.

88. Cf. Andrew of St. Victor, *In Leviticum*, line 856, *CCCM* 53, p. 179.

89. Letter 80, in *Anselmi Opera Omnia*, p. 204; Letter 329, in *Anselmi Opera Omnia*, p. 262.

90. *Neque in baptismo neque in aliqua ordinatione mea promisi me servaturum legem vel consuetudinem patris vestri aut Lanfranci archiepiscopi, sed legem dei et omnium ordinum quod suscepi.* Letter 319, in *Anselmi Opera Omnia,* p. 247, cf. p. 261.

91. Letter 319, in *Anselmi Opera Omnia*, p. 424.

92. *Facite ut abbas monasterii Sancti Ebrulfi revocet monachos suos quos contra legem dei et ordinem suum in ecclesiam praedictam ingessit, et es eiusdem ecclesiae, quas inde abstulit sacrilegia rapina, iuste restituat.* Letter 269, in *Anselmi Opera Omnia*, p. 184. An interesting usage implying that there are rules for genres, and perhaps indicating that Anselm had a knowledge of the new *ars dictaminis* is: *Nisi lex epistolae cogeret me.* Letter 101, in *Anselmi Opera Omnia* 3, p. 233.

93. Letter 355, in *Anselmi Opera Omnia*, p. 297.

94. Letter 311, in *Anselmi Opera Omnia*, p. 236.

95. Letter 391, in *Anselmi Opera Omnia*, p. 336.

96. Letter 391, in *Anselmi Opera Omnia*, p. 336.

97. Letter 472, in *Anselmi Opera Omnia*, p. 420.

98. *PL* 178.335–40.

99. *Diversis* 124.2.

100. *Sent.* 3–4, 19, and 86.

101. Letters 148 and 151, in *Anselmi Opera Omnia*.

102. *Qua causa quod adiutores me oportuerat habere in causa dei, terribiliter offensos patior; et quae per me crescere debuerat, me praesente deperit causa dei.* Letter 198, in *Anselmi Opera Omnia*, p. 89.

103. Letter 340, in *Anselmi Opera Omnia* 5, p. 278.

104. Letter 331, in *Anselmi Opera Omnia* 4–5, pp. 264, 277, 210, and 229.

105. Letters 338, 388, and 339, in *Anselmi Opera Omnia* 4–5, pp. 276, 31, and 277.

106. *Nullatenus igitur per me aliquid habebit de tota pecunia totius archiepiscopatus, nisi prius me canonice revestierit et ea quae abstulit mihi reddiderit.* Letter 349, to Ernulf, in *Anselmi Opera Omnia* 5, p. 288.

107. *Si hoc tempore factus fuerit monachus, concedo uxori eius, dum vivit, terras quas de me habet; et si quis eas ab alio acceperit nisi ab archiepiscopo Cantuariensi, vel me vel mihi canonice succedente.* Letter 331, to Ernulf, in *Anselmi Opera Omnia* 5, p. 266.

108. *Councils and Synods*, p. 675.

109. *Councils and Synods*, p. 675.

110. Letter 435, in *Anselmi Opera Omnia* 5, p. 383.

111. Letter 442, in *Anselmi Opera Omnia* 5, p. 389.

112. *The Letters of Lanfranc*, pp. 150–51.

113. Eadmer, *Historia Novorum*, pp. 48–49.

114. Morris, p. 450.

115. Morris, p. 453.

116. Morris, p. 458.

117. Brett, p. 152.

118. Brett, p. 158.

119. Brett, p. 155.

120. Brett, p. 151.

121. Three kinds of episcopal judgement could be identified: assemblies in which a bishop issued a public judgement; chapters (held in a fixed place) at which as bishop in chapter the bishop delivered a jdgement; judgements in synod, which could be given in a variety of locations. Brett, pp. 13–14.

122. Morris, p. 449.

123. He issued an ordinance before 1085:

Propterea mando et regia auctoritate precipio ut nullus episcopus vel archidiaconus de legibus episcopalibus amplius in hundret placita teneant, nec causam que ad regimen animarum pertinet ad iudicium secularium hominum adducant. Sed quicunque secundum episcopales leges de quacmque causa vel cupla interplellatus fuerit ad locum quem ad hoc episcopus elegerit et nominaverit veniat, ibique de causa vel culpa sua respondeat, et non secundum hundret sed secundum canones et episcopales leges rectum Deo et episcopo suo faciat. (Councils and Synods, pp. 623–24)

124. Brett, p. 151.

125. *Henrici Primi,* p. 5.

126. Morris, p. 451.

127. Brett, p. 159.

128. *Csi* I.iii.4.

129. *Csi* I.iv.5.

130. Bernard mentions Justinian in *Csi* I.5.

131. *Csi* I.vi.7.

132. *Csi* I.vi.7.

133. *Csi* I.x.13.

134. Morris, p. 453.

135. *Henrici Primi,* chap. 5.1, pp. 84–85.

136. *In omni discussione probitatis ydonei nullaque simul exactione permixt*i. *Henrici Primi,* chap. 5.1, pp. 84–85.

137. *Henrici Primi,* chap. 5.2.

138. *Henrici Primi,* chap. 5.5.

139. *Henrici Primi,* chap. 5.3.

140. Letter 52, to Pope Honorius.

141. *Henrici Primi,* chap. 5.3.

142. *Henrici Primi,* chap. 5.5a.

143. *Henrici Primi,* chap. 5.9a.

144. *Henrici Primi,* chap. 5.7a.

145. *Henrici Primi,* chap. 5.13a.

146. *Si in testibus et iudicibus et personis satisfactum sit ei, si iudicibus consentiat' [si iudice suspectos habeat] advocet aut contradicat. Henrici Primi,* chap. 5.3a.

147. *Csi* III.ii.6.

148. *Csi* III.ii.6.

149. *Csi* III.ii.8–9.

150. *Csi* III.ii.10.

151. *Csi* III.iv.18.

152. *Henrici Primi,* chap. 5.10.

153. *Henrici Primi,* chap. 5.11.

154. *Henrici Primi,* chap. 5.11a.

155. *In ecclesiasticis vero dicta causa recedere licet si necesse fuerit, si iudicem suspectum habuerit vel si se sentiat pregrava. Henrici Primi,* chap. 5.4.

156. Letter 1.

157. Letter 1.1.

158. *Csi* I.x.13.

159. *Csi* I.x.13.

160. *Csi* II.xiv.23.

CHAPTER 8

1. *Csi* V.iv.10.

2. The fifth-century author known as Dionysius the Areopagite or Ps.-Dionysius is edited in Migne, *Patrologia Graeca*, 3. His interest in the celestial hierarchies made him attractive to some medieval readers, who knew his work through Eriugena's Carolingian translation, *PL* 122. See, too, R. Roques, *L'Univers Dionysien* (Paris, 1954).

3. He will almost certainly have got these from Gregory the Great's list in the *Homilies on the Gospels* (34, *PL* 76.1249).

4. *Csi* V.iv.9.

5. *Csi* V.v.12.

6. *Csi* V.iv.10.

7. The Latin *virtus* carries the double sense.

8. *Csi* iv.10

9. *Csi* I.vii.8.

10. *Csi* I.vii.8.

11. *De Diligendo Deo* VIII.23–24.

12. *De Diligendo Deo* VIII.25.

13. *De Diligendo Deo* II.3.

14. *De Diligendo Deo* VI.15.

15. *De Diligendo Deo* VII.16.

16. *De Diligendo Deo* VII.17.

17. *De Diligendo Deo* VI.15.

18. *De Diligendo Deo* VII.18.

19. *De Diligendo Deo* VII.21.

20. *De Diligendo Deo* IX.26.

21. *De Diligendo Deo* X.27.

22. *De Diligendo Deo* VII.19.

23. *De Diligendo Deo* VII.21.

24. J. Lipkin, 'The Entrance of the Cistercians into the Church Hierarchy, 1098–1227: The Bernardine Influence', *Chimaera*, pp. 62–75.

25. Letter 256.1–2.

26. Baldwin of Ford, *Sermones* 18.90, *CCCM* 99, p. 287.

27. In Pope Gelasius I, and in Ambrose, *Expositio Secundum Lucam*, book 10.

28. Letter 183.

29. See pp. 000.

30. See my *Problems of Authority in the Reformation Debates* (Oxford, 1992).

31. Letter 255.1.

32. Letter 255.1.

33. Letter 255.2.
34. *On Conversion* I.1.
35. *Precept and Dispensation* IV.10.
36. *Precept and Dispensation* VI.12.
37. Letter 182.
38. Letter 97.1.
39. Letter 97.1.
40. Letter 97.2.
41. Letter 124.1.
42. Letter 78.11.
43. Letter 78.12.
44. Letter 331.
45. Letter 180.
46. Letter 42.i.1.
47. *Apologia*.
48. Malachy, 14.
49. *Ite nunc ergo, resistite Christi Vicario, cum nec suo adversario Christus restiterit; autt dicite si audetis, sui praesulis Deum ordinationem nescire, cum Romani praesidis potestatem Christus super se quoque fateatur fuisse caelitus ordinatam.* Letter 42.ix.36.
50. Letter 189.4.
51. Malachy, 14.
52. Proverbs 31.19.
53. Letter 42.i.1.
54. Letter 9.
55. Letter 42.i.3, *Csi* V.ii.9.
56. Letter 42.i.1.
57. Letter 42.i.3.
58. Letter 42.i.3.
59. Letter 190, *De Erroribus Petri Abaelardi*.
60. *Csi* V.ii.13.
61. Letter 42.ii.4 and 42.iii.8–9.
62. Letter 42.ii.4.
63. Letter 42.iii.11.
64. *Petri et Pauli* 2.
65. Letter 42.iii.9–10.
66. Letter 42.iii.9–11.
67. Letter 42.iv.13.
68. Letter 7.5.
69. Letter 7.9.

70. *Co-abbates*, Letters 4.3, 6.1, 63.1, et al.

71. *Csi* IV.vii.23.

72. *Csi* III.6, and cf. Letter 198.2.

73. Letter 240.1: *unici huius vestri primatus*.

74. Letter 42.

75. Letter 131.

76. *Sent.* 3.125.

77. *Sermo in Dominica infra Octavam Assumptionis Beatae Mariae* 13; and cf. *Sermones in Adnuntiatione Dominici* 2.2 on the *praerogativae Mariae* in particular.

78. *SS* 76.4.

79. *Csi* III.i.2.

80. *Csi* III.iii.13.

81. *Csi* II.vi.10.

82. *Csi* II.vi.11.

83. *Csi* II.vi.9.

84. *Csi* II.viii.15.

85. *Csi* II.vi.12.

86. *Csi* II.viii.15.

87. *Csi* II.ix.17.

88. *Csi* II.ix.17.

89. *Csi* II.ix.18.

90. *Csi* II.iv.14.

91. See my *Anselm and Talking about God* (Oxford, 1978).

92. *Csi* III.iv.15.

93. *Csi* III.v.19.

94. *SS* 7.12.

95. *Csi* III.v.19.

96. *Csi* IV.i.1–2.

97. *Csi* IV.ii.3–5.

98. Presumably a Bernardine conflation of Song of Songs 1.2; 4.10; 7.8–9.

99. Gregory the Great, in William of St. Thierry's *Excerpta*, *PL* 180.443.

100. *Csi* IV.vii.23.

101. *Petri et Pauli* 3.

102. *Csi* II.vi.9.

103. *Csi* II.vi.12.

104. *Csi* III.i.4.

105. Letter 8.1.

106. Letter 202.

107. Letter 43.

108. *Sermones in Festo SS Apostolorum Petri et Pauli*, LTR 5.188.

109. Letter 152.

110. Letter 178, to Innocent II, on behalf of the archbishop of Trèves.
111. Letter 152.
112. Letter 200.1.
113. Letter 200.2.
114. Letter 200.2.
115. *Templars* I.
116. See chapter 5.
117. Psalm 143.1.
118. Letter 2.12, Letter 535, *Templars* XXXI.
119. Letter 331.
120. Letter 330, to Pope Innocent.
121. *Templars* III.5.
122. *Templars* III.6.
123. *Csi* II.i.1–4.
124. *Templars* I.2.
125. *Templars* II.
126. *Templars* III.
127. *Templars* III.4.
128. *Templars* III.6.
129. *Templars* V.10.
130. *Templars* III.6.
131. *Templars* III.6, Jeremiah 31.11–6, and Psalm 76.16.
132. *Templars* IV.7.
133. *Templars* IV.7.
134. *Templars* IV.8.
135. *Templars* IV.8.
136. *Adversus spiritum concupiscens. Quam domesticus hostis, quam periculosa lucta, quam intestinum bellum. Sermones in 6 Dominica post Penecosten* 2.5.
137. *Festivitate* 5.8.
138. *Sermones in Dedicatione Ecclesiae* 2.3.

SELECT BIBLIOGRAPHY

PRIMARY SOURCES

Texts of patristic and medieval authors not otherwise listed in the bibliography are cited from the *Corpus Christianorum Series Latina* (*CCSL*) and *Corpus Christianorum Continuatio Medievalis* (*CCCM*) editions (Turnhout: Brepols).

Ailred of Rievaulx. *De Spiritali Amicitia*. Ed. A. Hoste and C. H. Talbot. CCCM 1. Turnhout, 1971.

Benedict. *The Rule of St. Benedict*. Ed. G. Holzmer. Dublin, 1994.

Berengar of Poitiers. 'The Satirical Works of Berengar of Poitiers: An Edition with Introduction'. Ed. R. Thompson. *Mediaeval Studies* 42 (1980), pp. 89–138.

Bernard de Clairvaux. *Lettres*. Vol. 1. Ed. and tr. M. Duchet-Suchaux and H. Rochais, Sources chrétiennes, no. 425. Paris, 1997.

Bernard of Clairvaux. *Bernard of Clairvaux: Selected Works*. Tr. G. R. Evans. Classics of Western Spirituality. St. Paul, 1986.

Bernard of Clairvaux. *Five Books on Consideration*. Tr. John D. Anderson and Elizabeth T. Kennan. Cistercian Fathers (series). Kalamazoo, Mich., 1976.

Bernard of Clairvaux. *The Life and Death of St. Malachy*. Tr. Robert T. Meyer. Cistercian Fathers (series). Kalamazoo, Mich., 1978.

Bernard of Clairvaux. *On Loving God*. Tr. Emero Stiegman. Cistercian Fathers (series). Kalamazoo, Mich., 1995.

Bernard of Clairvaux. *Magnificat: Homilies in Praise of the Blessed Virgin Mary.* Tr. M.-B. Said and G. Perigo. Cistercian Fathers (series). Kalamazoo, Mich., 1979.

Bernard of Clairvaux. *Sermons on Conversion.* Tr. M.-B. Said. Cistercian Fathers (series). Kalamazoo, Mich., 1981.

Bernard of Clairvaux. *On the Song of Songs.* Tr. Kilian Walsh and Irene Edmonds. 4 vols. Cistercian Fathers (series). Kalamazoo, Mich., 1971–80.

Bernard of Clairvaux. *Treatises.* Tr. Michael Casey, Conrad Greenia, C. Waddell, Martinus Cawley, B. McGinn, Ambrose Conway, and Robert Walton. 3 vols. Cistercian Fathers (series). Kalamazoo, Mich., 1970–77.

Bernard of Claivaux. *Sancti Bernardi Opera.* Ed. J. Leclercq, C. H. Talbot, and H. Rochais. 8 vols. Rome, 1957–.

Chalcidius. *On Timaeus.* Ed. J. H. Waszink. Leiden, 1962. Pp. 264–71.

Councils and Synods I (871–1204). Ed. D. Whitelock, M. Brett, and C. N. L. Brooke. Oxford, 1981.

Crispin, Gilbert. *The Works of Gilbert Crispin.* Ed. A. S. Abulafia and G. R. Evans. London, 1986.

Gilbert of Poitiers. *Commentaries on Boethius.* Ed. N. M. Häring. Toronto, 1969.

Guibert of Nogent. *De Vita Sua.* Ed. G. Bourgin. Paris, 1906.

John of Salisbury. *Historia Pontificalis.* Ed. M. Chibnall. Oxford, 1986.

Lanfranc of Canterbury. *The Letters of Lanfranc.* Ed. and tr. H. Clover and Margaret Gibson. Oxford, 1979.

Libellus de Diversis Ordinibus. Ed. G. Constable and B. Smith. Oxford, 1972.

SECONDARY SOURCES

Auberger, J. B. 'La législation cistercienne primitive'. In *Bernard de Clairvaux: histoire, mentalités, spiritualité.* Colloque de Lyon-Cîteaux-Dijon. Sources chrétiennes, no. 380. Paris, 1992. Pp. 181–208.

Barber, Malcolm, *The New Knighthood.* Cambridge, 1994.

Brague, R. *Saint Bernard et la philosophie.* Paris, 1993.

Bredero, Adriaan H. *Bernard of Clairvaux: Between Cult and History.* Grand Rapids, Mich., 1996.

Burnett, C. 'Confessio Fidei "Universis": A Critical Edition of Abelard's Reply to Accusations of Heresy'. *Mediaeval Studies* 48 (1986), pp. 111–39.

Camargo, Martin. '*Ars dictaminis, ars dictandi*'. *Typologie des sources du moyen âge occidental* (series), no. 60. Turnhout, 1991.

Châtillon, F. 'Regio dissimilitudinis'. In F. Lavalée, ed., *Mélanges E. Pochédard.* Lyon, 1945. Pp. 85–102.

Clanchy, M. *Abelard: A Medieval Life.* Oxford, 1997.

Constable, Giles. 'Letters and Letter-Collections'. *Typologie des sources du moyen âge occidental* (series), no. 17. Turnhout, 1976.

Dondaine, A. 'Aux origines du Valdéisme: une profession de foi de Valdes'. *Archivum Fratrum Praedicatorum* 16 (1946), pp. 191–235.

Evans, G. R. *Augustine on Evil*. Oxford, 1983.

Evans, G. R. 'A Change of Mind in Some Scholars of the Eleventh and Twelfth Centuries'. *Studies in Church History* 15 (1978), pp. 27–38.

Evans, G. R. *The Mind of Bernard of Clairvaux*. Oxford, 1983.

Evans, G. R. *Old Arts and New Theology*. Oxford, 1983.

Evans, G. R. *Philosophy and Theology in the Middle Ages*. London, 1993.

Javelet, R. *Image et ressemblance au douzième siécle*. 2 vols. Paris, 1967.

Klibansky, R. 'Peter Abailard and Bernard of Clairvaux'. *Medieval and Renaissance Studies* 5 (1961), pp. 1–27.

Lawless, George. *Augustine of Hippo and His Monastic Rule*. Oxford, 1987.

Leclercq, J. 'Autour de la correspondance de S. Bernard'. In *Sapientiae doctrina. Mélanges de théologie et de littérature médiévales offerts à Dom Hildebrand Bascour. Recherches de théologie ancienne et medievale* (series), no. 1. Louvain, 1980. Pp. 185–98.

Leclercq, J. *La femme et les femmes dans l'oeuvre de S. Bernard*. Paris, 1982.

Leclercq, J. *A Second Look at Bernard of Clairvaux*. Kalamazoo, Mich., 1990.

Louf, André. 'Bernard abbé'. In *Bernard de Clairvaux: histoire, mentalités, spiritualité*. Colloque de Lyon-Cîteaux-Dijon. *Sources chrétiennes*, no. 380. Paris, 1992. Pp. 349–79.

Luscombe, D. E. *The School of Peter Abelard*. Cambridge, 1969.

Marenbon, J. *The Philosophy of Peter Abelard*. Oxford, 1997.

Marilier, J. *Chartes et documents de Cîteaux*. Rome, 1961.

Michel, Bruno. 'La considération et l'unitas spiritus'. In R. Brague, *Saint Bernard et la philosophie*. Paris, 1993. Pp. 109–27.

Pranger, M. B. *Bernard of Clairvaux and the Shape of Monastic Thought: Broken Dreams*. Leiden, 1994.

Quillet, J. 'Aspects de la doctrine Bernardine de l'obéissance'. In R. Brague, *Saint Bernard et la philosophie*. Paris, 1993. Pp. 165–77.

Rassow, P. 'Di Kanzlei s. Bernhards von Clairvaux'. *Studien und Mitteilungen zur Geschichte des Benediktiner-Ordens* 34 (1913).

Reiter, J. 'Bernard de Clairvaux, philosophe malgré lui entre coeur et raison'. In R. Brague, *Saint Bernard et la philosophie*. Paris, 1993. Pp. 11–25

Rivière, J. 'Les "capitula" d'Abélard condamnés au concile de Sens'. *Recherches de théologie ancienne et médiévale* 3 (1933), pp. 5–22.

Southern, R. W. *St. Anselm and His Biographer*. Cambridge, 1963.

Williams, Rowan. *Arius*. London, 1987.

Williams, Watkin. *Monastic Studies*. Manchester, 1938.

INDEX

abbot, 34, 35

Abelard, Peter, 15, 18, 42, 47, 48, 50, 59, 74, 77ff., 82, 86, 87, 101, 106ff., 108, 113, 115, 117, 118ff., 121, 122, 125, 126, 127, 129, 136, 138, 190

acceptance of persons, 23

accusers, 147

action, 53
  and contemplation, 20–21, 131ff.

Adam, 80, 81, 83, 84

Adam, monk of Clairvaux, 10

Ailred, 180

Alan of Lille, 4, 68, 128, 135, 193

Alberic of Rheims, 125

allegorical, 63

Ambrose of Milan, 10

Anacletus II, 13ff.

anagogical, 63

Anastasius IV, Pope, 19

Andrew of St. Victor, 108

angels, 31ff., 53, 80, 84, 89, 150ff., 168

anima, 42

animus, 42

Anselm of Canterbury, 5, 12, 12, 20, 37, 42, 65, 68, 78, 81ff., 103, 104, 108ff., 125, 140, 141ff., 148
  Cur Deus Homo, 81ff.

Anselm of Laon, 71, 83. *See also* Laon; Ralph of Laon

Antichrist, 100

apostates, 90ff.

appeal, 147

Apuleius, 178, 198

Aquinas, Thomas, 74, 104

Aquitaine, 138

archdeacon, 144

argumentum, 45

Aristotle, 52, 76, 135, 188

armour, 169

Arnaud de Bonneval, 6ff., 20

Arnold of Brescia, 18, 30, 128, 129

ars dictaminis, 20

ars praedicandi, 68

Augustine of Hippo, 45, 52, 58, 65, 68, 74, 76, 88, 91, 101, 128, 136, 156, 181, 192, 159
  City of God, 156